Peace Corps Volunteers and the Making
of Korean Studies in the United States

Edited by SEUNG-KYUNG KIM *and* MICHAEL ROBINSON

CENTER FOR KOREA STUDIES PUBLICATIONS

The Northern Region of Korea: History, Identity, and Culture
Edited by Sun Joo Kim

Reassessing the Park Chung Hee Era, 1961–1979:
Development, Political Thought, Democracy, and Cultural Influence
Edited by Hyung-A Kim and Clark W. Sorensen

Colonial Rule and Social Change in Korea, 1910–1945
Edited by Hong Yung Lee, Yong-Chool Ha, and Clark W. Sorensen

An Affair with Korea: Memories of South Korea in the 1960s
By Vincent S. R. Brandt

South Korea's Education Exodus: The Life and Times of Study Abroad
Edited by Adrienne Lo, Nancy Abelmann, Soo Ah Kwon, and Sumie Okazaki

Spaces of Possibility: In, Between, and Beyond Korea and Japan
Edited by Clark W. Sorensen and Andrea Gevurtz Arai

Beyond Death: The Politics of Suicide and Martyrdom in Korea
Edited by Charles R. Kim, Jungwon Kim, Hwasook Nam, and Serk-Bae Suh

International Impact of Colonial Rule in Korea, 1910–1945
Edited by Yong-Chool Ha

This publication was supported by the Academy of Korean Studies Grant (AKS-2017-P-15).

The Center for Korea Studies Publication Series is dedicated to providing excellent academic resources and conference volumes related to the history, culture, and politics of the Korean peninsula.

Clark W. Sorensen | Director & General Editor | Center for Korea Studies

Peace Corps Volunteers and the Making of Korean Studies in the United States

Edited by

SEUNG-KYUNG KIM

and

MICHAEL ROBINSON

 A CENTER FOR KOREA STUDIES PUBLICATION

Peace Corps Volunteers and the Making of Korean Studies in the United States
Edited by Seung-kyung Kim and Michael Robinson
© 2020 by the Center for Korea Studies, University of Washington
Printed in the United States of America
23 22 21 20   5 4 3 2 1

CENTER FOR KOREA STUDIES
Henry M. Jackson School of International Studies
University of Washington
http://jsis.washington.edu/Korea

CATALOGING-IN-PUBLICATION DATA IS ON FILE WITH THE LIBRARY OF CONGRESS
ISBN (HARDCOVER): 978-0-295-74812-2
ISBN (PAPERBACK): 978-0-295-74813-9
ISBN (EBOOK): 978-0-295-74814-6

The paper used in this publication meets the minimum requirements of American National Standard for Information Sciences–Permanence of Paper for Printed Library Materials, ANSI Z39, 48-1984.

TO THE PEOPLE OF KOREA

Contents

Acknowledgments

The Institute for Korean Studies (IKS) at Indiana University was established in order to expand and strengthen the field of Korean Studies in the Midwestern region of the United States. In conjunction with its opening in September 2016, the Institute held an inaugural conference, titled "Peace Corps Volunteers and the Making of Korean Studies in the US." The conference was especially timely because 2016 marked the fiftieth anniversary of the Peace Corps–Korea program. Returned volunteers from this program went on to become a major component of the cohort of Korean studies scholars who established the field in the United States. These scholars either have retired or are approaching retirement age and are at a point in their careers when it is possible for them to reflect on what they have accomplished and what directions they expect the field to take in the future. This anthology contains the revised and expanded versions of the papers presented at the conference.

In their presentations, the participants brought together reflections on their own introduction to Korea, their understandings of the context within which the Peace Corps operated, and their professional accomplishments in Korean studies. What has emerged is an interesting and complex reflection on an important time in their own lives, and in Korea's historical development, as well as on the US-Korea relationship, and the growth of an academic field. The editors would like to thank the Academy of Korean Studies for supporting both the conference (AKS-2016-C-13) and the publication of this volume (AKS-2017-P-15). The Institute for Korean Studies and the Hamilton-Lugar School of Global and International Studies at Indiana University provided important material and logistical support for this project as well. We would like to thank Dr. John Finch, associate director, and Mr. Keith Seidel, assistant director, for their work on the publication of this anthology.

Although she was not able to participate in the conference, Ambassador Kathleen Stephens graciously agreed to write an Afterword to this volume, and we would like to thank her. We would also like to thank the anonymous reviewer for their insightful comments. Finally, we owe an important debt to our colleague, Clark W. Sorensen, for guiding this volume through the publication process.

Illustrations

Introduction

SEUNG-KYUNG KIM and MICHAEL ROBINSON

The chapters in this anthology present the history and impact of the Peace Corps program in South Korea (1966–82) from a variety of individual perspectives. Most of the authors (Don Baker, Edward Baker, Donald N. Clark, Carter Eckert, Bruce Fulton, Laurel Kendall, Linda Lewis, Michael Robinson, and Edward J. Shultz) were volunteers who served in the Peace Corps in South Korea (Peace Corps–Korea), and, in their chapters, they have addressed not only their experiences, but also how their time in the Peace Corps led to subsequent careers involving lifetime engagements with Korea. We have rounded out the volume with chapters by contributors, one American (Clark W. Sorensen) and one Korean (Okpyo Moon), who were not part of the Peace Corps, but as members of the same cohort of Korean studies scholars, are able to provide outsiders' perspectives on what Peace Corps–Korea has meant to Korean studies in the United States.

A surprisingly diverse set of experiences is revealed in the chapters included in this anthology, given that the authors came from mostly similar, middle-class American backgrounds and went to South Korea as part of the same organization at about the same time; however, three broad issues connect all of the chapters. First, the authors pose questions about how their experiences reflected the broader cultural and political relationship between South Korea and the United States at a particular historical moment. For the most part, these reminiscences encompass the period between 1966 and 1975. This was an important time for US–Republic of Korea (ROK) relations, and it was a period of transition for the Peace Corps as well. After its early support from the Kennedy administration (1961–63), then creeping criticism during the Johnson years (1963–69), the Peace Corps found itself under attack after 1968, under President Nixon (1969–74). Moreover, the idealistic fervor characterizing the early years of the Peace Corps was waning along with the numbers of college graduates applying for spots in its programs. Despite this, the Peace Corps persevered and even expanded during the 1970s.

Second, each chapter also contains a vivid account of the cross-cultural encounter with Korea and Koreans, as well as each author's take on the Peace Corps itself as an institution. What emerges is an illustration of how such an experience internationalizes individuals. Finally, the authors comment on how their experiences led to their choice of careers. For most of the authors, teaching or researching Korea became their life's work. In this sense, they represent the fruition of one of the principle goals of the Peace Corps—to transmit cultural knowledge of the outside world back to the American homeland. The chapters that follow reveal how, as the result of their immersion in Korea through the Peace Corps, this cohort became an important strand in the development of the academic field of Korean studies.

The chapters also demonstrate the power of "the Peace Corps experience" to affect an individual volunteer's life and career. This is now a cliché driven by Peace Corps recruiting materials that promise that the Peace Corps experience will do nothing less than change your life. The participants' experiences varied, but their accounts all describe intense reactions to their time living in South Korea during the first years of the Peace Corps program. Their experiences affected their worldviews, individual politics, aesthetic sensibilities, and views on gender discrimination. Service in the Peace Corps revised their relationship to their home culture and profoundly shaped their choice of careers.

Each of our authors who served in the Peace Corps developed his/her connection to Korea into his/her primary career. Those who became academics contributed to the creation of knowledge about Korea, trained new specialists in Korean studies, and taught Korean studies at different universities and colleges while others went into university administration, government service, or work with NGOs. Whether academic, administrative, or service, these careers added immeasurably to the United States' understanding of Korea. Looking back at their initial training in the Peace Corps, all remarked about how little information was available about Korean society, culture, or politics. Indeed, this group helped broaden the knowledge base on Korea through their own teaching, research, and development of Korean studies programs.

Today the literature available on Korea is no longer limited to studies of the Korean War, economics, or international relations. Peace Corps–Korea thus helped to expand the small cadre of experts and interpreters of Korean culture that had come out of the long-standing missionary connection and the later involvement of the US Army in Korea. This small cohort of returned Peace Corps volunteers worked to develop Korean studies in the United States and directly addressed one of the primary goals of the Peace Corps, namely, "to help promote a better understanding of the American people on the part of the peoples served" and "to help promote a better understanding of other peoples on the part of the American people."[1] Their Peace Corps experiences unfolded within a unique political context in the Republic of Korea.

Volunteers were witness to South Korea's rapid and tumultuous economic and social development. In particular, Peace Corps volunteers worked in a South Korea in the grip of authoritarian politics and considerable conflict between US political interests and those of the South Korean elites. This combination was then overlaid with social tensions caused by the notable US Army presence. This experience radicalized some volunteers and deepened the political engagement of others, which had a concomitant effect on their subsequent research and writing on Korea. Some Korean scholars have noted the critical tone of this early groups' scholarship on Korea (see chapter 10 by Okpyo Moon in this volume).[2] That criticism might be, in part, an extension of their early experiences.

Peace Corps memoirs often hold fast to a normative description of the Peace Corps experience, one that acknowledges its transformative effect on volunteers, while fitting a general template of praise for its intention to spread goodwill and to make friends for the United States around the world. These chapters certainly do that, but they also reveal more complex and ambiguous encounters. In the context of the post–World War II spread of US political and economic hegemony and its confrontation with the Union of Soviet Socialist Republics (USSR) for the hearts and minds of the so-called Third World, the Peace Corps represented the use of soft power to achieve these ends. How could service, understanding, and international friendship be bad? But the Peace Corps also served as an adjunct to serious US political and economic interests and US competition during the Cold War for influence throughout the world. Accordingly, from its inception the Peace Corps fought, sometimes unsuccessfully, to maintain its independence from the foreign policy arms of the US government. Thus, while volunteers committed themselves to being immersed in the society of their postings, living as some put it "on the local economy," they still enjoyed a privileged status supported by US power. This was obviously the case in South Korea with its sizable Embassy/USAID contingent (at the time the US Embassy in Korea was among the top five in numbers of diplomats attached) and the substantial US Army presence. Peace Corps volunteers in South Korea provided a small counter example by eschewing the artificial comforts of these compounds.

Volunteers were afforded a clear view of the contradictions within US propaganda about its mission in the "Third World" and how US power and wealth contrasted with everyday conditions in South Korea.[3] This unmasked the neo-colonial aspects of the US–ROK relationship and placed volunteers in ambiguous positions as exemplars of US values and goodwill, while the United States simultaneously fostered the ugliness of military camp towns and supported the authoritarian dictatorships of Park Chung Hee (Pak Chŏnghŭi, 1961–79) and Chun Doo-hwan (Chŏn Tuhwan, 1979–88).

During the Cold War, the United States supported a number of authoritarian regimes around the world. South Korea was of vital strategic importance to US interests in East Asia. While the US continued to urge a loosening of authoritarian practices in the ROK, its treaty obligations with both the ROK and Japan necessitated looking the other way as constitutional norms were eroded in the 1970s and 1980s. This engendered resentment among pro-democracy protesters throughout the period. Indeed, one returned volunteer, Ed Baker (chapter 2), recounted seeing the well- known clasped hands symbol of the USAID program stamped on trucks ferrying riot police.[4] Given the political protests of the late 1960s in the United States, Peace Corps volunteers, arriving from campuses where their fellow students were demonstrating against US imperialism, felt more empathy with the South Korean protesters than with the South Korean government.

While the Peace Corps had benevolent goals, it was still a US institution that had been designed to advance US political interests. In addition, many volunteers who served during the first five years of Peace Corps–Korea had been politicized by the campus protests against the United States' Cold War policies. Indeed a few of our authors were actively avoiding the draft at the height of the Vietnam War.[5] Unlike most countries that hosted Peace Corps programs, South Korea was on the front line of the Cold War divide, and

Peace Corps–Korea was implicated in US support of an authoritarian anti-communist government. Volunteers in South Korea participated actively, if quietly, in anti–Vietnam War protests by sending a representative to a global Peace Corps contingent that went to Washington to protest the bombing of Cambodia on May 8, 1970. Returning volunteers who moved into Korean studies positions maintained a critical stance against South Korea's authoritarian government even while promoting understanding of Korean culture and society. Furthermore, scholars of modern history and contemporary society sometimes faced hostility toward their research from the South Korean government. Nevertheless, this critical stance stood as a countervailing force within the broader stream of journalistic and popular information in the United States often dominated by conservative politics and a continuing distrust of North Korea.

The Peace Corps was also a creation of 1960s America, and, as such, it brought that generation's prevailing mores with it into the "Third World." The Women's movement had thus far made few inroads into the US bureaucracy, and Peace Corps policies for male and female volunteers cleaved along a divide that privileged males and discriminated against females (in both cases overwhelmingly white). The sexism still imbedded in US culture continued to operate in Peace Corps–Korea, and the more blatant patriarchy of South Korean culture as well as the obvious power differential between the United States and South Korean society set these differences in stark relief. Women and men, as a consequence, experienced very different Koreas to the point where Laurel Kendall (chapter 6) asks "Did Women Have a Peace Corps Experience?" The struggle for women to be seen and heard even in the Peace Corps might seem anachronistic save for our awareness that the same struggle continues to be fought within all institutions in American life, no less so the academy where the majority of these volunteers sought careers.

What began as a few professors at a handful of universities in the 1960s has grown into a substantial body of scholars doing serious research and writing about Korea today as an increasingly affluent South Korea has begun to generously fund Korean studies programs in North America and around the world. The subjects of study have expanded beyond the earlier historical and anthropological work to include art, music, literature, cultural studies, film studies, and social science. The rather uniform white, male domination of the field of Korean studies has given way to a much broader representation of women, Korean Americans, native Koreans, and scholars trained in Europe to the betterment of the field. And the experience of Korean culture and society these scholars bring to the field is substantially broader than that of the small group of graduate students studying South Korea in the late 1960s and 1970s of which this cohort of Peace Corps volunteers were a part.

In closing, two themes emerge from these accounts of the Peace Corps experience and involvement with South Korea. The first is "witness." We think it is notable that Korean studies began to expand around the time of this group's return from South Korea. These young scholars were witness to a South Korea on the cusp of rapid development which took the country on a revolutionary ride for the next twenty-five years. During their service they witnessed a proud peoples' encounter with the indignities of American power and influence in the face of their dependence. They also observed a South Korea very different from that of the prevailing news reels and journalistic accounts dominated by the Cold War mentality. Thus, this experience of witnessing these moments in an as-yet-to-develop South Korea became formative in the minds of these volunteers when they returned to enter graduate school and prepare for careers in the academy.

The second theme throughout this volume is "cultural awareness." There is something about the Peace Corps experience or any other deep cultural immersion that instills appreciation of difference and international connection. In this volume, we encounter the stories of young Americans going abroad to serve in the Peace Corps and extend their hand in friendship in foreign lands. Make friends they did, but perhaps the more important result of this service was the knowledge brought back in the form of first-hand experience and later expertise on societies that were little known or appreciated in the United States. These chapters also reveal an awakening to the constricting mores and gendered power hierarchy and a clear resolution to confront this in one's life's work. In this instance, it formed part of a nucleus of expertise on Korea. Returning volunteers from other programs became part of a growing expertise on the Middle East, Southeast Asia, Africa, and Latin America. In the case of Peace Corps–Korea, the total experience was more than hands across the seas; it was a multifaceted experience that engaged deep elements of cultural identity, social practice, and politics on both sides of the encounter.

NOTES

1. Peace Corps (United States), Office of World Wise Schools, *Looking At Ourselves And Others* (Washington, DC: Peace Corps, World Wise Schools, 1998). https://files.peacecorps.gov/wws/pdf/LookingatOurselvesandOthers.pdf?_ga=2.224670172.731701389.156 9854334-528674421.1569854334.

2 See chapter 10 of this volume, Okpyo Moon, "A Korean Perspective: Peace Corps Volunteers, Europe, and the Study of Korea," *Peace Corps Volunteers and the Making of Korean Studies in the United States*, edited by Seung-kyung Kim and Michael Robinson, 175–90 (Seattle: Center for Korea Studies, 2020).

3 General Park Chung Hee (Pak Chŏnghŭi) took over control of the government of South Korea in a military coup that began on May 16, 1961. He installed himself as acting president in 1962 and, following the election of 1963, held the office of president of the Republic of Korea until his assassination in October 1979. General Chun Doo Hwan led a military coup on December 12, 1979. His consolidation of power included the notorious Kwangju Massacre on May 18, 1980, when troops under his leadership killed numerous pro-democracy demonstrators. Chun arranged to be elected president of the Republic of Korea later that year and held office until 1998.

4 See chapter 2 of this volume, Edward J. Baker, "How the Peace Corps Changed Our Lives," in *Peace Corps Volunteers and the Making of Korean Studies in the United States*, edited by Seung-kyung Kim and Michael Robinson, 36 (Seattle: Center for Korea Studies, 2020).

5 See chapters 2, 3, 4, and 8 of this volume, Edward J. Baker, "How the Peace Corps Changed Our Lives"; Donald Clark, "On Being Part of the Peace Corps Generation in Korean Studies"; Carter J. Eckert, "A Road Less Traveled: From Rome to Seoul"; and Michael Robinson, "Empathy, Politics, and Historical Imagination: A Peace Corps Experience and Its Aftermath," in *Peace Corps Volunteers and the Making of Korean Studies in the United States*, edited by Seung-kyung Kim and Michael Robinson. (Seattle: Center for Korea Studies, 2020).

BIBLIOGRAPHY

Baker, Donald. "Kwangju, Trauma, and the Problem of Objectivity in History-Writing." In *Peace Corps Volunteers and the Making of Korean Studies in the United States*, edited by Seung-kyung Kim and Michael Robinson, 9–30. Seattle: University of Washington Center for Korea Studies, 2020.

Baker, Edward. "How the Peace Corps Changed Our Lives." In *Peace Corps Volunteers and the Making of Korean Studies in the United States*, edited by Seung-kyung Kim and Michael Robinson, 31–52. Seattle: University of Washington Center for Korea Studies, 2020.

Clark, Donald N. "On Being Part of the Peace Corps Generation in Korean Studies." In *Peace Corps Volunteers and the Making of Korean Studies in the United States*, edited by Seung-kyung Kim and Michael Robinson, 53–76. Seattle: University of Washington Center for Korea Studies, 2020.

Eckert, Carter J. "A Road Less Traveled: From Rome to Seoul." In *Peace Corps Volunteers and the Making of Korean Studies in the United States*, edited by Seung-kyung Kim and Michael Robinson, 77–92. Seattle: University of Washington Center for Korea Studies, 2020.

Kendall, Laurel. "Did Women Have a Peace Corps Korea Experience?" In *Peace Corps Volunteers and the Making of Korean Studies in the United States*, edited by Seung-kyung Kim and Michael Robinson, 111–26. Seattle: University of Washington Center for Korea Studies, 2020.

Lewis, Linda. "At the Border: Women, Anthropology, and North Korea." In *Peace Corps Volunteers and the Making of Korean Studies in the United States*, edited by Seung-kyung Kim and Michael Robinson, 127–40. Seattle: University of Washington Center for Korea Studies, 2020.

Moon, Okpyo. "A Korean Perspective: Peace Corps Volunteers, Europe, and the Study of Korea." In *Peace Corps Volunteers and the Making of Korean Studies in the United States*, edited by Seung-kyung Kim and Michael Robinson, 175–90. Seattle: University of Washington Center for Korea Studies, 2020.

Peace Corps (United States). Office of World Wise Schools. *Looking At Ourselves And Others*. Washington, DC: Peace Corps, World Wise Schools, 1998. https://files.peacecorps.gov/wws/pdf/LookingatOurselvesandOthers.pdf?_ga=2.224670172.731701389.1569854334-528674421.1569854334.

Robinson, Michael. "Empathy, Politics, and Historical Imagination: A Peace Corps Experience and Its Aftermath." In *Peace Corps Volunteers and the Making of Korean Studies in the United States*, edited by Seung-kyung Kim and Michael Robinson, 141–58. Seattle: University of Washington Center for Korea Studies, 2020.

Sorensen, Clark W. "Cultural Immersion, Imperialism, and the Academy: An Outsider's Look at Peace Corps Volunteers' Contribution to Korean Studies." In *Peace Corps Volunteers and the Making of Korean Studies in the United States*, edited by Seung-kyung Kim and Michael Robinson, 191–220. Seattle: University of Washington Center for Korea Studies, 2020.

1

Kwangju, Trauma, and the Problem of Objectivity in History-Writing

DON BAKER

Forty-nine years ago, in 1971, I flew to Korea for the first time. At that point in my life, I wasn't very much interested in Korea. I was much more interested in China and Taiwan. I had already studied Chinese in Hawai'i and Taiwan, from 1965 to 1966, on a US government grant for undergraduates from educationally deprived environments. Louisiana State University (LSU), because it didn't teach any Asian languages then, was considered such an environment. I couldn't go to China on an US passport at the time and, after three years working as a psychiatric aide in a mental hospital for children in the Boston area (a position that was in lieu of military service during the Vietnam War), I hadn't saved up enough money to go to Taiwan to live and study. Instead, I joined the Peace Corps. I planned to have Peace Corps training give me the marketable skill of teaching English as a second language. I originally had planned to spend about a year in Korea, to gain some teaching experience and to grow accustomed to what I mistakenly had thought was a culture not all that different from what I had experienced in Taiwan, before quitting and moving to Taiwan.

I was able to visit Taiwan once while I was a Peace Corps volunteer in South Korea but, by then, Korea was in my blood. I don't know if it was the good food in Kwangju or the many good friends I made there, but I ended up extending for a third year as a Kwangju Peace Corps volunteer and then, in 1974, I joined Mike Robinson as a graduate student in Korean history at the University of Washington. Those three years as a Peace Corps volunteer in Kwangju definitely changed my life forever. It might have been the memories of good food (and drink, usually makkŏlli) and the good times with friends in

Kwangju, or just a desire to learn more about a country that few people in the United States knew much about back then (other than what they saw on the popular TV show M*A*S*H), but Korea pushed China aside and became the focus of my life's work. If the Peace Corps had not sent me to South Korea when it did, I may have ended up a historian of China or even just a small-city lawyer like my father back in Louisiana.

Peace Corps service in Korea changed my life by pulling me away from Chinese studies and putting me on the path toward a life-long academic involvement with things Korean. The specific city the Peace Corps sent me to ended up influencing the way I study Korea. Kwangju back then was the fifth largest city in the Republic of Korea (ROK), with a population of around 500,000. However, it felt more like a small town than a large city, since it was behind Seoul and Pusan in the amenities the larger and more modern cities provided. I lived in a small inn near the center of town. My room was about the size of a large dining table (I could just about touch both side walls at the same time!) and, if I wanted to take a bath, I had to go down the street to the public bathhouse. I was provided delicious meals in my room (Kwangju was then, and still is, famous for its cuisine) but if I wanted to eat some chicken or beef I had to go to either a Chinese restaurant or to the one Western restaurant in town that was not located in a tourist hotel. Moreover, having grown up in Louisiana, where the weather is a lot warmer than it is in Korea,

Fig. 1.1 Don Baker drinking a cup of cheap Korean rice wine. Kwangju, Chŏlla Province, 1972. Photo by Michael Brady.

I was cold from October until around March or April. Wearing long johns day and night was how I survived.

I still remember a Korean Peace Corps staff member offering condolences as he informed me that I was being assigned to a hardship post far away from Seoul in the countryside—though Kwangju was then the capital of Chŏlla Namdo, one of South Korea's nine provinces. I also learned fairly quickly that many of the people in other parts of South Korea not only thought of Kwangju as akin to an undeveloped village in a remote mountain valley but also thought of the people of Kwangju as being much less sophisticated, much less educated, and even much less trustworthy than people elsewhere on the peninsula. On my first trip from Kwangju in the southwest to Pusan in the southeast, several months after I had arrived in Kwangju and begun to speak in the local dialect, I was asked by a merchant in a Pusan market where I had learned to talk Korean like that. When I replied that I lived and worked in Kwangju, he looked at me and, in a paternalistic tone, warned me to be careful because "everyone knew that Kwangju was full of thieves."

Despite the disdain I sometimes heard other Koreans express toward Kwangju and its inhabitants, I came to love that city and its people. The lady who ran the inn in which I lived treated me like a member of her family, even teasing me when I had a little too much to drink, and I began to look upon her as almost a second mother. Her nephew, who also lived in that inn so he

Fig. 1.2 Don Baker looking at Dongshin Middle School. Mount Mudŭng is in the background. Kwangju, South Chŏlla Province, 1972. Photo courtesy of Don Baker.

could attend a prestigious high school in Kwangju, treated me like his older brother. (We are still in frequent contact forty-nine years later, and he still calls me his older brother!) For my first two years in Kwangju, I taught English conversation at a middle-school and became drinking buddies with quite a few of the teachers there. My third year was spent working at the provincial Board of Education and traveling around Chŏlla Namdo Province to see how English conversation was being taught in the countryside. The English-language supervisor I traveled with also became a close friend (though I couldn't call him a friend because he was quite a few years older than me and the term "friend" is reserved in Korea for those who are close in age and status).

The personal connections my Peace Corps service in Kwangju provided—the people I lived and worked with—were the primary reason I decided to devote my life to studying Korea. I was so at home in Kwangju after three years that I was somewhat reluctant to leave. (One of my fellow Peace Corps volunteers from that time is still there, having retired a few years ago from teaching English at a South Korean university.) However, I realized that, if I wanted to become a scholar of Korea so that I could share my love of Korea with others, I needed to return to the United States and obtain a graduate degree. In 1974, I said goodbye to my friends in Kwangju, and to those who had become like family, and moved to Seattle to pursue graduate degrees in Korean history at the University of Washington.

At that time, I had no idea how much my connection to Kwangju would affect my academic stance, even though I brought a little bit of Kwangju back to the United States with me (I had married a Kwangju woman just before I left South Korea). I intended to take advantage of the fact that I already had some familiarity with classical Chinese to focus on premodern Korean history (that is why I chose to study under James Palais). Since I didn't plan to work on regional history, I didn't expect Kwangju to be in any way relevant to my future scholarly endeavors.

That changed in May 1980. After four years of coursework in Seattle, I returned to South Korea in late 1978 to do the research necessary to write a dissertation on the Confucian persecution of Korea's first Catholics in the late eighteenth century. Since most of the materials I needed, and the Korean scholars I needed to consult with, were in Seoul, I rented an apartment in Seoul, not Kwangju. Though I spent most of my time with my head in docu-

ments almost two centuries old, or in books and articles about those documents, I couldn't ignore what was happening around me in Seoul. I still
vividly remember the phone call from the US Embassy on the morning of
Saturday October 27, 1979, advising me to stay indoors because President
Park Chung Hee (Pak Chŏnghŭi, 1961–79) had been "incapacitated." (That
was how I learned Park Chung Hee had been assassinated.) I still can see in
my mind's eye the demonstrations that started on Seoul's campuses in April
1980, and then began spilling off campuses onto the streets of Seoul in early
May. What had begun as demands for campus autonomy had grown into
demands for an end to compulsory military training for male students and
finally—this is when the students took to the streets—grew into demands for
a free election to select a replacement for the late President Park.

Fig. 1.3 Don Baker and Confucian scholar outside of a Confucian academy (sŏwon)
somewhere in the countryside in South Chŏlla Province, 1973. Photo courtesy of
Don Baker.

Not wanting to miss the history that was happening all around me, I
sometimes shut my books and headed out onto the streets to watch what was
going on. That is why, late on the afternoon of May 15, 1980, I found myself
standing on the sidewalk of the Namdaemun rotary, on the other side from
the road that rose toward Mt. Namsan. A group of riot policemen, in what we
might now call "Darth Vader" uniforms, were pushing a group of demonstrating students up the hill in front of what was then the Tokyu Hotel.
Because of the police attempt to rid that area of demonstrators, there was no

traffic around Namdaemun at the time—until I noticed a city bus with no passengers coming from the southwest. It circled Namdaemun and then plowed into the group of unsuspecting riot policemen who had their backs to the rotary so they could face off against the demonstrators.

I saw what looked like five or six riot policemen fall. After it ran over them, the bus continued moving up the hill and then stopped. The demonstrators then pulled the driver off the bus and turned him over to the surviving policemen. However, they forgot to set the brake, and the bus rolled back down the hill toward the other side of the rotary where I was standing. It didn't hit any of the small group of us standing there, since we could see it coming. I then turned my attention back to where the policemen had fallen. I watched as five or six of them were picked up and thrown onto the back of a pickup truck and driven away. (It was definitely a pickup, not an ambulance.) Shaken up after watching what I thought was the killing of five or six defenseless men, I returned home. The next day I read in a newspaper that only one policeman had died there, and the other five were seriously wounded. (I also read that the driver had been arrested, and the authorities had discovered he was from Kwangju. I didn't see any news reports about him after that, so I don't know if he was put on trial for what he did.) Many years later I read then Ambassador William Gleysteen's account of his time in South Korea, and he also reported that "a policeman was killed when protestors [notice the plural] drove a truck into police lines."[1] I assume he was relying on US intelligence reports for that statement.

That was the first time I learned through personal experience something I had only been theoretically aware of before: primary sources such as eyewitness accounts cannot be trusted to give us an accurate account of what happened. I was sure several of those policemen were killed. They didn't appear to be alive when they were thrown onto the bed of that pick-up truck. Yet the press reported only one of them died. Did my eyes deceive me or was the press told, for some reason I can't understand, to downplay the actual number of those killed?

The press also reported that there were about 100,000 people demonstrating in downtown Seoul that day. I can't confirm that. I was too shaken up by watching people (or one person?) killed right in front of me that I could not stick around to watch any more of the protests that day. Instead, I left Namdaemun and returned to the books in my apartment. The next couple of days were much quieter, though the atmosphere was tense. On Sunday morning, May 18, suddenly everything changed. General Chun Doo-hwan (Chŏn Tuhwan) seized control of the government, suspended all political activity, shut down the parliament, and declared nationwide martial law. A few hours later violence broke out in Kwangju when Chun's martial law forces began violently suppressing the peaceful calls there for free elections.[2]

I was still in Seoul, so I didn't learn what was going on down south in Kwangju for a few days. Eventually, I was able to listen to short-wave radio broadcasts that reported that special forces troops were killing dozens of people there. Since I had in-laws living there at that time, as well as many close friends, I decided to check it out for myself to see if the people I knew were ok. To get to Kwangju, I had to go around the city, since the military was blocking all of the roads into Kwangju. I first went further south, to Haenam along the southwestern coast, spent the night there, and then the next morning caught a country bus that promised to get me within walking distance of Kwangju.

Since I didn't leave Haenam until May 27, shortly after Chun's army suppressed the uprising and seized the city of Kwangju, I cannot claim to be an actual eyewitness to the violence there. However, I saw plenty of evidence that violence had occurred. For example, on the way to Kwangju, as we passed an intersection near the town of Naju, I noticed some buses (they looked like highway buses) laying on their sides on the edge of the road. They looked like they had been on fire and maybe even shot at. Unfortunately, the bus I was on didn't stop, so I couldn't investigate to try to get a better idea of what had happened.[3]

To get into Kwangju, I had to hike over a mountain path, following some older ladies who were carrying rice into the cut-off city. (The army was still blocking the roads into Kwangju.) Once I got there, I checked on my family and friends, including a couple of Americans there—David Shaffer (who is still living there) and Linda Lewis who was there as a Fulbright-funded researcher—and found that everyone I checked on, including my former landlady and her nephew, had survived, though they were traumatized.[4] Soon after arriving, I began to hear stories about what had happened between May 18 and May 27, 1980, when Kwangju was under siege. I also saw evidence of how terrible those ten days had been in the eyes of the Kwangju people I talked with and in the traces of blood that could still be seen on downtown streets.

Some of what I personally witnessed remains as fresh in my mind as it did in 1980, and this fact makes it difficult for me to write about what Koreans now label the "May 18 Democratization Movement" in an unemotional, objective manner. For example, I will never forget seeing the long line of grandmother-aged women waiting to enter a downtown gymnasium to see if they could locate their grandson or granddaughter among the many corpses awaiting identification there. Nor can I forget seeing a mother chasing a coffin that was being carried away to a make-shift cemetery on the outskirts of town. As she was running behind the coffin, she was crying out "don't leave me, son!" I was told by her neighbors that he had been attending college in Seoul and had returned home when Chun Doo-hwan closed all the colleges there, only to be shot and killed by Chun's troops because they suspected he might be part of the armed resistance a few Kwangjuites had mounted.

I wasn't able to confirm whether what I was told about how that young man in the coffin had died was accurate or not. Nor was I able to confirm most of the other stories that were related to me as first-person accounts or as accurate retellings of eyewitness accounts. One such unconfirmed story I heard was that a few busloads of students from Seoul had tried to reach Kwangju to join the uprising, but had been stopped by the military near Naju and killed. I have never seen this story confirmed in any of the published reports on the May 18th Uprising so it may have simply been a rumor started by people who saw the buses that I saw. It's hard to believe that such a deadly incident would not have been mentioned once it became legal to talk about what really happened in May of that year. But that still raises the question: why were those buses on their side by that intersection? And why did they appear to have been burnt and possibly shot at? I am still hoping to find some reliable primary sources which can clear up that mystery for me. One informant, who works for the May 18 Memorial Foundation in Kwangju, told me in a personal communication recently that there definitely were deaths at that intersection near Naju where I saw those buses. He said at least seven young people were killed, but he did not, or could not, tell me if they were students from Seoul. Nor did he provide any details about how those young people died.[5]

While I was in Kwangju, I also heard the tragic story of the "young lady in the sound truck." I was told by several people that on May 27 at 4:30 in the morning, as the army was beginning its final assault on Kwangju, a sound truck had driven through the city with the voice of a young woman coming out of the loudspeaker on its roof calling for the people of Kwangju to come to the Provincial Office Building (which had become the headquarters of the armed resistance) to "save the students." However, according to the story, the voice had stopped suddenly, which meant that the army had shot at that truck and killed her. I believed what I was told and repeated that story many times over the years that followed—until I found out that it wasn't true.

Around twenty years ago, I was visiting a friend who was teaching at Andong University. He knew my Kwangju connection and asked me if I wanted to go with him to a bar that was run by a woman originally from Kwangju. I said yes, of course, and off we went. When we got there, the middle-aged lady who owned the bar greeted me in the Kwangju dialect. As we drank her makkŏlli, she remarked that she had heard that I believed the young woman in the sound truck had been killed. I replied that was what I had been told. She then informed me that, yes, there had been a woman in a sound truck that morning trying to rally the citizens of Kwangju to defend the citizen's militia. And, yes, the army had forced her to stop mid-broadcast. However, she was not killed. The proprietor confided that she knew she had survived because they had spent five years in jail together in the aftermath of the Kwangju Uprising. Moreover, she told me that, like her, that lady had not returned to Kwangju after she was released from prison and instead lived in another part of the country, where few knew of her radical past. That is why many people in Kwangju still don't know she survived.

At the risk of overdoing it, let me give another example of first-person testimony that is not necessarily reliable. Lee Jae-eui, who was in Kwangju during those bloody days in May, writes that the violence began Sunday morning when special forces troops charged the two hundred or so demonstrators who had gathered that morning at the front gates of Chŏnnam University to protest martial law. According to Lee, those soldiers used clubs to beat many of those students into unconsciousness.[6] Linda Lewis was also in Kwangju that day. However, in her published account of what happens, she states that the uprising began when about two hundred college students marched Sunday morning to the Provincial Office Building in central Kwangju and were attacked at first by riot police using nothing worse than tear gas.[7] Neither Lee nor Lewis were at the front gate of Chŏnnam University that morning. Nor were they in front of the Provincial Office Building that morning. However, they both recounted what they had heard about what happened from people who were there (or from people who had heard from people who had heard from people who were there). Both accounts, therefore, should count as primary sources. Yet these accounts contradict each other, which is not uncommon with primary sources. (That is why careful journalists try to have more than one source for a story.)

What does what happened in Kwangju in May 1980 have to do with the impact of the Peace Corps on Korean Studies in North America? I would not have gotten this close to the Kwangju Uprising, and would not be so concerned about what really happened, if the Peace Corps had not sent me to Kwangju in 1971. If I had not seen what I saw in Seoul on May 15, 1980, and had not then gone down to Kwangju on May 27, I would not have learned first-hand how difficult it is to get an objective and accurate grasp of history. After all, I was an eyewitness to the May 15 killing(s) and, I talked with eyewitnesses in Kwangju right after the incident was over. However, I can't trust what people told me, and I can't even trust my own eyes.

The connection I forged with Kwangju thanks to the Peace Corps has made me a much more skeptical—and hopefully more careful—historian, more aware of how tentative the conclusions are that we draw about the past. The short time I spent in Kwangju in the immediate aftermath of the ten days of violence there did more than merely wake me to that fact that eyewitness accounts are not always reliable. I also learned how messy history is, how difficult it can be to get a clear picture of what happened no matter how hard we try to learn the details of what transpired. I also learned that it is impossible for me to convey, either orally or in writing, the complexity of what happened that month in South Korea. The only way to make sense of what happened, to myself and to others, is to simplify it. My experiences in Seoul and Kwangju showed me that if we want to draw a coherent picture of a historical event, if we want to construct a coherent narrative, we have to leave out some details, overlook some discrepancies, and even downplay inconsistencies in first-person accounts. As much as I—as a historian who strives for objectivity—hate to admit it, telling the truth sometimes requires us to refrain from telling the whole truth since it may be too complicated for readers to grasp.

Even if historians could get all the details right about a traumatic incident such as the Kwangju Uprising on May 18, we still cannot reproduce what it was like to actually live through such an event. Filmmakers, screenwriters, and fiction authors do a much better job of letting readers know what it is like to exist inside an important historical moment than a dry historical account can. The most realistic and accurate portrayals of what it was like in Kwangju that May in 1980 are not narratives authored by historians but rather the play *Owŏl sinbu* (May bride), which I saw performed in Seoul in 1980, and the novel *Sonyŏni onda* (*Human Acts: A Novel*), by the acclaimed author Han Kang.[8]

Fiction cannot be relied upon to tell us *why* things actually happened, of course. That is the job of historians. However, in trying to determine the cause of a traumatic event, academic historians often run the risk of designating certain people as victims and others as villains (though we are reluctant to use such value-laden terms). Such black-and-white academic portrayals make it easier to construct a coherent narrative and explanation of an event, but they overlook the murkiness of what it was like to live through a traumatizing incident.

Fiction, on the other hand, since it can provide a way for us to look into the minds of individuals, can offer a more accurate account of what it was like to experience an important historical event. Fiction can show us, in ways it is difficult for academic historians to accomplish, how people caught up in traumatic and emotionally or physically disturbing events are often not clear about what is going on at the time and therefore are not sure what they should do or what role they should play. They may do something that in retrospect looks quite heroic, though they were simply acting instinctively at the time, or they may end up acting in a way that appears cowardly when recalled days or years later, though again they may have been acting without thinking. It is popular these days for people living in Kwangju, especially those who were not there in 1980, to praise the people in the city at that time as brave fighters for democracy who all came together to form an absolute community, in which individual self-interest was put aside so they could join together in the struggle against Chun Doo-hwan's coup.[9]

However, this was not what was conveyed to me when I talked with people in Kwangju in the days immediately after the fighting in the streets had ended. There was a strong sense of community, born from having shared a terrible experience, but I didn't hear much about fighting for democracy. The people I talked to told me that their primary concern was survival.

Experiencing Kwangju both while in the Peace Corps and after the Kwangju Incident in May 1980, taught me to be more careful in how I use data from the past, even eyewitness accounts. Hopefully that caution is reflected in my recent translation of a first-person account of the anti-Catholic persecution of 1801.[10] These experiences have also provoked me to question what exactly historians mean when we talk about an historical narrative being "objective." In recent years, historians have come to realize how difficult it is to separate objectivity from subjectivity in history-writing. For example, Tessa Morris-Suzuki argues that "historical truthfulness is something that is expressed (more or less fully) through a series of relationships between participants in historical events, the people involved in recording and representing the events, and the people who consume the accounts that are subsequently produced."[11] Dominick LaCapra made a similar point in "History, Language, and Reading: Waiting for Crillon," when he calls for a "dialogic reading" of the material used to narrate and explain the past.[12]

Since I still feel unable to produce an "objective" account of what happened in Kwangju forty years ago, I am still grappling, even after more than forty years working as an historian, with what objectivity means in history writing. Is it our job as historians simply to produce at best a *plausible* account of what happened and why it happened, or should we raise the bar a little higher and strive for *probability*? Is a claim to objectivity always tentative, in that it is merely a prediction that our narrative will be confirmed later by as yet uncovered data? Maybe someone someday will discover documents that will tell us exactly why an order to shoot unarmed demonstrators in Kwangju was given, and who gave that order. In turn, those documents might then either confirm or refute what historians have said about why those killings happened. Can a historical narrative qualify as an objective account if it is not contradicted by the evidence available to us and others at the present time? Should we be modest in our definition of "objectivity," and thus bring objectivity within reach, by saying that it means nothing more than that other scholars are likely to reach similar conclusions if they ask the same questions of the same data?

These are questions I may have asked myself anyway in the course of trying to make sense of the past from the limited number of documents that are available to answer any historical inquiry. However, these questions are made more urgent by my connection to Kwangju and my need to find out what "really" happened there.

One thing that has become clear to me when reading what other scholars have written about May 18–27, 1980, is that to understand what any historian is trying to say we need to understand the question that the historian is trying to answer. Not every account of May 18 is directed toward the question that motivates me. I want to know "why Kwangju?" why were the people of that city, whom I had come to known so well thanks to the Peace Corps, singled out for such brutality. Other scholars focus on why the paratroopers acted the way they did, or why the people of Kwangju resisted the brutality the way they did. In recognizing that different people bring different questions to the same data, I have had to admit that I do the same thing, and that any claim of objectivity is compromised by the fact that the question leads me to overlook, or at least pay insufficient attention to, some other important bits of data.[13]

How should we try to explain important historical events, such as the May 18 Uprising? Can we suggest that it was predictable, given the way the Kwangju region had begun falling economically behind the southeast under the policies of Park Chung Hee? The people I talked to in Kwangju in May 1980 didn't appear to feel that what happened on May 18, 1980, was inevitable. Such violence definitely did not feel foreseeable to me when I lived there from 1971 to 1974.

Another possibility is to try to determine the intentions of the people in Kwangju—did the uprising break out because a few radicals had planned for it in advance? Even if there were such radicals, it appears unlikely they alone could have been responsible for nearly the entire city rising up. The people I talked to didn't talk about trying to bring about a revolutionary transformation of government and society. They were just trying to stay alive.

A third possible way to explain the May 18 Uprising is to ask why it only happened in Kwangju. The popularity of Kim Dae-jung (Kim Taejung, 1998–2003) is one possible explanation, but no one told me they were fighting for Kim Dae-jung (though I'm sure some of the protestors were driven to protest in the beginning by their anger over his arrest by Chun Doo-hwan on May 17). Or Kwangju may have been singled out because the people of Kwangju had been consistently discriminated against by many people in other parts of South Korea. That hypothesis gains some support from the many reports I heard that the troops who perpetrated the worse violence spoke in the dialect of Korea's southeastern Kyŏngsang Namdo Province, a traditional rival of the

Chŏlla Namdo region. But this rivalry existed long before 1980 and continues to this day. Regional rivalry alone, therefore, cannot explain why horrendous violence erupted in May 1980, and only in May 1980. I had never seen before, and have never seen since, the animosity between peoples of Chŏlla and Kyŏngsang result in anyone resorting to physical violence solely because they did not like where another person came from.

None of these possible explanations fit into my own personal experience, so how do I try to explain why the May 18 Uprising happened? Do I give up and say, "it just happened"? Do I blame Chun and his co-conspirators, who apparently deliberately left most of the student leaders in Kwangju alone even though they arrested student leaders in Seoul, Pusan, and other cities? Could they have wanted to provoke an incident in Kwangju to provide a pretext for arresting and executing Kim Dae-jung? This is a plausible hypothesis, but there is no solid proof that was the government's original intention.

The May 18 Uprising and my Peace Corps connection to the city in which it occurred, therefore, forces me to recognize the limits of my ability as a historian to explain historical events, suggesting that it is much easier to explain specific incidents in the past if we have not experienced them ourselves and therefore are less reluctant to oversimplify.[14]

That noted, personal experience can provide information we can use to invalidate some hypotheses, such as the suggestion that the May 18 Uprising was caused by three hundred North Korean soldiers who had managed to sneak into Kwangju that month and ferment the protests that began on May 18.[15] Since there is no documentary evidence to support such a claim—no North Korean bodies were identified among the hundreds killed that May, and no one in Kwangju said anything to me about seeing or hearing any North Koreans—we can confidently throw that rumor out as complete nonsense.

Perhaps if we combine first-hand accounts with the documentary record, both government and military records and records from hospitals and other sources in Kwangju at the time, we can come closer to an accurate narrative of what happened.[16] But exactly how close can we come? And does it matter if our account is incomplete and therefore somewhat misleading? Is it acceptable if our account presents nothing more than a probable narrative and explanation—a narrative that not only helps later generations understand what a tragedy May 18 was but may also inspire people to make sure such a tragedy never happens again?[17]

Normally, I deal with events too far in the past for me or anyone I know to have personal knowledge of what happened. For example, there is no one alive today who can tell me about their personal experience with the anti-Catholic persecution of 1801. Although I have always been aware of deficiencies in the accuracy, precision, and completeness of what I write about that persecution, that awareness is more of an intellectual awareness than a gut

Fig. 1.4 Don Baker (front) participating in a Confucian ritual honoring the Korean Confucian sages of old. This was an event held in Andong, North Kyŏngsang Province as part of the Twenty-First–Century Human Value Forum in July 2014, sponsored by Andong University and the Center for Advanced Korean Studies. Photo courtesy of Don Baker.

feeling based on personal experience. If it were not for the connection I forged with the people of Kwangju thanks to Peace Corps, I would not be as acutely aware of how unreachable the historian's goal of objectivity really is.

My memories and my close ties with the people of Kwangju create emotional baggage that make it difficult for me to write about May 18 in an "objective" manner that will convince readers that I am letting the facts speak for themselves (which, of course, facts never do). It is much easier to adopt the historian's favored dispassionate stance when writing about the Chosŏn Dynasty, since I have no personal connection with what happened there. Thanks to the influence Kwangju and May 18 have had on me, however, and thanks to the constant reminders Kwangju has given me over the years about the unreliability of even first-person accounts, I believe I have grown more careful in the historical narratives I construct and the claims I make and therefore have come closer to being more "objective" than I would be otherwise.

The personal connection the Peace Corps gave me when they sent me to Kwangju and having been witness to one of the most important events in modern South Korean history has also broadened the areas within the field of history I have developed a professional interest in. I still tend to focus on traditional philosophy and religious change. However, because of my inability to trust my own memories of that traumatic event, I have become more interested in questions of memory and trauma. That is why for many years I taught a graduate seminar at the University of British Columbia on the reproduction (though histories, fiction, film, and art) of traumatic events in modern Asian history. That seminar always began with a discussion of the May 18 Uprising and how it has been remembered and reproduced in political discourse as well as in literature and film. Using that as a starting point for discussions of how memory and history can sometimes be in conflict, and how both history and memory change with growing temporal distance from the events under examination, the seminar moved on to discuss other instances of contested memories and histories. We looked at first-person accounts and then literary and cinematic depictions of other tragic events such as the bombing of Hiroshima, the Nanjing Massacre, and the Partition of India. The students often told me at the end of that seminar that it had changed the way they thought about history. In particular, they gained a better understanding of why historical narratives are never encased in concrete but are constantly open to challenges.

Having encountered over the years the many different ways the events of May 1980 have been portrayed, I have developed a broader interest in historiography and in how and why different histories are constructed. That is why I published a short survey of history-writing during the Chosŏn Dynasty a few years ago.[18] Without the need to grapple with my own awareness of conflicts between my own memories and what sources report about the events I was a partial eyewitness to, I doubt I would have paid as much attention to how historians pick and choose not only which events to focus on in their narratives of the past but also how they both portray the unfolding of those events and identify their causes and impacts. I am not claiming to be a great historian or even a better-than-average one. However, I am convinced that I would be a worse historian if Kwangju had not taught me to be careful in how much trust I place in my sources.

Fig. 1.5 Don Baker in 2009 at the place where Tasan Chŏng Yagyong (1762–1836) lived when he was in exile in Kangjin, South Chŏlla Province. Tasan has been the subject of Don's academic research for over forty years. Photo courtesy of Don Baker.

It is clear to me, and I hope it is clear to you as well now that I have shared my memories and reflections with you, that I owe a lot to the people of Kwangju. I owe them for the way they introduced Korea to me in early 1970s. They inspired me to dedicate my life to studying and teaching Korean history, and I owe them for the bravery they showed in resisting Chun Doo-hwan's coup in 1980. Because their actions, and the way they and others have interpreted them, I have been forced me to think more deeply about what it means to be a historian. I therefore have to also say thank you to the Peace Corps for sending me to Kwangju forty-nine years ago. Kwangju and the Peace Corps gave me my career, and gave my career more meaning, and for that I will always be grateful.

NOTES

1. William H. Gleysteen, *Massive Entanglement, Marginal Influence: Carter and Korea in Crisis* (Washington, DC: Brookings Institute, 1999), 120.

2. One of the best English-language accounts of what happened in Kwangju in May 1980, is Jae-eui Lee, *Gwangju Diary: Beyond Death, Beyond the Darkness of the Age*, translated by Kap Su Seol and Nick Mamatas (Kwangju: May 18 Memorial Foundation, 2017).

3. I wasn't the only one who saw those buses. Paul Courtright, a Peace Corps volunteer at the time, also saw them. See Bo-gyung Kim, "Former Peace Corps Member Courtright Recollects Gwangju Uprising," *Korea Herald* May 13, 2019. www.koreaherald.com/view.php?Ud=20190512000161.

4. Linda Lewis, "At the Border: Women, Anthropology, and North Korea," in *Peace Corps Volunteers and the Making of Korean Studies in the United States*, edited by Seung-kyung Kim and Michael Robinson, 127–40 (Seattle: University of Washington Center for Korea Studies, 2020).

5. May 18 Memorial Foundation employee, email message to author, June 3, 2018.

6. Jae-eui Lee, *Gwangju Diary*, 42–43.

7. Linda Lewis, *Laying Claim to the Memory of May: A Look Back at the 1980 Kwangju Uprising* (Honolulu: University of Hawai'i Press, 2002), 3.

8. A brief description of the play can be found in my chapter "Victims and Heroes: Competing Visions of May 18," in *Contentious Kwangju: The May 18 Uprising in Korea's Past and Present*, edited by Gi-wook Shin and Kyung Moon Hwang (Lanham, MD: Rowman and Littlefield, 2003), 97–98; and Han Kang, *Human Acts: A Novel*, translated by Deborah Smith (London: Portobello Books, 2014).

9. For example, see Choi Jungwoon, "The Kwangju People's Uprising: Formation of the 'Absolute Community,'" *Korea Journal* 39, no. 2 (Summer 1999), 238–82. The same issue includes a useful correction to that view, Kim Doo-sik, "'Meaning Construction' of the Kwangju Pro-Democracy Movement and Futuristic Frame," 205–37.

10. Don Baker and Franklin Rausch, *Catholics and Anti-Catholicism in Late Chosŏn Korea* (Honolulu: University of Hawai'i Press, 2017). This text is an analysis and translation of the *Hwang Sayŏng paeksŏ* (Silk letter of Hwang Sayŏng). Hwang Sayŏng was an eyewitness to the anti-Catholic persecution of 1801.

11. Tessa Morris-Suzuki, *The Past Within Us: Media, Memory, History* (New York: Verso, 2005), 237.

12. Dominick LaCapra, "History, Language, and Reading: Waiting for Crillon," *American Historical Review* 100, no. 3 (June, 1995): 824–28, https://doi.org/10.1086/ahr/100.3.799.

13. I also need to occasionally remind myself that it is nearly impossible to be apolitical, and therefore "objective" in dealing with recent history. As Harman Paul notes in his recent work *Key Issues in Historical Theory*, "Historians therefore need not wonder whether they want to be politically involved: the questions rather is which political aims they serve." Harman Paul, *Key Issues in Historical Theory* (New York: Routledge, 2015), 78. Statements about the recent past always reflect on the present and therefore always have political implications.

14. Recently scholars of history have begun to ask how much weight they should give to memory vis-a-vis written documents in narrating modern history. See, for example, Dominick LaCapra, "Trauma, History, Memory, Identity: What Remains?" *History and Theory* 55, no. 3 (October 2016), 375–400, https://doi.org/10.1111/hith.10817.

15. Kim Taeryŏng [Daniel Kim], *Yŏksa rosŏ ŭi 5.18: 5.18 chaep'an pŏmni ŭi mosun* [Looking at May 18 in historical perspective: Legal contradictions in the trials related to the May 18 incident] (Sŏul: Pibong Books, 2013). A similar claim can be found in a recently published primary document, Chun Doo-hwan, *Chun Tu-hwan hoegorok I* [The memoirs of Chun Tu-hwan, vol. I] (Sŏul: Chajak namusŭp, 2017), 535. A particularly vocal advocate of the assertion that many of the Kwangju citizens who appear in photos taken in May 1980, were actually North Korean special forces soldiers in disguise is Chi Manwŏn. He defends that claim in *The Lonely Seeker in the Fog* (Seoul: System Publishing, 2018).

16. The 5.18 Memorial Foundation (5.18 kinyŏm chaedan) published several volumes of first-person accounts in the *5.18 ŭi kiŏk kwa yŏksa* [Memories and history of 5.18] series. The series is available on the 518 Memorial Foundation [5.18 kinyŏm chaedan] website, http://www.518.org/sub.php?PID=0404, date accessed August 27, 2019. A recent publication of first-person accounts by medical personnel who treated many of those injured over the course of those ten days is also valuable. No Sŏngman and twenty-nine others, *5.18 sibilgan ŭi yajŏn pyŏngwŏn* [A field hospital over the ten days starting May 18], (Kwangju: Chŏnnam Taehak Pyŏngwŏn, 2017).

17. Paul Ricoeur's *Memory, History, Forgetting* (Chicago: University of Chicago Press, 2004) provides a sophisticated argument that history is constructed, not found, and that therefore there is an unresolvable competition between history and memory. Stanley Cohen's *States of Denial: Knowing about Atrocities and Suffering* (Malden, MA: Blackwell, 2001) examines the particular difficulties we face when we try to understand, and either explain or explain away, particularly egregious examples of the inhumanity of humanity.

18. Don Baker, "Writing History in Korea, 1400–1800," *Oxford History of Historical Writing* (New York: Oxford University Press, 2012), 103–18.

BIBLIOGRAPHY

Baker, Don. "Victims and Heroes: Competing Visions of May 18." In *Contentious Kwangju: The May 18 Uprising in Korea's Past and Present*, edited by Gi-wook Shin and Kyung Moon Hwang, 87–107. Lanham, MD: Rowman and Littlefield, 2003.

Baker, Don. "Writing History in Korea, 1400–1800." *Oxford History of Historical Writing Volume 3*: 400–1800, edited by Jose Rabasa, Masayuki Sato, and Edordo Tortarolo, 103–18. New York: Oxford University Press, 2012.

Baker, Don, and Franklin Rausch. *Catholics and Anti-Catholicism in Late Chosŏn Korea.* Honolulu: University of Hawai'i Press, 2017.

Chi Manwŏn. *The Lonely Seeker in the Fog*. Seoul: System Publishing, 2018.

Choi, Jungwoon. "The Kwangju People's Uprising: Formation of the 'Absolute Community.'" *Korea Journal* 39, no. 2 (Summer, 1999): 238–82.

Chun Doo-hwan [Chun Tuhwan]. *Chun Tuhwan hoegorok I* [The memoirs of Chun Doo-hwan, vol. I]. Sŏul: Chajak namusŭp, 2017.

Cohen, Stanley. *States of Denial: Knowing about Atrocities and Suffering*. Malden, MA: Blackwell, 2001.

Gleysteen, William H. *Massive Entanglement, Marginal Influence: Carter and Korea in Crisis*. Washington, DC: Brookings Institute, 1999.

Han, Kang. *Human Acts: A Novel*. Translated by Deborah Smith. London, UK: Portobello Books, 2014.

Kim, Bo-gyung. "Former Peace Corps Member Courtright Recollects Gwangju Uprising." *Korea Herald* May 13, 2019. http://www.koreaherald.com/view. php?ud=20190512000161.

Kim, Daniel. *See* Kim Taeryŏng

Kim, Doo-sik. "'Meaning Construction' of the Kwangju Pro-Democracy Movement and Futuristic Frame." *Korea Journal* 39, no. 2. (Summer, 1999): 205–37.

Kim Taeryŏng [Kim, Daniel]. *Yŏksa rosŏ ŭi 5.18: 5.18 chaep'an pŏmni ŭi mosun* [Looking at May 18 in historical perspective: Legal contradictions in the trials related to the May 18 incident]. Sŏul: Pibong Books, 2013.

LaCapra, Dominick. "History, Language, and Reading: Waiting for Crillon." *American Historical Review* 100, no. 3 (June 1995): 799–28. https://doi.org/10.1086/ahr/100.3.799.

LaCapra, Dominick. "Trauma, History, Memory, Identity: What Remains?" *History and Theory* 55, no. 3 (October 2016): 375–400. https://doi.org/10.1111/hith.10817.

Lee, Jae-eui. *Gwangju Diary: Beyond Death, Beyond the Darkness of the Age*. Translated by Kap Su Seol and Nick Mamatas. Kwangju: May 18 Memorial Foundation, 2017.

Lewis, Linda. *Laying Claim to the Memory of May: A Look Back at the 1980 Kwangju Uprising.* Honolulu: University of Hawai'i Press, 2002.

Lewis, Linda. "At the Border: Women, Anthropology, and North Korea." In *Peace Corps Volunteers and the Making of Korean Studies in the United States,* edited by Seung-kyung Kim and Michael Robinson, 127–40. Seattle: University of Washington Center for Korea Studies, 2020.

Morris-Suzuki, Tessa. *The Past Within Us: Media, Memory, History.* New York: Verso, 2005.

No Sŏngman, et al. 5.18 *sibilgan ŭi yajŏn pyŏngwŏn* [A field hospital over the ten days starting May 18]. Kwangju: Chŏnnam Taehak Pyŏngwŏn, 2017.

Paul, Harman. *Key Issues in Historical Theory.* New York: Routledge, 2015.

Oilp'al kinyŏm chaedan [5.18 Memorial Foundation]. 5.18 *ŭi kiŏk kwa yŏksa* [Memories and history of 5.18]. http://www.518.org/sub.php?PID=0404. Accessed August 27, 2019.

Ricoeur, Paul. *Memory, History, Forgetting.* Chicago: University of Chicago Press, 2004.

2

How the Peace Corps Changed Our Lives

EDWARD J. BAKER

In the spring of 1966, during my second year at Yale Law School, my wife Diane and I decided it was time for a break. We thought that we would like to do something really different and interesting that might, at the same time, contribute in some small way to international understanding and peace. The intensifying war in Vietnam was a daily reminder of how badly the world needed more understanding among peoples. The Peace Corps sounded promising, having been established in 1961 "to promote world peace and friendship which shall make available to interested countries and areas men and women of the United States qualified for service abroad and willing to serve, under conditions of hardship if necessary, to help the peoples of such countries and areas in meeting their needs for trained manpower and to help promote a better understanding of the American people on the part of the peoples served and a better understanding of other peoples on the part of the American people."[1]

Having applied, taken the test, and passed, we specified that we were interested in being assigned—in descending order of preference—to a country in Africa, Latin America, or Asia. Nevertheless, we were offered and accepted a program teaching English in Thailand, but that was soon cancelled. After a brief wait, we were offered a program teaching English in South Korea. Although we knew nothing about Korea except that the United States had fought a war there and that the winters were cold, we decided to accept the offer and began to read about Korea and to prepare to take off for training in Hilo, Hawai'i.

Being country bumpkins from small towns in Maine, Hawai'i was a revelation. The climate, vegetation, food, and people were all very different from what we were accustomed to. Hawai'i is, of course, also very different from South Korea, but the total change of scenery was useful conditioning for living in South Korea where the change would be even more extreme. By the end of the three-month training program, we knew a bit more about South Korea, a little Korean language, and a smattering about teaching English as a second language. Nevertheless, we thought we were ready. We were excited but uncertain of what lay ahead.

I was assigned to the English Department in the College of Education (COE) at Seoul National University, which at that time was located on a small separate campus in the eastern part of the city. My colleagues were mostly young professional linguists and literature specialists with American master's degrees, on their way to obtaining their PhDs. They took me in and made me feel welcome, as did my students, who were younger, but not that much younger, than I was. Being a foreigner with rudimentary Korean, I was of course outside the system, but that also meant that I could participate in the social activities of both the teachers and the students without being a full member of either group. South Korea was a very poor and rather authoritarian place at that time, but I was immediately struck by the energy and dili-

Fig. 2.1 Ed and Diane Baker on a picnic with College of Education faculty and students at T'aerŭng, a royal tomb in northeastern Seoul, South Korea, in the fall of 1967. Photo courtesy of Ed Baker.

gence of the people and the intelligence and democratic ideals of my colleagues and students. It seemed clear to me from the beginning that South Korea would one day be a prosperous, democratic country. Diane was assigned to the high school attached to the COE, located just inside of Tongdaemun (East Gate).

Diane's school placed us with a family that had a daughter in the high school. The house, a newly built, not-quite-finished, "Western-style" house, was located in a redeveloping neighborhood. From our bedroom we had a view of nearby, shabby, older houses, shops, and a hillside of shacks that had no electricity or running water. There was poverty in Maine for sure, but this was on a different level—the South Korean national per capita income hovered around $100 per year.

The family was prosperous, with a shop and a small sweater factory in P'yŏnghwa Sijang (Peace Market). They were an extended, merchant family from Kaesong, a city located just over the Demilitarized Zone (DMZ) in North

Fig. 2.2 Diane and Ed Baker with Diane's high school students at Kyŏngbokkung, a royal palace in Seoul, South Korea, autumn 1966. Photo courtesy of Ed Baker.

Korea. Eventually we learned that the father had grown tired of the suspicion and surveillance he endured because of his northern origins and had gone back to the north when the opportunity presented itself during the war. Although the house was new and plumbed for hot water and ondol heat to warm the floors, neither worked all that well. We were soon introduced to the public bathhouse and in the winter had to purchase a kerosene space heater. Being from Maine, we were familiar with long underwear and had worn it for outdoor activities at home, although we soon realized that because of the lack of central heating in South Korea we would need to wear it all winter, indoors and out, especially while teaching in our frigid classrooms. Although we bonded with the daughter who was Diane's student, the rest of the family remained reserved and distant, and by the end of the first year everyone realized it was time for us to move.

The second family had two children in high school—a boy in the third year and a girl in the first—and another boy in the sixth grade of primary school. They lived in a traditional, Korean-style house. We lived in a room next to the front gate. The father owned a wholesale chemical shop in the Namdaemun Sijang (South Gate Market). They too were prosperous, but apparently not as well off as the first family.

The very welcoming atmosphere in this family was completely different. We all ate together, sitting on the floor around a common table. The head of the household—an older man we called "Father," who had been born before the Japanese Colonial Period, had both a traditional, Chinese classics–based education and had graduated from Kyŏnggi Middle School, the best school in Korea during the Japanese occupation. He was a thoughtful, intelligent person skilled at making the most of our still limited Korean. We learned a lot of the language and a lot about Korea from these dinner table conversations. Mother was much younger. She was a warm, kindly country woman and a great cook who gardened avidly until the end of her long life in 2012.

We have remained in close contact with this family over the years. The younger son has celebrated his sixtieth birthday and is a grandfather. We know their children's children, and they know our children and grandchildren. We often visit them in South Korea, and they have visited us in Boston. Our ties with them and those with other Korean friends made through the years are important reasons why we remain so attached to Korea after more than fifty years.

Because of my interests, I often discussed history, politics, and law with both my colleagues and my students. My colleagues, although not activists, were quite critical of President Park Chung Hee's government (Pak Chŏnghŭi, 1961–79). My students, in the time-honored tradition of Korean students, felt an obligation to demonstrate against any and all governmental repression or corruption. University and high school students had risen up and overthrown the Syngman Rhee (Yi Sungman, 1948–60) government only six years earlier during the April 19, 1960 Student Revolution, and their example was very much on the minds of my university students. We would occasionally visit the 4.19 Memorial Cemetery, a memorial graveyard commemorating the uprising that was located nearby in the northeastern part of the city, with the students on weekend hikes.

In the summer of 1967, the Korean Central Intelligence Agency (KCIA) announced the so-called East Berlin Spy Case. Officials arrested more than 150 people who were studying or had studied in Europe. The most well-known was the composer Yun I-sang who, along with a number of others, had been kidnapped from Germany, brought back to South Korea, and tried for espionage. Having read about the announcement in the English-language Korean press over breakfast, I went to school and dropped in at the office of the head of the English department. Professor Chang asked me to step out into the hallway where he pointed at the name on the door of the adjacent office and asked me if I knew the occupant, Professor Ch'un, who taught French literature. When I replied that I did not, he motioned me back into his office where he announced quietly, "He's the bright young star of the French Department, and he has been arrested in the East Berlin Spy Case." Chang did not pronounce Ch'un innocent but gave me the clear impression that he was skeptical about the charge. Of course, this case was the talk of the entire COE and stimulated my awakening to the role of the KCIA in South Korean life.

During our second Peace Corps year, 1967, I was reclassified by my draft board and faced the possibility of being conscripted into the Vietnam War at any time. Sargent Shriver, the director of the Peace Corps, and Kevin O'Donnell, the Korean country director, anxious not to lose their volunteers, tried in vain to get the draft board to reconsider, but it refused. At the same time, Diane and I began to consider starting a family. As I thought about the prospect of being sent to fight in Vietnam, I made up my mind that I would go to prison first. As my resolve hardened, I decided to submit a conscientious objector petition. My petition seemed unlikely to be accepted because I was not raised in a religion that opposed all war, and if my country or loved ones were attacked, I would join the fight to defend them.

Before we knew it, our Peace Corps service was drawing to a close and, having already concluded that we wanted to extend our Korean experience, we searched for other ways to stay. In the end, the Fulbright Commission offered me a two-year position. The first year would, in effect, be an extension of my Peace Corps service; I continued to teach at the COE and added classes at the Hankuk University of Foreign Studies. During the second year, I worked in the Fulbright Office counseling people who were interested in applying for graduate study in the United States. Soon thereafter, on a short trip home, my draft board, ignoring my conscientious objector petition, informed me that I had again been deferred. Greatly relieved, we returned to Seoul to take up our new jobs and prepare for parenthood. With the help of Fulbright, we were able to place a key money deposit on a small house near Hanguk University where I would soon be teaching.[2] We settled down to work and awaited the birth of our first child who turned out to be a son born in January 1969 at Severance Hospital.

During the spring and summer of 1969, as rumors spread that Park Chung Hee was planning to amend the constitution so that he could run for a third term (or even perhaps three more terms), the students at the COE and other universities began to demonstrate daily and to confront riot police on the street in front of the campus. The riot police fired a lot of tear gas, and we all had to learn to deal with it. At that time, when the students ran into the campus and closed the gates, the riot police did not follow them in. Soon I noticed that the riot police were arriving daily in the COE neighborhood and at nearby Korea University in brand new trucks emblazoned with the USAID emblem of hands shaking in front of the US shield on the doors. Until I saw those trucks, I had confined myself to observing the actions and discussing them with my students, but seeing these trucks led me to conclude that, as a US citizen, I had a right and an obligation to address my own government. The sense that I needed to try to stop my government from supporting the South Korean dictatorship became a principal motivating factor for me from then on.

During the summer of 1969, an American missionary called a meeting at his home for Americans concerned about the apparent US support of the

South Korean government's plans to amend the constitution. Fifty or sixty people, mostly Christian missionaries with a scattering of Fulbrighters, former Peace Corps volunteers, and other expatriates, gathered to discuss the issue. The position of the US Embassy was that this was a South Korean domestic political matter upon which the United States took no stand. Most of the group felt strongly that, in light of the degree of involvement of the United States in South Korea, saying nothing on the matter amounted to supporting the South Korean government's actions, particularly in light of the fact that the riot police were being ferried daily to the university demonstrations in new trucks conspicuously marked with an official US government emblem indicating that they were a gift from the American people to the South Korean people. In the course of several meetings we composed a petition to the US government arguing that the United States should make it clear that it disapproved of the constitutional amendment. The next question was whether we should sign it with our own names. Most members of the group felt they should not sign their names on the petition because doing so would bring their Korean colleagues to the attention of the South Korean government with potentially harmful results. It did not occur to any of us to think that there was any possibility that the US embassy would protect our names and not give them to the Republic of Korea (ROK) government. In the end five of us signed the letter as the steering committee of "The Group of 50." The signers included Rev. George Ogle, Rev. Herb White, Faye Moon—the wife of well-known democracy activist Rev. Moon Dong-hwan—and me. The next day I delivered the petition, with a polite bow, into the hands of a surprised US Marine guard at the US Embassy.

A few days later the steering committee was invited to meet with Ambassador William Porter. We stressed our view that, in light of the tremendous support the United States was giving the Republic of Korea, ordinary Koreans could not help thinking the United States supported the third-term amendment, especially since they had seen the trucks. Ambassador Porter took note of our arguments but seemed much more interested in getting a list of the names of all of the members of "The Group of Fifty." We explained that we could not and would not provide such a list because of the danger to Korean colleagues. The ambassador then suggested that he meet with the whole group in a week, and we agreed.

At the next meeting the ambassador announced that the problem of the trucks had been solved—by repainting them in the colors of the Korean National Police at the body shop of the US Eighth Army. We pointed out that this was too little too late since thousands of Koreans had already seen these trucks in action. Again, the officials seemed most interested in who the members of the group were and again we refused to give them a list, although by then they had probably figured out who most of us were. Needless to say, we did not reach a meeting of the minds with the ambassador.

On through August and into September student demonstrations continued, and the opposition in the National Assembly struggled to prevent the passage of the amendment; however, since the government had a two-thirds majority, the enactment of the amendment could not be prevented. On September 14, 1969, the constitutional amendment bill, that would allow Park Chung Hee to run for a third term, passed the National Assembly, and on October 17 the third-term amendment was approved in a national referendum.

During the fall of 1969 another event further changed my life and career path. Professor Jerome A. Cohen, the director of the East Asian Legal Studies Program (EALS) at Harvard Law School, visited Seoul and met with current and former Peace Corps volunteers interested in law school at a Chinese restaurant. I sat next to him and explained my situation—I had completed two years at Yale Law School and had spent nearly four years in South Korea. I explained that I hoped to finish law school, but that I had also become interested in doing graduate work in Korean history. He encouraged me to do both, informing me that there was an agreement between Harvard Law School and Yale Law School under which I could spend an "Intensive Semester" at the EALS program at Harvard, write a paper on the South Korean legal system for credit at Yale, and return to Yale to complete the spring semester of 1971 and graduate. It seemed perfect, and the arrangements were soon made.

I spent a very interesting semester at EALS at Harvard Law School before returning to Yale for a final semester. I then returned to Boston where I took and passed the Massachusetts Bar Exam. Meanwhile I had come to know Professor Edward W. Wagner, who taught Korean history at Harvard, and had applied for the Regional Studies East Asia AM Program. While wrestling with the question of whether to practice law or go into a PhD program in Korean history, I interviewed at an international law firm. Without much hesitation I chose to go to graduate school. After receiving my AM, I went into the PhD program in History and East Asian Languages at Harvard where I took courses taught by John K. Fairbank, Edwin O. Reischauer, Albert Craig, and Ed Wagner and kept in close touch with Jerry Cohen when I became a research fellow at EALS.

When it became clear in 1971 that rapprochement between the United States and the Peoples Republic of China (PRC) was underway, South and North Korea, fearing possible abandonment by their respective patrons, tempered their hostility and began to talk to each other. In 1972, this culminated in the July 4 South-North Joint Communique, a history-making agreement.

During the spring, summer, and into the fall of 1971, students, university professors, journalists, laborers, resettled slum dwellers, Christians, opposition politicians, and even National Assembly members of Park Chung Hee's party protested on many issues including, but not limited to, labor problems, student military training, and the actions of the KCIA and the military against students. In this new era, the riot police and even the military did not hesitate to enter the campuses and detain students. Many students were forcibly conscripted into the army. Park reacted to this unrest and the rapprochement with the North by declaring the Yusin Constitution, a so-called reform that made him president for life, and established "Korean-style democracy."

In the spring of 1974, after passing general examinations for my PhD, I prepared to take my family back to South Korea with a Fulbright grant to do dissertation research. By that time the Yusin Constitution had been in effect for two years, and its critics were getting restive. Kim Dae-jung (Kim Taejung, 1998–2003), a popular democratic politician, had been kidnapped by the KCIA from his hotel in Tokyo in August 1973 and had been narrowly saved by US and Japanese pressure from being thrown into the ocean.[3]

After my first couple of days in Seoul, I was asked to meet with Mr. George Lichtblau, the labor attaché at the US Embassy. As he firmly informed me that I and other Americans were not to become involved in South Korean domestic politics, I felt certain that he knew about the "Group of 50" petition. I assured him that I would be mindful of the fact that I was not a South Korean citizen. I left without getting into a discussion of my intention to talk with any and every interesting Korean I was fortunate enough to meet or my intention to petition my own government if I felt it was out of line.

In the spring of 1975, a number of us Fulbrighters were introduced to Kim Dae-jung, then under house arrest, but still able to receive visitors, by a former

Peace Corps volunteer, Doug Reed, who was Kim's English tutor. I was very impressed with Mr. Kim and made it a point to visit him periodically, a practice that I kept up whenever I was in Korea until the end of his life in 2009. Throughout the fall of 1974 and all of 1975 there were frequent demonstrations on university campuses, and many intellectuals and activists were arrested and tried for violations of a panoply of restrictive laws: the Anti-Communist Law, the National Security Law, the emergency decrees Park issued under the Yusin Constitution, and various provisions of the Criminal Code.

One day when we learned that a session of the poet Kim Chi Ha's trial was to be held at noon in a nearby court, David McCann (Peace Corps–Korea, K-1), also then in South Korea as a Fulbrighter, and I decided to stop by and have a look. When we got to the courtroom the doors were closed and locked. When the appointed time arrived and the doors swung open, we were surprised to see that most of the seats had already been filled with sturdy looking men in leather jackets who decidedly did not look like nor act like the poet's supporters. We stepped inside and, standing, watched as Kim was brought in, hands tied behind his back, a very brief hearing was held, and Kim was led away. We hoped he had seen us.

Late March and early April 1975 were filled with excitement for me. A British barrister and a Danish doctor came to Seoul on an Amnesty International mission. While they were there, coincidentally, US House of Representatives Congressman Donald M. Fraser (D-Minnesota, 1963–79), chair of the Subcommittee on International Organizations of the Committee on International Relations, came to Seoul on a brief visit during which he paid a call on Kim Dae-jung, still under house arrest. During the approximately two-week Amnesty International mission visit and the four- to five-day stay of Congressman Fraser and his aide, Mr. Robert Boettcher, I and a couple of other Fulbrighters made ourselves available as guides and interpreters. Amnesty International issued an excellent report, still worth reading, and Congressman Fraser and Mr. Boettcher firmed up their opinion that the US Congress needed to look more closely at the question of US government support for the Park Chung Hee government.[4]

When we arrived in Seoul in August 1974, we were a family of three: Diane, our son, Hayden—who was born at Severance Hospital in Seoul in 1969, and me. Ever since Hayden's birth, Diane and I had been thinking about adoption. We felt that with the earth facing a population problem, there was no reason for us to have another child, especially since there were so many orphans in South Korea. In Korea's Confucian society adoption is rare, and orphans in general have rather dim prospects in life. Particularly dim were the prospects of orphans of mixed parentage, for the most part the offspring of American soldiers and Korean women living on the edges of US bases. At first, we thought we should try to adopt a mixed-race child to help with a societal problem created by the US military presence in South Korea. However, in 1970, when we inquired with the Holt Adoption Agency about the possibility of such an adoption, they replied that in fact American couples were adopting such children at such a rate that we would be on a waiting list for at least a year and a half.

Contemplating that, we decided that, if we adopted, we should adopt a Korean child. However, we decided to put off the decision for the time being.

As time passed—and returning to Seoul became more likely and as Hayden became more verbal—we began to talk with him about the prospect of adopting a sister just a year or so younger than he was. It is impossible to know at what level he understood this prospect, but he expressed enthusiastic agreement. As a result, during our first year back in Seoul, we started to look into adoption seriously. After inquiring with friends, Korean and American, we went to the Korean Social Welfare Society (Taehan Sahoe Pokchihoe) where we met a social worker. After several meetings during which she explained the legal situation and the availability of children for adoption and interviewed us to determine our suitability as adoptive parents, she sent us to an orphanage that had a five-and-a-half-year-old girl who was ready to be adopted. In much shorter order than would have been possible if we were making an international adoption from the United States, the arrangements were made, and we—Diane, Hayden, and Ed—became the family of Kim Meejin, soon to be called Elizabeth Meejin Baker. We lived in Seoul for another year during which we maintained a partially Korean-speaking household. Hayden's Korean in particular was very good. Hayden and Meejin attended an international school where the language of instruction was English, but each classroom had a Korean-speaking assistant. By the summer of 1976, we were ready to return to Cambridge as a four-member family. Forty-five years later we still regard this as one of our best decisions ever.

When we returned to the United States in the fall of 1976, the "Koreagate" scandal involving businessman Tongsun Park's attempts to influence the US

Congress in favor of the objectives of the government of the Republic of Korea was much in the news and was being investigated by the House and Senate ethics committees. In the spring of 1977, I was once again a researcher at EALS and working on my thesis, when Jerry Cohen recommended me to Congressman Fraser, who was about to launch an eighteen-month investigation of ROK government activities aimed at influencing American opinion. Offered a job, I jumped at the opportunity and plunged into the most intense and one of the most interesting periods of my life.

At the beginning I was the only investigator on the team who had lived in Korea, could speak Korean, or had studied about Korea. One of my first assignments was to interview former KCIA Director Kim Hyung Wook who was living in exile in the United States. I spent many days questioning Kim on a wide range of topics. Having been the chief of the KCIA for six years, he was a goldmine of information, but for me the most interesting thing I learned was that Kim was very proud of his role as the planner and executor of the East Berlin Spy Case and the third-term constitutional amendment operation—the two things that had so stimulated my interest in South Korean politics and the US role in South Korea.

My experience with the Fraser subcommittee deepened my interest in ROK repression and human rights violations, and I turned enthusiastically to volunteer work with Amnesty International. Amnesty International made me the coordinator for the South Korean cases assigned to US Adoption Groups. We worked on dozens of cases in the United States and many more worldwide. The International Secretariat in London kept in close contact with my team about specific cases and more general research topics. The Amnesty International South Korea coordinators met a number of times in London and in other European cities. I continued to work intensively for Amnesty International until the great improvements to the human rights situation under President Kim Young-sam (Kim Yŏngsam, 1993–98) came to pass in the mid-1990s.

I also became a member of the board of Asia Watch, established in 1985 in affiliation with Helsinki Watch (now Human Rights Watch). Between 1985 and 1991 Asia Watch published half a dozen in-depth reports on the human rights situation in South Korea, based on thorough research and, in some cases, missions to South Korea. I worked closely with the staff and went on an Asia Watch mission to South Korea in 1990.

In addition to these volunteer activities, from 1979 to 1991, I worked intensively with Professor Choi Sung-il of Hobart and William Smith Colleges who was an extremely energetic and effective advocate for democracy and the protection of human rights in South Korea. Choi organized the Council for Democracy in Korea and, with me and a few others, worked mightily to publish the *Monthly Review of Korean Affairs* and *Korea Scope* until his untimely death in 1991.

In August 1980, when Kim Dae-jung and his co-defendants were on trial for allegedly instigating the May 18 Kwangju Uprising, the Amnesty International secretariat sent Assistant Secretary General Dick Oosting and

Fig. 2.3 Choi Sung-il and Ed Baker on Choi's wedding day at Stony Brook, Long Island, New York, in November 1987. Photo courtesy of Ed Baker.

me on a mission to South Korea. In Tokyo we called on the ROK Embassy where we saw the charge d'affaires. He suggested that we should go to Seoul at a less troubled, more convenient time, but we pointed out that, as a human rights organization, we had the obligation to visit at difficult times. As we rose to leave, we asked if we would be allowed to enter the country if we followed our plan and went to Seoul the next day. "No," he replied. Politely stymied, we headed back to London to work on the ROK situation.

With my devotion to activism I was not making much progress on my dissertation, and even though Diane was working full time in family planning services at Somerville Hospital, our family's financial situation was suffering as time dragged on without me finishing my degree and getting a job. At this juncture, Professor Albert M. Craig, the director of the Harvard-Yenching Institute (HYI), invited me to join the Institute as assistant director. Professor Craig knew of my intense interest in Korea from my time in his classes. He needed an assistant director and felt that having someone seriously interested in Korea would be an asset to the Institute. I was to remain with the HYI for twenty-five years. A number of the best universities in China, Japan, South Korea, Taiwan, Thailand, and later Vietnam were invited to nominate faculty members in the humanities and social sciences for the HYI's visiting programs. The Institute's practice was to have each candidate interviewed by a representative of the Institute, and the most rewarding part of my job was traveling every fall to East Asia to interview the candidates. Having narrowly focused on Korea from the Peace Corps onward, I found this a tremendously deepening experience. I became acquainted with these countries and their universities while, at the same time, I traveled every year to interview the candidates in South Korea, broadening my knowledge of South Korean academia. These visits also gave me a chance to see our Korean family and friends, personal and political, regularly.

In the fall of 1981, as I made my way through my first interviewing trip for the HYI, I finished my meetings in Taipei and flew to Seoul only to find out that I was on the ROK Minister of Justice's list of people not to be admitted to the country—clearly a leftover from the Amnesty International mission. My visa was cancelled, and I was put on the same airplane back to Taipei. By telephone I was able to mobilize the Fulbright Commission, the president of Korea University—later to be prime minister—and Professor Han Seung-joo of Korea University—later to be foreign minister. With this assistance I was able to get a visa four days later. As he handed me my passport, the consular officer said, "I hope someday to have a chance to study at Harvard." For the next five years I was on a watch list. This meant I had to get a new fifteen-day visa for each trip to South Korea and sign a pledge to do only the work of the HYI while there. Although I did not follow that pledge and was often tailed, I was never again refused entry to or expelled from the country.

After the assassination of Park Chung Hee on October 26, 1979, General Chun Doo-hwan (Chŏn Tuhwan, 1980–88) cracked down on demonstrators on May 18, 1980, during the Kwangju Uprising, in which apparently many more than the officially acknowledged 200 people were killed, and later in 1980 made himself president. The Kwangju Uprising had another consequence that I only became aware of many years later. Rather suddenly in 1981, the Chun Doo-hwan government decided it was time for the Peace Corps to leave South Korea. Of course, since the Peace Corps is in a country only at the invitation of the host country, it left very soon after that. Those of us who had been in the Peace Corps in South Korea were disappointed by this, but we knew that the South Korean government and people were sensitive to anything that might be taken to indicate that South Korea, a rapidly developing country, was still underdeveloped. I, and I think most of us Peace Corps–Korea alumni, assumed that the Chun regime was calling for an end to the Peace Corps mission because its continuing presence implied that South Korea was still an underdeveloped country. Our sense that the Peace Corps was asked to leave because of nationalistic pride—rather than because its mission was no longer valued by the ROK government—was reinforced by the fact that the Fulbright program was now asked to supply a substantial number of young Fulbright grantees to do exactly what most Peace Corps volunteers had done—teach English in middle and high schools. I learned of this in the mid-1990s when visited in my office by a young woman who had just finished up as a Fulbright in Kwangju. As she described her responsibilities there teaching English to middle school students, I realized that she had done exactly what most Peace Corps–Korea volunteers had done. When I asked how many such Fulbrights were sent to South Korea each year, she replied "forty or fifty." I believe this continued for some years although I do not know how many.

In recent years, I had heard stories to the effect that the Peace Corps had been asked (or ordered) to leave because President Chun Doo-hwan was furious over public statements critical of his government made by Peace Corps volunteers who had been in Kwangju at the time of the uprising. This was confirmed to me recently by Kenneth Quinones, an old friend from graduate school, who had been stationed in Seoul as a US Foreign Service officer. According to Ken, Chun was furious and insisted that the volunteers had to leave, despite the strong arguments to the contrary made by Ken and other US diplomats.[5]

As Chun solidified his control, I testified in September 1982 for the US House of Representatives Subcommittees on Asian and Pacific Affairs and International Organizations that there was a consistent pattern of gross violations in South Korea; contrary to the testimony of William H. Gleysteen, former ambassador to South Korea and Richard Holbrooke, former assistant secretary of state for East Asian affairs. Quiet diplomacy was insufficient by itself as a means to promote democracy and respect for human rights in South Korea; and many formerly pro-American Koreans, especially university students, had become very anti-American because they blamed the United States for Chun's oppression.[6]

For me one of the high points of the decade came in December 1982, when Kim Dae-jung, who had been sentenced to death in connection with the Kwangju Uprising, had his sentence commuted to life and then reduced to twenty years, was suddenly released from prison and sent into exile in the United States. A few days after he arrived, I met Mr. Kim in Washington, DC and introduced him to Professor Philip Kuhn, then director of the Fairbank Center, that was on the record as having extended a standing invitation to Kim to come to Harvard to do research. Kuhn and Kim were very cordial, and Kuhn repeated the invitation. A few days later Professor Kuhn withdrew the invitation on the grounds that "Kim is not a scholar." Fortunately, I was able to get Mr. Kim invited as a fellow of the Center for International Affairs starting in the fall of 1983. After a year at Harvard and a year in Washington, in the spring of 1985, Mr. and Mrs. Kim returned to Seoul with a large delegation of supporters including two US congressmen and Professor Bruce Cumings (Peace Corps–Korea, K-3) of the University of Chicago.

In 1985 and 1986, the political situation in South Korea grew steadily more tense. In April 1986, I again testified in a congressional hearing, this time on behalf of Asia Watch. My main points were that the United States should link any military assistance to South Korea with public statements to the effect

that democratization was integrally related to South Korean security and sta-
bility and thus of paramount interest to the United States and that Asia Watch
favored a congressional resolution making specific points in support of
democracy and encouraging President Reagan to speak forcefully, publicly in
support of Korean democracy. In June 1986, the House passed such a resolution, but unfortunately it did not call for a presidential statement nor did
it mention conditioning US military aid on the ROK military not interfering
in politics.[7]

By the fall of 1986, the situation had grown bad enough that Professor
Edwin O. Reischauer and I published "A Time Bomb is Ticking in South
Korea" in the *New York Times Magazine*. We argued that the Korean people had
clearly demonstrated their desire for democracy; that many South Koreans
had become convinced that the United States favored military dictatorship
over democracy; and for historical reasons, the United States had "a duty to
work for the establishment of a stable democratic society" there; and it was
in our own interest to make such an effort. We stressed that "We must not
just stand idly by, waiting for South Korea to blow."[8]

In January 1987, a Seoul National University student named Pak Chong-
chŏl was killed while undergoing interrogation by the anticommunist police.
This set off a series of events that culminated in June 1987, when popular
demonstrations forced the government to accept a new constitution providing
for the direct, popular election of the president, the lifting of the prohibition
on Kim Dae-jung's participation in politics, and other democratic reforms.
Throughout this period, I continued to work with Amnesty International, Asia
Watch, and Choi Sung-il as we attempted to improve the human rights situation and promote democracy in South Korea, including focusing on the
notorious torture case of Mr. Kim Keun-tae. During the spring of 1987, I was
frequently called on by radio, television, and the print media to comment on
the situation in South Korea. The high point was a confrontation with the
ROK ambassador to the United States, Kim Kyungwon, on ABC Nightline.[9] I
had known Kim from the days when he was a professor of political science at
New York University. He was summoned to the ABC studio in Washington DC
and I to a studio in Boston. When he entered the green room, I was told by
ABC staff, he asked, "Where's Ed?"

As part of this effort, in December 1987 Carter Eckert (Peace Corps–
Korea, K7/K8) and I joined an election observer mission organized by Choi

Sung-il.[10] Unfortunately, two democratic leaders, Kim Young-sam and Kim Dae-jung, competed in the 1987 presidential election giving Roh Tae-woo (No T'aeu, 1990–92), Chun's chosen successor, a narrow victory. However, in 1992 Kim Young-sam won the presidency, and Kim Dae-jung won the office in 1998. It was with great satisfaction that I attended the inauguration of President Kim Dae-jung. In my view Kim Dae-jung's greatest achievement was his Sunshine Policy that brought about ground-breaking improvements in relations with North Korea for which he won the Nobel Peace Prize. Although Kim's successor, Roh Moo-hyun (No Muhyŏn, 2003–8), continued to improve relations with North Korea, Roh was succeeded by two conservative presidents: Lee Myung-bak (Yi Myŏngbak, 2008–13) and Park Geun-hye (Pak Kŭnhye, 2013–17), the daughter of Park Chung Hee, under whom South-North relations deteriorated sharply. After President Park was removed from office for abuse of power and corruption in 2017, she was succeeded by the current president, Moon Jae-in (2017–present). President Moon has succeeded in significantly improving relations with North Korea and in promoting dialogue between the United States and the Democratic People's Republic of Korea (DPRK, North Korea).

Fig. 2.4 Ed Baker showing President Kim Dae-jung, also a grandfather, photos of his grandchildren at the Blue House (the official Presidential residence), Seoul, South Korea in 2000. Photo courtesy of Ed Baker.

Over the years my interest in Korea has led me to make three trips to North Korea—in 1988, 1999, and 2013. I made these trips out of curiosity about the North and a desire to contribute to the understanding between the United States and the DPRK. The first two trips each lasted for four nights and five days. The first was facilitated by the International Center for Development Policy, a Washington, DC think tank dedicated to improving international understanding, and Food for the Hungry, an organization that participated in the international effort to provide food aid during North Korea's famine in the mid-1990s, managed the second visit. Diane and I went together on the third trip in 2013, joining a multi-drug resistant tuberculosis (TB) mission led by Dr. Stephen Linton of the Eugene Bell Foundation, an organization that has been involved in providing humanitarian aid to North Korea since 1996 and TB support in particular since 1998. In recent years, I have focused my attention on advocating for a peaceful settlement of the standoff between North Korea on the one side and the United States and South Korea on the other.

In 2006, I retired from the HYI and finally became a professor when I accepted an invitation to teach both East Asian and Korean history for the

Fig. 2.5 Ed and Diane Baker with Madame Lee Hee Ho, the widow of President Kim Dae-jung, in the Kims' home in Tonggyodong, Seoul, South Korea, in May 2015. Photo courtesy of Ed Baker.

International Division of Hanyang University in Seoul. Then in 2010, I joined the College of Liberal Studies at Seoul National University, teaching the same two subjects plus human rights in Korea. Unfortunately, this second career was cut short by a health crisis in late 2010 that impelled me to retire for a second time and return home to Massachusetts. Nevertheless, since then our lives have continued to revolve around Korea with frequent trips there— including ones with our children and their children—and with visits from Korean friends and family. I have to stress that Korea has been "our lives." Our attention to Korea was greatly influenced by the fact that we went to Korea as a couple and that our children both entered our lives in Korea.

Back in 1966, tired of law school and anxious to have a chance to think about what we might try to do with our lives, we searched for a way to spend a couple of years doing something worthwhile and interesting that might, at the same time, contribute in some small way to international understanding and peace. The needless, misguided US war in Vietnam was a daily reminder of how badly the world needed more understanding among peoples. Thus, we decided to give the Peace Corps a try, never expecting our experience to shape the rest of our lives. We wound up as Peace Corps volunteers in South Korea largely by chance, yet our experience, as has been the case with other returned Peace Corps volunteers who have followed careers related to Korea, has to a large extent shaped almost every aspect of the rest or our lives and strongly influenced the lives of our children and grandchildren.

NOTES

1. US Government Publishing Office, Public Law 87–293. Title 1—The Peace Corps, Declaration of Purpose, September 22, 1961, Washington DC, https://www.govinfo.gov/content/pkg/STATUTE-75/pdf/STATUTE-75-Pg612.pdf.

2. Interest rates in the informal lending market were so high that landlords would let a room or house for a deposit (called *chŏnsae*), the full amount of which was to be returned at the end of the lease.

3. This has been widely reported and credit has been claimed by several people. Kim Dae-jung, in his autobiography, gives credit to Prof. Jerome A. Cohen, who was alerted by Prof. Channing Liem, and especially to the US ambassador at the time, Philip Habib, with the assistance of CIA Station Chief Donald Gregg. This was confirmed by the US House of Representatives in the report of the Subcommittee on International Organizations of the Committee of International Relations, H.R. Rep. *Investigation of*

Korean-American Relations, 95th Cong, 2nd Session (October 31, 1978). When I met Mr. Kim for the first time at his home where he was under house arrest in April 1974, he told me that weights had been attached to him, and he had been told he would be thrown overboard. Then, he said, they heard an airplane of unknown provenance (although he later concluded it was Japanese), and the man returned and untied him! The kidnaping incident is described in detail in Kim Dae-jung, *Conscience in Action: The Autobiography of Kim Dae-jung*. Translated by Seung-hee Jeong (London: Palgrave Macmillan, 2019), 187–205.

4. Amnesty International, *Report of an Amnesty International Mission to the Republic of Korea March 27–April 9, 1975* (London: Amnesty International, 1976).

5. Kenneth Quinones, personal communication with author, March 2018.

6. *Reconciling Human Rights and U.S. Security Interests in Asia: Hearings Before the Subcommittees on Asian and Pacific Affairs and on Human Rights and International Organizations of the Committee of Foreign Affairs*, US 97th Cong. 102–41 (1982) (statement of Edward J. Baker, Harvard University).

7. *Political Developments and Human Rights in the Republic of Korea: Hearings on H. Con. Res. 345 and H. Con. Res. 347, Before the Subcommittee on Human Rights and International Organizations and the Subcommittee on Asian and Pacific Affairs of the Committee on Foreign Affairs*, 99th US Cong. 47–100 (1986) (statement by Edward J. Baker, Assistant Director, Harvard-Yenching Institute). An erratum was issued regarding this hearing: "On page iii and 47, Edward J. Baker was wrongly identified as a professor at Harvard University. He is in fact the assistant director of the Harvard-Yenching Institute, which is an independent foundation affiliated with Harvard University. The error is regretted."

8. Edwin O. Reischauer and Edward Baker, "A Time Bomb is Ticking in South Korea," *New York Times Magazine* (November 16, 1986): 50–51, 80–88.

9. Syracuse University Libraries Special Collections Research Center, Inventory, Nightline 1980–2005, Box 143, 06/17/1987 *Nightline: Protests in South Korea* Videotape, VHS, dub (ID#: koppel_nl87061701). https://library.syr.edu/digital/guides/k/koppel_t.htm#series3.

10. Carter Eckert has detailed his experiences in the Peace Corps in Chapter 4 of this volume. See Carter J. Eckert, "A Road Less Traveled: From Rome to Seoul via the Peace Corps," in *Peace Corps Volunteers and the Making of Korean Studies in the United States*, edited by Seung-kyung Kim and Michael Robinson, 77–92 (Seattle: University of Washington Center for Korea Studies, 2020).

BIBLIOGRAPHY

Amnesty International. *Report of an Amnesty International Mission to the Republic of Korea March 27–April 9, 1975*. London: Amnesty International, 1976.

Eckert, Carter J. "A Road Less Traveled: From Rome to Seoul via the Peace Corps." In *Peace Corps Volunteers and the Making of Korean Studies in the United States*, edited by Seung-kyung Kim and Michael Robinson, 77–92. Seattle: University of Washington Center for Korea Studies, 2020.

Political Developments and Human Rights in the Republic of Korea: Hearings on H. Con. Res. 345 and H. Con. Res. 347, Before the Subcommittee on Human Rights and International Organizations and the Subcommittee on Asian and Pacific Affairs of the Committee on Foreign Affairs, 99th US Cong. 47–100 (1986) (statement by Edward J. Baker, Assistant Director, Harvard-Yenching Institute).

Reconciling Human Rights and U.S. Security Interests in Asia: Hearings Before the Subcommittees on Asian and Pacific Affairs and on Human Rights and International Organizations of the Committee of Foreign Affairs, 97th US Cong. 102–41 (1982) (statement of Edward Baker, Harvard University).

Subcommittee on International Organizations of the Committee of International Relations, H.R. Rep. *Investigation of Korean-American Relations*, 95th US Cong, 2nd Session (October 31, 1978).

Syracuse University Libraries Special Collections Research Center, Inventory. Nightline 1980–2005. Box 143. 06/17/1987 *Nightline: Protests in South Korea* Videotape, VHS, dub (ID#: koppel_nl87061701). https://library.syr.edu/digital/guides/k/koppel_t.htm#series3.

US Government Publishing Office, Public Law 87–293. Title 1—*The Peace Corps, Declaration of Purpose*, September 22, 1961, Washington DC, https://www.govinfo.gov/content/pkg/STATUTE-75/pdf/STATUTE-75-Pg612.pdf.

3

On Being Part of the Peace Corps Generation in Korean Studies

DONALD N. CLARK

In 1987, an Association for Asian Studies (AAS) panel on the Kwangju Uprising, chaired by Linda Lewis, included presenters David McCann and me, plus Mark Peterson and our discussant, Chongsik Lee.[1] During the question and answer session, our senior colleague Chaejin Lee prefaced his comment by referring to the American academics on the panel as representing what he called the "thin second echelon of Korean studies in the United States." We were a handful of scholars following the founding generation of American Koreanists who had missionary or military backgrounds, plus Lee's own cohort of Korean-born political scientists who had received degrees at US institutions after the Korean War and stayed on in the United States to teach. Calling us the "thin second echelon" reflected Lee's concern that Korean studies always seemed to be on the brink of extinction, facing headwinds in matters of tenure, enrollments, and budgets. It was not at all certain that we could sustain ourselves. This volume is proof positive that our "thin second echelon" survived and succeeded in planting roots across the United States and Canada, and that Korean studies is here to stay.

"KOREA IS AN INTERESTING PLACE! GET OUT AND SEE IT!"

The Peace Corps grounded me in Korea, but I had a bit of a head start. My parents and grandparents had been Presbyterian missionaries in Korea going back to 1902, and I spent the 1950s growing up in Seoul immediately after the Korean War. My first encounter with South Korea was in April 1954 at the age of ten, when my parents and I flew from Tokyo on the CIA-proprietary Civil

Air Transport airline, which consisted of a rattling, twin-engine Curtiss C-46 Commando, and landed on a gravel runway near Pusan. We then traveled to Seoul on the US military train known as the KCOM-Z Comet, a twelve-hour ride through the mountains in a railroad car protected by metal grates on the windows to keep grenades out as we passed between Taegu and Taejŏn. Our house in Seoul—the one built by my grandfather in 1907—had just been vacated by US Army officers who were using the former Seoul National University (SNU) campus as one of their bases and our nearby compound as their billet. There was no school that year, so I spent the second half of fifth grade riding my little bike around Seoul all day where the only traffic consisted of oxcarts, bicycles, and the occasional military Jeep.

The South Korea that I discovered at the tender age of ten was a suffering country. Wounded people were everywhere, subsisting by selling second-hand goods and castoffs from the US military supply system. On my bike I had to dash through gauntlets of beggar children and submit to being handled by adults who were endlessly curious about my age, skin, hair, weight, and wrist circumference (for some reason). When I rode city buses, I ran the risk of being crushed and suffocated and, as it happened, developing new immunities such as having my tuberculosis (TB) skin test turn positive. The prevalence of parasites in the South Korean population in the 1950s meant learning not to eat Korean food, to recoil from summer kimch'i, and to never drink un-boiled water or to eat uncooked anything, shellfish of any kind, or unpeeled fruit. For me, therefore, enjoyment of Korean food came much later, beginning in the Peace Corps, though we still had some of the precautions at that time. Even so, as a child I was always healthier than two of my father's brothers who died in infancy, and my father who nearly died of typhoid in 1912, all while in Seoul.

These were reasons why missionaries and other foreigners lived on compounds, grew their own vegetables and kept milk cows, and met daily needs by buying selectively in the local markets. They sent their kids to special foreign schools and summered away from the disease-ridden cities at isolated beach resorts. Having been raised in this extraterritorial bubble myself, I found it more difficult than other volunteers to practice local customs, eat local foods, and appreciate the wonderful strangeness of the tiny country village where I ended up doing Peace Corps health work.

During my childhood, even though I lived on a protected mission compound and attended a foreign school, there was no way to avoid witnessing the miseries of the South Korean people. I knew my parents were there to "help," and I absorbed a certain sense that South Koreans were to be pitied and also the feeling that Americans were to be envied, as if my obvious material advantage was an entitlement, somehow. My parents did not teach me this. In fact, they regularly chided me when they saw signs of my expat kid's assumption of superiority. They unfailingly tried to teach me to regard Koreans with respect. At the time, though, the rubble and desperation of South Korea were all I could see. Later, after working for South Korean organizations and having Korean colleagues and superiors, this childhood tendency—I would call it a handicap—slowly dissipated. The Peace Corps experience knocked a lot of it out of me. However, while other volunteers soaked up Korean culture, I still had to work on losing some of my earlier baggage.

This process of un-learning negative things about South Korea started while I was still a student at Seoul Foreign High School. Our teachers were well aware of our ignorance and attitudes, and they worked to purge us of them. First came the annual, week-long field trips caravanning by Jeep and Land Rover across the entire country—traveling unpaved roads and fording streams to get to South Korea's greatest historical sites—eating Korean food, bathing in Korean bathhouses, and sleeping in yŏgwans and monasteries along the way, all the while accompanied by adults who explained things to us. Our lead social studies teacher, Hope Diffenderfer, was a particular inspiration. Sometimes she would taunt us about keeping to our foreigners' compounds—our extraterritorial ghettoes—that were meant to keep us safe but also suffocated our ability to learn about where we were. "Korea is an interesting country," she would tell us. "History is being made right in front of you. Get out and watch it happen!"

Among other things, Mrs. Diffenderfer introduced me to a group of students from Kyŏngbok Boys' High School who were starting an English club and needed a native speaker. These English club students were from prominent families, and when they invited me to their homes, I suddenly came in contact with the refinements of upper-class South Korean culture. Many of their parents were VIP's. They had traveled and knew languages. They had fine art in their homes, and the food was delicious. Out in the city, my

Kyŏngbok High School friends opened my eyes to so many things: historic sights, social movements, different sections of the city, the market environment, tea rooms and coffee shops, politics, and even new religions—a Saturday trip to the headquarters of the Olive Tree Cult (commonly known in Korea as Pak Changno-kyo) was one such memorable outing.[2] With them I witnessed the April 1960 Revolution that ousted President Syngman Rhee (Yi Sŭngman, 1948–60) during my junior year, and then the 1961 military coup that brought in General Park Chung Hee (Pak Chŏnghŭi, 1961–79). Many of my American classmates who stayed in their missionary, military, and embassy compounds missed all of this. I credit Hope Diffenderfer, my Kyŏngbok High School friends, and of course my parents, for not letting me waste my years growing up in South Korea.

From the April 1960 (4.19) Revolution I also learned one really important lesson about the American empire and what it has meant to the world. After a week of demonstrations, martial law, and dithering in President Syngman Rhee's inner circle, President Eisenhower (1953–61) sent a demarche essentially telling the disgraced South Korean president to resign. A large excited crowd lined Sejongno waiting for Ambassador Walter McConaughy's motorcade as it passed en route to Kyŏngmudae (now Ch'ŏngwadae) to deliver the message. Everyone in the crowd seemed to know what was about to happen. "How amazing," I thought on the sidewalk, "to watch an American diplomat force the leader of another sovereign nation to resign."

Later on, as a diplomatic history student, I learned about the regime changes forced by the American empire in Latin America, Africa, Iran, the Congo, Vietnam, Indonesia, and elsewhere. I came to interrogate the connection between the empire and what my parents as missionaries were doing in South Korea, and later what I myself was doing in the Peace Corps. Eventually I wrote a book that reflected that issue, in which American missionaries who once had stood against Japanese imperialism in Korea became complicit in the division of Korea and the consequences that came from the Korean War and after.[3]

"IF YOU WANT TO STUDY KOREA, STAY AT UW."

After high school my parents shipped me to Whitworth College in Spokane, Washington, a denominational school known for producing Presbyterian ministers. They meant for me to follow in their footsteps and to represent the third generation of our missionary family in Korea. However, my explorations in high school had already shown me that there was more to Korea than the church. My hero-worship of Ambassador McConaughy gave rise to a fascination with diplomatic work, and I was determined to join the US Foreign Service. This was not to be. When I failed the US Foreign Service exams on the first try, I was forced to take stock and face the fact that if there was anything unusual about me, it was my Korea–missionary kid background, and I should probably figure out how to make that the key to my future. I knew the Korea missionary McCune family and the brothers George and Shannon McCune who had built academic careers on their childhoods in P'yŏngyang. I also knew of Edwin O. Reischauer, the Harvard history professor whom President Kennedy (1961–63) had appointed to be ambassador to Japan. Reischauer was a "BIJ" (born in Japan) missionary kid. I was inspired by the idea that I could carve out a career that blended academic and diplomatic work. Buoyed by this inspiration, newly graduated, and married, I started studying Korea at the University of Washington (UW) in Seattle.

This was in 1966, just after the UW had won a Ford Foundation grant to develop a Korean studies program. The University of Washington library was in the process of expanding its Korea collection, and a flock of visiting professors had taken up residence, among them historian (and later SNU President) Koh Byŏng-ik, political scientist (and later Republic of Korea National Assemblyman) Cho Soon-sŭng, and the noted linguist Lee Ki-moon. When added to the resident Korea faculty—literature scholar Suh Doo-soo and linguistics professor Fred Lukoff—and the strong support of Far Eastern and Russian Institute Director George Taylor, the University of Washington became a Korean studies powerhouse overnight. There were four advanced graduate students. The rest of us were a mixed lot of undergraduates, first year MA students, assorted yuhaksaeng (overseas Korean students), and ringers including one ex-serviceman who told Dr. Lukoff that he wanted to study Korea "because it's there."

Studying in this environment was a joy that year. I loved the subject matter and having a teaching assistantship to help pay the bills. However, in the distance was the Vietnam War and the fact that my draft board had reclassified me "1-A," which in the year 1967, before the draft lottery, meant likely conscription at any moment. One day that summer, the UW student newspaper announced that the UW School of Public Health had won a contract to train a group of Peace Corps volunteers to go to South Korea to do rural health work. I knew nothing about public health, but I did know that Peace Corps service brought with it deliverance from the draft. My wife Linda and I applied, were accepted to the program and, in October 1967, we reported to the training site to be part of the Peace Corps–Korea Group Six (K-6). Back at the university, Dr. Lukoff was annoyed with me. He had no interest in my draft board problem and was not impressed by my argument that it was really a choice between Peace Corps–Korea and the US Army in Vietnam. "If you want to study Korea, stay at UW," he said. But I ignored his advice and, on a snowy day in February 1968, a World Health Organization (WHO) driver dropped Linda and me off at Poksu, our assigned village in the mountains of Kŭmsan, south of Taejŏn.

"WHAT GOOD ARE YOU ANYWAY?"

The University of Washington School of Public Health had taught us some of the bare essentials regarding maternal and child health, family planning, communicable disease control, and environmental sanitation. In theory, we knew how to give shots, promote contraception, deliver babies, dig wells, and give lessons on how to avoid malaria and such. We had also been given fourteen weeks of intensive Korean-language training, enough to survive but hardly enough to converse on complicated topics or to counsel our Korean neighbors on the delicate details of their health in general, let alone their sex lives.

For starters, when we got to South Korea the skeptical US ambassador forbade us to practice any form of medicine on any Koreans. Thus, our real functions were not clear to anybody. The Republic of Korea (ROK) Ministry of Health and Social Affairs had established health centers with doctors and nurses in county towns across the nation. In 1968, the effort was extended to put health subcenters in each of the townships (myŏn) that comprised the counties (kun). The Peace Corps volunteers of the two newly arrived health groups, K-4 and K-6, were assigned to various myŏn subcenters to augment the skeleton crews that were already in the district. Most had two Korean employees, one for family planning, and one for tuberculosis (TB) control and prevention. The family planning employee's job was to know all of the fertile women in the *myŏn*. They were also to counsel them on birth control and to persuade the wives to use IUDs and birth control pills, and the husbands to get vasectomies. The TB employee's job was to identify TB patients with skin tests, track TB patients as they took their meds, and mass-vaccinate the *myŏn*'s schoolchildren with Bacillus Calmette–Guérin (BCG) shots.

The K-6 group therefore faced the task of trying to be useful to our two Korean co-workers, preferably without burdening them with the need to take care of us on top of their regular jobs. In our case, as one of the group's few married couples, we had been assigned to a tiny two-room house. The *myŏn* office had gone to the effort and the expense to protect our gated "property"

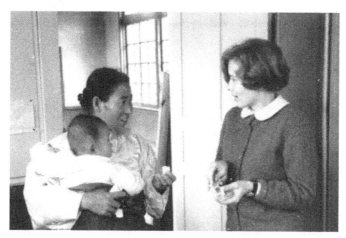

Fig. 3.1 Linda Clark at the Well Baby Clinic, Poksu Village, Kŭmsan County, South Ch'ungch'ŏng Province, South Korea, 1968. Photo by Don Clark.

with a mud wall and to make the house habitable with amenities like a new outhouse complete with a splendid ceramic urinal. It seems that this investment was made with the idea that these two young Americans would accomplish some good for the villagers. When we arrived with our baggage, our *chim*, which consisted of our suitcases, two good-sized trunks—the standard Peace Corps book locker full of reference books and things to read—and assorted bags and bundles, we looked to the locals like we were bearing cargo, presumably medical cargo, to benefit our neighbors. There was disappointment when we explained that all this stuff just belonged to us, and that there was nothing for them. It also had to be explained that we weren't doctors. The village carpenter, a rough-hewn neighbor who would become our main interlocutor, put his first question to us, in *panmal* (low talk) "Amudo ŏpsi, muŏ harŏ wassŏ," "You have nothing, so what did [you] come to do?" Or, as I took it, "What good are you, anyway?"

In time, we found more-or-less useful things to do. We taught English at the local school, helped the TB worker give BCG shots to school children, invented a record-keeping system for the health center, and organized the village library. We were given in-service training in TB control and began taking surveys and sputum samples to improve patient identification. But mostly we just lived in the village, took walks, learned the names for things, discovered things to photograph, and experienced South Korea's four seasons with its varieties of foods, fruits, and rituals. Time seemed to go more slowly, there was time to read, study, and observe our surroundings. We went to weddings and funerals, learned of the relationships among our neighbors, and occasionally had long conversations with people who dropped by, curious, to exchange stories. Our Korean got better, though never good enough. We listened a lot.

My wife Linda did not have the advantage (or handicap) of having any sort of Korea background. Everything was new and even fascinating to her in ways that it was not for me. Her quality was to take things as they came, while I still had "fixing Korea" in my DNA, something I'm sure I displayed in my weaker moments. Her job was to help the family planning employee, in the course of which she learned much from the village women: a vocabulary of family things, of foods and growing things, and of health issues as well as an overlay of village gossip. Our fellow K-6 volunteers demonstrated great differences in their abilities to accept the realities of South Korea without trying to change them. Between us, Linda and I also experienced this difference. Her mind was always more open than mine, and she enjoyed the village much more than I did.

Instead, I tried to use the experience in K-6 as a Korean studies practicum. In boyhood I had known the missionary-scholar Richard Rutt and had read his *Korean Works and Days*, a book that followed the seasons of his first year living in a village near Suwŏn.[4] By the time Linda and I were in the Peace Corps, Richard Rutt was the Anglican Bishop of Taejŏn just to the north of our assignment in Kŭmsan. On our visits with the bishop and his wife Joan, he urged me to seek out elements of higher culture in our village. He had me read his article "The Chinese Learning and the Pleasures of a Country Scholar," from which I drew an inkling of the importance of classical Chinese in Korean culture.[5] A Peace Corps study allowance enabled me to hire a tutor, a man my age who had been schooled in a valley *sŏdang*. He started me out on our first day, seated on the floor, rocking back and forth, singing/chanting the *Thousand Character Classic* (千字文), the primer used by generations of Chinese and Korean young people to memorize essential Chinese characters, starting with "*Hanŭl-ch'ŏn, Tta-ji, Kŏmŭl-hyŏn, Nurŭl-hwang* . . . ." (天, 地, 玄, 黃).[6]

Fig. 3.2 Linda Clark and her garden at the Poksu Health Center, Poksu Village, Kŭmsan County, South Ch'ungch'ŏng Province, South Korea, 1968. Photo courtesy of Don Clark.

My tutor introduced me to prominent families in the valley, who traced their ancestries through their *chokpo* genealogies, which they showed me. One family in particular was proudly descended from the sixteenth-century official Cho Hŏn, who with his Buddhist monk–friend Yŏnggyu Taesa, had organized a militia of common folk in Kŭmsan County to fight the oncoming Japanese invaders in 1592. Their story and the chronicle of the Battle of Kŭmsan, the county's signature historical story commemorated at the Shrine of the Seven

Fig. 3.3 Don Clark with the most senior Poksu Village elder, Poksu Village, Kŭmsan County, South Ch'ungch'ŏng Province, South Korea, 1968. Photo courtesy of Don Clark.

Hundred Martyrs (Ch'ilbaek Ŭich'ong), is inscribed on part of an elaborate tomb site, which had just been dedicated as part of President Park Chung Hee's effort to honor Korea's military heroes. Through my tutor, Linda and I became acquainted with a line of Cho Hŏn's descendants who maintained a beautiful country home across the stream behind our house, complete with a tablet shrine on the grounds for the annual family chesa rituals. I'm very grateful for these lessons and connections with Korean history and society.

Our village had a central square that included a makkŏlli house where the men gathered every afternoon in the closest thing we had to a local Rotary Club. The social skills required to survive these sessions included more language than I had, a ready supply of jokes and profanity, the ability to sing, detailed memories for things I couldn't remember, and astonishing capacities for alcohol consumption. I was invited—and sometimes I went of my own volition—but when I didn't, I would often get a visit from one of the Rotarians, often the carpenter-interlocutor, who would pull me out of my house or the health center and hustle me to the gathering. When this happened, it was usually because they were wondering something about my wife

Fig. 3.4 Don Clark with the Poksu Village executive committee, Poksu Village, Kŭmsan County, South Ch'ungch'ŏng Province, South Korea, 1968. Photo courtesy of Don Clark.

and me and wanted answers. For example, one day I was summoned to discuss the following:

CARPENTER. "Welcome, we don't see you often enough. Have some *makkŏlli*. Drink up!"

ME. "Thank you, I appreciate your warm hospitality. I'm glad to be living in this village." [*They pour, I raise my cup and drink.*]

SOMEONE. "You didn't bring your wife, did you?" [*laughter all around*]

ME. "No she's at home preparing dinner."

SOMEONE. "Then we know you'll have to leave soon. American wives don't like to wait." [*more laughter*]

CARPENTER. "What we wanted to ask you is, how long have you been married?"

ME. "Two years."

THEY. [*Gasp, intake of breath through clenched teeth.*]

CARPENTER. "Then your wife must be pregnant, yes?"

ME. "No. We are waiting to have babies until later."

Fig. 3.5 The Poksu Village Makkŏlli Club, Kongnamni Hamlet, Poksu Village, Kŭmsan County, South Ch'ungch'ŏng Province, South Korea, 1968. Photo by Don Clark.

CARPENTER. "What, why? Of course, you know what to do, right? Everybody knows that. Are you, you know, doing it?"

ME. [pride wounded] "Yes of course we do it. We're just planning our family."

SOMEONE. "Family planning? What good is family planning?"

ME. "Yes, we are here to encourage family planning. We want to be an example."

SOMEONE. "What kind of an example is that?"

CARPENTER. "Maybe you're not doing it right. Are you sure you're doing it right?"

ME. "Yes, no doubt. Also, we work for the Peace Corps, and there is a rule that if we have a child, we have to leave our jobs."

SOMEONE. "That's a rule?"

ME. "Yes, it's a rule put out by the government, which employs us."

CARPENTER. "Wow, if we had that rule, the people would overthrow *our* government! No one can stop Koreans having babies."

SOMEONE. "Another cup of *makkŏlli*? Or do you need to go home to your wife?" [*raucous laughter*]

Such was the effectiveness of me, a twenty-three-year-old American male, long-enough married but with no prospect of sons or even daughters, speaking Korean like a toddler, trying to teach family planning in a South Korean farming village in 1968. I am one of the many Peace Corps volunteers who recognized that what changed in our Peace Corps encounters was not our host countries, but ourselves.

"KOREANISTS CAN STEP UP TO THE BAR BUT THEY CAN'T DRINK"

In 1969, the leading historians of Korea gathered for an international conference at Academy House in the then-suburb of Suyuri. Among the Americans present were many of our mentors—that is, the "first echelon" of Korean studies—among them Gari Ledyard, Edward Wagner, Michael Rogers, Jim Palais, William Henthorn, and Spencer Palmer, together with their closest Korean colleagues such as historians Song June-ho and Lee Ki-baek.

I managed to get myself in the door of this distinguished assemblage, sitting in the back of the room while they shared their papers. When it was all over, Ledyard and Wagner stayed on in South Korea for a couple of days to hold sessions for interested Peace Corps volunteers and others who might want to apply to their programs at Columbia and Harvard. This was the golden age of Cold War area studies and there was serious federal funding for new Asian studies centers. Quite a few Peace Corps–Korea volunteers had applied and spent the next several years starting, and in many cases finishing, Korea-related graduate programs.

I applied to both Columbia and Harvard, and also Berkeley, professing to want to study North Korea and security issues since I had been an international relations major in college. My only acceptance came from Harvard, along with indirect word from Ed Wagner that I should forget about North Korea and come prepared to study what we then called "Yi Dynasty" society. I responded that I would love to study Yi Dynasty society, and in January 1971 Linda and I moved to Boston, and I enrolled in Harvard's Regional Studies East Asia program. Quite a few Peace Corps–Korea volunteers were already there, including Ed Baker, David McCann, and Beverly Nelson, all of whom had been members of the Peace Corps–Korea K-1.[7]

My boot camp introduction to Yi Dynasty social history was an Ed Wagner seminar that spent a semester studying a census register from the year 1663 that covered the Seoul neighborhood of Hapchang-ri (today's Hapchŏng-dong). Listed were the householders and their families, tenants, and slaves. The householders were often people with titles; and through this I learned the Korean for official titles. Korean families could be looked up in the genealogies, and this experience exposed me to Korean *chokpo* clan registers. The language of the document was Classical Chinese, but since many characters repeated and were names and titles, the vocabulary was not impossible to master. My village studies of the *Thousand Character Classic* were just enough to keep me afloat.

I spent more than seven satisfying years at Harvard, taking courses in Korean language and literature and was continuously supported by Edward Wagner with funding, eventually completing my dissertation on Ming-Korean relations in the late fourteenth-century transition from Koryŏ to Chosŏn.[8] Like others in my cohort, I spent dissertation research time in South Korea on Fulbright and Social Science Research Council (SSRC) fellowships, working under Korean professors. I finished in 1978. By then, our having two children greatly focused my mind on graduating and venturing into the job market.

Graduate study at Harvard deepened my knowledge of Korea while it broadened my knowledge of East Asia, inspired by the leading faculty in Chinese and Japanese history. My teaching fellowships were in "rice paddy" courses and US–East Asian relations, working for Edwin O. Reischauer, Albert Craig, John Fairbank, Benjamin Schwartz, and James C. Thomson, who served as my mentors alongside Ed Wagner. These teachers and the work in their courses steered me into a life teaching what I call "East Asia–General," a specialty that I hoped would suit me for a position in a liberal arts college somewhere. For Linda and me both, Whitworth College had been a wonderful undergraduate experience with small classes and dedicated teachers who knew our names and often invited us to dinner at their houses. Moreover, I remembered a remark by Harvard's Al Craig, speaking to several of us in Korean studies, about our chances of finding Korea jobs when we finished our PhDs. He said, "Koreanists are people who can step up to the bar, but they can't drink." I studied Korea, but I also took classes in Chinese and Japanese history, hoping to make myself believable as a possible tenure-track teacher of East Asia–General in a liberal arts college history department.

The job hunt in 1977 and 1978 came during a desperately dry season for hiring in the humanities across the nation. Harvard graduates were accustomed to launching themselves into jobs at fine universities. My more modest ambition to teach at a liberal arts college was met by disbelief by some in my student cohort; but in those years, all of us were competing for just a handful of jobs at schools of any kind. Harvard's Graduate School of Arts and Sciences organized a series of afternoon meetings with representatives from industry to sell the idea that we might try transferring our skills to the corporate sector. I remember one session in particular, led by a representative from Maidenform, telling us we might excel at selling ladies' underwear. With visions of an alternative career in lingerie in mind, I competed for jobs at Carleton, Colby, Grinnell, Sarah Lawrence, St. Johns, and Trinity University in San Antonio. The one offer came from Trinity, which turned out to be a well-funded, private liberal arts school with exactly the kind of teaching environment I was searching for. I went there and stayed for thirty-eight years. I started teaching courses on China and Japan, and after several years I put together a new course on the history of Korea. To the astonishment of my department and administration, it filled with students from the start and continued to be packed full every spring until my retirement in 2016. The students came with various interests and backgrounds: Korean school friends, the Korean War, Korean business, then Korean films and dramas, Korean food, and finally K-pop. Trinity did not have a large Korean American student population; most of my students were not heritage students. In that teaching environment, comparing notes with colleagues at other, larger universities, I became convinced that there was a great need to teach Korea studies as a "mainstream" curriculum subject and that Korean studies classes need not be reliant just on Korean heritage students for enrollments. I still feel strongly about this. People in graduate programs like Harvard's Regional Studies—East Asia MA program ought not be able to get away with not taking a single course on Korea. They should be prepared to teach units and courses on Korea, and undergraduate departments with Asian concentrations must include Korea-relevant material. When I became East Asian Studies director at Trinity, I attempted to put this into practice across the entire program.

"IF WE HAVE A KOREA COMMITTEE, WHY NOT AN OKINAWA COMMITTEE?"

To stay afloat in the Korea field, from the start I took advantage of every chance to participate in Korea panels at the AAS and the American Historical Association. I also let my Harvard sŏnbae Marshall Pihl talk me into taking his place as head of the AAS/Northeast Asia Council Committee on Korean Studies (CKS) in 1982. At the time, nobody much wanted to chair the CKS, but I thought at the time that chairing the committee might keep me active and visible in the field, so I accepted Marshall's put'ak (assignment). Throughout the 1980s, I chaired the Korea Committee, served as vice-chair, or edited the committee newsletter that was meant to serve as a networking tool. It looks easier now, with a website and a Facebook page, but in those days, editing a newsletter was a lot of typing, printing, folding, and mailing not to mention persuading people to supply news in the first place.

The job of the CKS chair brought with it ex officio membership in the Northeast Asia Council (NEAC), a provision intended to guarantee that at least one Koreanist would always attend NEAC meetings even if there weren't enough Koreanists in the AAS to get any of us properly elected.[9] The CKS chair had his/her expenses reimbursed, could sit in on NEAC business, usually participated fully in giving grants to Japan scholars that were funded by the Japan Foundation or the US-Japan Friendship Commission. I attended enough NEAC meetings over the years to dread the inevitable explanation to new members, always Japan scholars, of why the Korea field deserved free CKS chair membership. The topic periodically came up during NEAC budget discussions, when people noticed that the Committee on Korean Studies was funded entirely by a subvention from the AAS. While the Japan side was generating income from Japanese sources, the Korea side was a charity case. At one memorable meeting, one NEAC Japanist was heard to grumble, "If we have a Committee on Korean Studies, why don't we have a Committee on Okinawa Studies?"

Experiences with the CKS and the NEAC made the Association for Asian Studies (AAS) my lifeline from south Texas to the wider world of Korean and Asian Studies, and over the years I served on the program committee, the Northeast Asia Council (NEAC), and the *Journal of Asian Studies* editorial board on top of chairing the Committee on Korean Studies for multiple terms.

The wisecrack about Okinawa Studies surfaced around 1992, before the Korea Foundation had made much of an appearance. When it came to South Korean funding, we had, in addition to the problem of finding funds, the political problem within the Korea field of having colleagues who objected to seeking or accepting support from the military dictatorships that had been ruling South Korea since 1961. This was an important issue. We had professional colleagues whose academic freedom in South Korea was under constant government pressure. We knew of instances when Republic of Korea (ROK) consular officials in the United States had intimidated colleagues, especially South Korean nationals, by warning them not to present politically sensitive topics such as labor relations at AAS meetings.

South Korean political interference also extended into the AAS. For example, in 1982 while serving on the AAS program committee, I was contacted by a ROK embassy official in Washington, DC who urged me to place some ROK spokespeople on a planned panel discussing Japanese textbooks. He offered me an expense-paid trip to South Korea "for a conference," as bait. Muscling government spokesmen into AAS panels is not done, of course; and after the program committee meeting, he called and asked how it had gone. I told him that we had not changed the panel as he'd requested. His response had a note of retaliation: "I regret that you will be unable to join us at the conference in Korea." My colleagues in the field can tell their own stories of attempts to influence our professional work for political purposes.

When NEAC and the CKS determined to try to infuse a little South Korean money into the AAS, we had only one source to approach: the Korean Research Foundation, headed by a director well known to us: Hong Samyŏng. In Seoul over dinner I recounted the CKS's funding and representation problems to Mr. Hong. I had in mind a grant of, maybe, $10,000. At AAS in Boston in the spring of 1993, Mr. Hong and I met in the lobby of the Copley Plaza Hotel, and he promised $30,000 to the AAS "in the near future." There was no application process, no deadline, no signatures —only a handshake. Weeks passed. I thought he might have failed or forgotten, when suddenly the AAS called to ask me if I could explain an envelope that had been delivered to NEAC Chair Josh Fogel at the University of California at Santa Barbara. The envelope was unsealed and contained no letter, but it did contain a check for $30,000 from the Korean Cultural Service in Los Angeles made out to the AAS.

My office-holding years with the AAS/NEAC/CKS ended in the late 1990s when I moved into international education administration at Trinity University. Two years after that first $30,000 check, the Committee on Korea Studies had attracted the attention of the newly formed Korea Foundation (KF). KF representatives became regular attendees at AAS, and they took over funding NEAC's Korea programs, beginning with a small grants program comparable to what the Japan side already had. The Korea Foundation provided funding for research trips, organizing panels, course development, and distinguished lecturers. Money flowing to NEAC—along with prizes to scholars publishing books on Korea and to those with maturing careers in the field—brought notice in AAS elections also, the result of which created a much better balance in the Northeast Asia Council between Korea and Japan.

Before the Korea Foundation eclipsed the Korea Research Foundation in the mid-1990s, the KRF set the course for several other Korean studies organizations that have improved networking in the field and created opportunities for productive collaboration among scholars. These include the Pacific Area Conference (PACS), the Association for Korean Studies in Europe (AKSE), and the British Association for Korean Studies (BAKS). These organizations have evolved over the years and are still ongoing. An exchange effort began between the AAS/NEAC Committee on Korea Studies and AKSE in the mid-1990s, enabling scholars to participate in each other's annual meetings. Added to the tendency for Koreanists to gather in South Korea during the summer, these international opportunities have produced a lively global community of scholars who know each other and enrich each other's work.

UNFINISHED BUSINESS: KOREAN STUDIES AND LIBERAL ARTS COLLEGES

Nowadays it seems normal to have Korea Foundation support for overseas Korean studies programs and libraries, professorships, museum development, and career development. It took a while for the KF to organize a North American advisory group to help direct its largesse to where it would do the most good. Not surprisingly the advisors turned out to be the leading Korea scholars from major US institutions—universities with established resources including PhD programs. In the big picture, the emphasis on PhD training, including laudable fellowship support for students at critical moments in their careers, seemed like a miracle compared to the former parlous state of Korean studies training.

However, students don't sign up for Korean studies graduate training without some earlier life experience. Undergraduates take the courses taught by our newly minted PhDs, and then they go on to study abroad in Korea as juniors. A significant number of such students—some of America's best and brightest undergraduates—attend the liberal arts colleges that produce top candidates for the United States' best graduate schools. Wesleyan, Smith, Williams, Amherst, Oberlin, Grinnell, Macalester, Carleton and St. Olaf, and my own Trinity University are just a few. Their graduates excel in law, business, and in PhD programs in all disciplines, their choices based on things that inspired them before they got their BAs. I argue that the Korea Foundation and its North American advisory board have missed an opportunity—failed in fact—to cultivate this population of students and to persuade them to study Korea.

There is a way to do better. The ASIANetwork is a consortium of 160 smaller colleges and universities (enrollments under 2,500) that develops Asian studies in a way that combines strengths. ASIANetwork schools work together and have had great success raising funds to share among member institutions for consortial purposes.[10] A Freeman-funded traveling program enables faculty from member institutions to take their students to Asia, including South Korea, for summer research. A Mellon-funded program enables groups of non-specialist faculty to study together in programs designed to develop new courses on their campuses—including courses on Korea. A Luce-funded program has enabled ASIANetwork faculty to study in China and Hong Kong. One sign of the eagerness of ASIANetwork schools to do more with Korea is Lewis and Clark's new post-doctoral fellowship in Korean social science. No doubt our PhD graduates would like to see more of these career-building opportunities. It would not be hard to do.

Post-docs like the position at Lewis and Clark are just one way that the Korea Foundation and its advisors can deepen the demand for Korean studies in North America. More study abroad support for undergraduates in South Korea also seems like an obvious thing. Also vital is support for Korean-language instruction in liberal arts colleges. At Trinity University where I taught, demand for Korean outran demand for Japanese for many years running, but it was hard to maintain quality and staff and sustain student commitment. Even modest funding for an adjunct instructor would have made a great difference. Trinity is an important member of the ASIANetwork, and its students would be prime candidates for Korean studies support. They are eagerly looking for direction and interesting futures. They are talented, ambitious, and likely to succeed. As has been the case with some of my students, there are some who might actually find futures in things related to Korea.

LEGACIES OF THE PEACE CORPS GENERATION

In September 2016, a large group of former Peace Corps–Korea volunteers returned on the fiftieth anniversary of the arrival of the first group (K-1) to help open an exhibit about the Peace Corps in Seoul's National Museum of Korean Contemporary History.[11] The group was extraordinary. It included scientists, artists, diplomats, novelists, teachers and academics in all fields, and major contributors to advances in medicine. For many, it was the first return since their experience in the Peace Corps, and the reunions that were arranged with former co-teachers, health center co-workers, students, and host family members and neighbors were occasions for tears and nostalgia The museum exhibit was titled "Beautiful Journey, Endless Friendship." The reunion itself is documented on the former Peace Corps Volunteer group website called "Friends of Korea."[12]

The overarching message of the return visit is in the exhibit's title: "Beautiful Journey, Endless Friendship." Certainly, for anyone who has been away from South Korea since the 1960s or 1970s, the material progress of the country is astounding and there was amazement and delight because of it. Towns and villages that once were accessible only by a rickety country bus on muddy mountain roads are now reached in minutes or just a few hours on superhighways and bullet trains. This remarkable development—a prosperous South Korea—came at great sacrifice by generations of Koreans working brutal hours in often-miserable conditions to make life better for their children and to win a sense of national pride. The reunion group's hosts' effusions of gratitude might have exaggerated the role of the Peace Corps in these developments, but credit is certainly appropriate for the work and, at times, sacrifices of the volunteers in adding to the momentum of South Korea's advance.

We who ended up making a career of Korean affairs, whose story with Korea has involved frequent return visits and sustained friendships over many decades, are no less astonished by what we have been privileged to witness since our service in the Peace Corps. Korea has remained a lifelong focus, and we have been present during many crucial events in modern Korean history: elections and strikes, the Park assassinations, the Kwangju Uprising, and moments of crisis with North Korea. During periods of study and teaching, during conference trips and Fulbright fellowships, our knowledge of Korea has deepened, always revealing that the more we learn the more we need to know. All of us are well aware of the agency of the Korean people in the making of their own destiny. Our job has been to make them real to our own people, not as objects of American foreign policy or pawns in our own global conflicts, but as people worth knowing on their own terms.

NOTES

1. Linda Lewis has contributed a chapter to this volume detailing her experiences with Peace Corps–Korea. See Linda Lewis, "At the Border: Women, Anthropology, and North Korea," in *Peace Corps Volunteers and the Making of Korean Studies in the United States*, edited by Seung-kyung Kim and Michael Robinson, 127–40. Seattle: University of Washington Center for Korea Studies, 2020.

2. Felix Moos, "Leadership and Organization in the Olive Tree Movement" *Royal Asiatic Society–Korea Branch* 43 (1967):11–27, accessed September 24, 2019, http://www.raskb.com/content/full-texts-volume.

3. Donald N. Clark, *Living Dangerously in Korea: the Western Experience, 1900–1950* (Norwalk, CT: Eastbridge Books, 2003).

4. Richard Rutt, *Korean Works and Days: Notes from the Diary of a Country Priest* (Rutland, VT: Charles E. Tuttle Co., 1964).

5. Richard Rutt, "The Chinese Learning and the Pleasures of a Country Scholar: An Account of Traditional Chinese Studies in Rural Korea," *Transactions of the Royal Asiatic Society, Korea Branch* 37 (1960): 1–100.

6. Zhou, Xingsi, *Ch'ien tzu wen: The Thousand Character classic, A Chinese Primer* (New York: F. Ungar Pub. Co, 1963).

7. See Ed Baker's chapter in this volume. Ed Baker, "How the Peace Corps Changed Our Lives," in *Peace Corps Volunteers and the Making of Korean Studies in the United States,* edited by Seung-kyung Kim and Michael Robinson, 31–52. Seattle: University of Washington Center for Korea Studies, 2020.

8. A condensed version of the dissertation appeared in Donald N. Clark, "Sino-Korean Tributary Relations under the Ming" in *The Cambridge History of China, Volume 8: The Ming Dynasty, 1368–1644, Part 2,* edited by Denis Twitchett and Frederick W. Mote (Cambridge: Cambridge University Press, 1998): 272–300 and 989–91.

9. There were exceptions such as Chongsik Lee, Jim Palais, Laurel Kendall, JaHyun Haboush, John Duncan, and me, all "properly" elected to NEAC in the 1980s and 1990s. With the CKS chair, that made room for two Koreanists at NEAC meetings, not a negligible presence but still a small minority.

10. The Asia Network: Promoting Asia in the Liberal Arts, www.ASIANetwork.org.

11. "What a Beautiful Journey Celebrating the Fiftieth Anniversary Peace Corps Korea," Peace Corps Stories, accessed September 24, 2019, https://www.peacecorps.gov/stories/what-beautiful-journey-celebrating-50th-anniversary-peace-corps-korea/.

12. Friends of Korea. "Seoul in September 2016. . . What a Week!", accessed October 2, 2019. www.friendsofkorea.net/seoul-in-sept-2016.html.

BIBLIOGRAPHY

Baker, Ed. "How the Peace Corps Changed Our Lives." In *Peace Corps Volunteers and the Making of Korean Studies in the United States,* edited by Seung-kyung Kim and Michael Robinson, 31–52. Seattle: University of Washington Center for Korea Studies, 2020.

Clark, Donald N. *Living Dangerously in Korea: The Western Experience, 1900–1950.* Norwalk, CT: EastBridge Books, 2003.

Clark, Donald N. "Sino-Korean Tributary Relations under the Ming." In *The Cambridge History of China*, Volume 8: *The Ming Dynasty, 1368–1644*, Part 2, edited by Denis Twitchett and Frederick W. Mote, 272–300 and 989–97. Cambridge: Cambridge University Press, 1998.

Friends of Korea. "Seoul in September 2016. . . What a Week!" Accessed October 2, 2019. www.friendsofkorea.net/seoul-in-sept-2016.html.

Lewis, Linda. "At the Border: Women, Anthropology, and North Korea." In *Peace Corps Volunteers and the Making of Korean Studies in the United States*, edited by Seung-kyung Kim and Michael Robinson, 127–40. Seattle: University of Washington Center for Korea Studies, 2020.

Moos, Felix. "Leadership and Organization in the Olive Tree Movement" *Royal Asiatic Society–Korea Branch* 43 (1967):11–27, accessed September 24, 2019. http://www.raskb.com/content/full-texts-volume.

Rutt, Richard. *Korean Works and Days: Notes from the Diary of a Country Priest.* Rutland, VT: Charles E. Tuttle Co., 1964.

Rutt, Richard. "The Chinese Learning and the Pleasures of a Country Scholar: An Account of Traditional Chinese Studies in Rural Korea." *Transactions of the Royal Asiatic Society, Korea Branch* 37 (1960): 1–100.

Zhou, Xingsi. *Ch'ien tzu wen: The Thousand Character classic, A Chinese Primer.* New York: F. Ungar Pub. Co, 1963.

4

A Road Less Traveled: From Rome to Seoul via the Peace Corps

CARTER J. ECKERT

"All roads lead to Rome," as the saying goes, and this certainly was the case for me in terms of my historical interests until the Peace Corps took me to Seoul on what I thought was a temporary detour but instead turned out to be a new and life-changing destination. In 1968, I was a student at Harvard University studying late Roman imperial political history. It was the height of the Vietnam War—to which, like many in my generation, I was strongly opposed—and I sought an alternative to the draft, which was in force at the time, by applying to the Peace Corps. I requested Tunisia, close to Italy and filled with Carthaginian and Roman ruins, as my country of choice, and I fully expected to serve out my Peace Corps service there and return to Harvard to complete my doctoral degree in Roman history with some on-site archeological knowledge and much-improved French in my academic quiver. The Peace Corps in its wisdom, however, had other plans for me. Much to my disappointment at the time, I was offered a position as a university English teacher in South Korea, a country and region I knew little about, and whose history, strange to think today, was a total blank, apart from some newsreels about the Korean War (1950–53) I had seen in movie theaters as a boy in the 1950s but only vaguely remembered. I had no choice but to accept the offer at the time, however, because my local draft board was aggressively in pursuit, doing everything possible to ensure my conscription, and the Peace Corps would guarantee a deferment.

In the fall of 1968, I found myself with a hundred or so other volunteers comprising Peace Corps–Korea groups 7 and 8 (K-7 and K-8) in an abandoned Boy Scout camp in Hilo, Hawai'i, studying Korean language and culture, as well as TEFL (Teaching English as a Foreign Language). The Korean-language curriculum was based on what was called the aural-oral method, essentially a technique of listening and repeating without any clear explanations of grammar. While such a method might have worked well with infants learning to speak for the first time, it was in my view not very effective with adults, or at least not with me, and when I finally arrived in Seoul in January 1969, after four months of training in Hawai'i, I was able to repeat whole swatches of dialogue but unable to understand or respond to any new patterns that I had not encountered before. We had also learned only the polite forms of speech, so my friendly attempts to communicate with Korean children and dogs using honorific forms were occasions of uproarious laughter from any Koreans observing the scene, including the children themselves, if not also the dogs.

The balmy Hawaiian weather in which we had trained had also failed to prepare us for winter in Korea. In fact, January 1969 saw the heaviest snowfall on the peninsula in fifty years, and on our way there, we were forced to lay over in Tokyo for several nights because Seoul's Kimp'o Airport had been closed because of the storms and snow. Once in Seoul, our first abode was a small inn (yŏgwan) just off Sinch'on Rotary. One by one over the next week or so we were given a tour of our respective universities where we would begin teaching English conversation that spring semester. We were also introduced to our South Korean host families, where we would be living. Unlike many of

Fig. 4.1 Carter Eckert at Hilo training camp with Korean-language teacher Sŏl Sŏnsaengnim in front of dormitory named "Peace House." Hilo, Hawai'i, Fall 1968. Photo courtesy of Carter J. Eckert.

my fellow volunteers, who were being sent out to often challenging situations in a still very undeveloped countryside, I was fortunate in being welcomed into a well-educated and artistic family in Seoul, whose oldest child and elder daughter was at that time a professor of music at Seoul National University, as well as the premier classical pianist in the country. Hardly what one thinks of as the typical Peace Corps experience, I often woke up in the morning to live Mozart—the sound of my Korean "older sister" (nuna) practicing or teaching one of her protégés. Through Nuna, I met many other outstanding Korean musicians and artists and attended the opening of the Café Theater (Kkap'e Tteattŭrŭ), an intimate coffee shop and experimental theater on Ch'ungmuro Street that became a gathering place for Seoul's intelligentsia in the 1970s, as well as my own favorite spot in the city to hang out and meet friends. I think these early encounters with South Korean intellectuals and artists were among the first things that kindled a growing interest in the country and its history. One often hears that Koreans are a people filled with han, a deep-seated sense of frustration, grievance, and injustice, and the politics of the 1970s in South Korea were certainly conducive to that, but for me then and now the dominant impression is of a people imbued with a profound understanding of and desire for human interaction, open, generous, curious, willing if not eager to engage and develop lasting relationships with

Fig. 4.2 Carter Eckert in Korean dress (hanbok) at a party with Korean host family (Korean mother and older sister/Nuna) and friends, including three other Peace Corps volunteers from K-7/8, Spring 1969. Photo courtesy of Carter J. Eckert.

others, including strangers like myself. This is a combination of traits that I later learned Koreans associate with the term "*chŏng*," which is difficult to translate with a single English word, though perhaps "empathy" comes close.

Chŏng was also something I felt as a teacher almost immediately from my students. The school where I taught was not in the top tier of South Korean universities, and its facilities at that time, including classrooms and libraries, left much to be desired. Apart from a couple of weeks of teaching-practice in an elementary school in Honolulu as part of our Peace Corps training, I was completely inexperienced as a teacher, as well as very young, not much older than the students I was supposed to be teaching. But the students not only greeted me with the extraordinary respect that Koreans reserve for teachers and demonstrated a contagious enthusiasm for learning, they also quickly included me in many of their extracurricular activities, from informal meetings and assemblies to mountain treks to the temples around Seoul.

The South Korea I encountered as a Peace Corps volunteer in the late 1960s and 1970s was a very different place than it is today. First of all, Seoul was relatively small compared to the city we see now. It still had not expanded much beyond its old colonial contours, and today's affluent Kangnam area south of the Han River, made famous by the South Korean singer Psy, existed largely as paddy fields. In the early 1970s, if you knew the city as well as I had come to know it by then, you could find and walk your way blindfolded to most of the major locations, something unimaginable today. Many streets of the city were still unpaved, including the street that ran east from the East Gate (Tongdaemun) to my university. During the summer rainy season, the mud of that street and others that were still unpaved, splattered on and clung to one's shoes and clothes and found its way onto the floors of the city's shops and buses.

Many of those shops were also only one- or two-story structures, again dating from the colonial era or rebuilt after the Korean War. The tallest building, which Korean friends always liked to point out with pride, was the thirty-one-story Samil Building in Kwanch'ŏltong, completed in 1970. Spreading out in different directions from the base of the Samil Building were the major business and recreation districts of the city, each very compact, and with its own distinctive clientele. Kwanch'ŏltong and the old Ch'ŏnggyech'ŏn area catered to the beer-drinking salarymen, many of whom worked in the vicinity. To the north lay the Chongno area, with its large, long, low-tabled *makkŏlli* houses, the favorite haunt of university students, who could be heard singing and rhythmically tapping their chopsticks on the tables to the beat of the songs on almost any night of the week. To the south lay Myŏngdong, the old colonial shopping and entertainment district, still the most fashionable and sophisticated part of the city, with trendy coffee houses, tearooms, restaurants, and drinking establishments of various kinds, boutique clothing and accessories shops, and cinemas and theaters, including the Café Theater mentioned above, as well as the old National Theater. Whereas today, Seoul's modish establishments are spread throughout a greatly enlarged geographical area, in the 1970s much of what constituted the city's urban chic, with a hint of the demimonde thrown in as well, was concentrated in the greater Myŏngdong area. Very early on in my first months in Seoul, I visited an American friend and fellow volunteer teaching at Ewha Womans University for a "high-tea" at the school with her students and other faculty in what was then known as the "English House," where the girls practiced their English-language conversation skills and Western social manners. Ewha has changed a great deal since then, as has the visibility and role of women in South Korean society, but at that time an almost nineteenth-century puritanical atmosphere seemed to pervade the English House, and when I asked one of the faculty what parts of the city she would suggest I visit, she replied that wherever I went, I must at all costs avoid Myŏngdong, which was decadent and full of unhealthy temptations. It was of course on that excellent advice that I made my first trip to Myŏngdong that very same evening.

Seoul was not only small in the 1970s. It was poor, and the poverty was palpable, something I personally had never seen on such a scale before. The Gross Domestic Product (GDP) per capita income in South Korea was still less than US $300 in 1970, while today it is more than one hundred times that. Despite the fact that the Korean War had been over for sixteen years when I arrived, the city still had a kind of postwar feel to it. Beggars were everywhere, asking for alms or proffering unwanted trinkets for sale wherever they could, on the streets, on the buses, and even in the tearooms and shops if they were allowed entry by a compassionate merchant. Not a few were, or claimed to be, veterans of the war, often squatting or lying on a piece of dirty cardboard, and displaying their wounds or limbless bodies to passersby in the hope of a handout. Street urchins, barefooted or wearing the cheap rubber shoes (komusin) often seen in those days, were also ubiquitous, running after pedestrians with their wares, usually gum or candy, especially enthusiastic and persistent if their quarry was a foreigner, whom they all invariably called "American" (*Miguk saram*). For many Koreans in those days of Cold War American hegemony in an impoverished South Korea, the United States was an almost fantastical imaginary of wealth and power. To be an American in that setting on the one hand carried great privilege, but it also evoked uncomfortable feelings of inequity and neo-colonialism. Such feelings were only exacerbated by the conspicuousness of an enormous new US embassy building on Seoul's main thoroughfare opposite the Republic of Korea's main government complex at Kwanghwamun, and by the presence of more than 60,000 US troops in the country, whose Post Exchange (PX) base stores with their abundance of consumer goods were the wellspring of a flourishing black market and a reminder of the great disparity in living standards that then existed between the two countries. Today there are about 30,000 US troops still stationed in South Korea, and one can still find the occasional vendor of PX items on side streets or in the larger markets, but such scenes seem oddly out of place or even archaic in a country where the United States now imports large amounts of consumer goods from South Korea.

Such goods today of course include South Korean–made cars, most notably those produced by Hyundai. In the 1970s, the production of Hyundai's

Fig. 4.3 Man with oxcart in Ch'ŏngju city, North Ch'ungch'ŏng, South Korea, Spring 1969. Photo by Carter J. Eckert.

first export car to the United States, the Excel, was still a quarter of a century away. Apart from three-wheeled delivery trucks and taxis and buses, the latter belching noxious black fumes, the number of vehicles on the streets of Seoul was limited. Army Jeeps from the war were still quite common sights, refitted for private use with beaded upholstery and the inevitable box of facial tissues enclosed in an embroidered doily for honored passengers in the rear; it was in one of these refurbished Jeeps that I was picked up and taken for the first time to meet the president of the university where I would be teaching. The colors of the vehicles on the streets were for the most part black and grey, a chromatic pattern that seemed to dominate in the city, whether in the drab buildings on often treeless streets, in the suits of the hurrying salarymen (perhaps the only suit they owned), or in the uniforms worn by the gaggles of middle and high school students, another residue of the colonial era. At night the city became even darker. Electricity was expensive, and the urban neon flash and glitter of today's Seoul was still nearly two decades in the future. As one moved from the center of the city to the suburbs, the darker it became, with single bulbs, or even kerosene or candles providing the only illumination in the few places that remained open. The only time I saw a brightly-lit Seoul in the entire time I lived there from 1969–77 was in the early 1970s when a North Korea Red Cross delegation made an unprecedented visit to the city, and the Park Chung Hee (Pak Chŏnghŭi, 1961–79) government ordered that all of the buildings of the city leave their lights on at night as a sign to the North of the South's economic growth and prosperity.

The temporary brightness of the Seoul nightscape during the North Korean visit was in sharp contrast to the growing and more pervasive political darkness that was descending on the capital and the country in the early 1970s. When our Peace Corps group arrived in January 1969, the Park Chung Hee government was in the process of revising the constitution to allow Park a third term as president, and when I began to teach at my university that spring, there were frequent campus clashes between students protesting the government's plan with shouts of "No constitutional change!" (Kaehŏn pandae!) and angry helmeted combat police with tear gas and clubs. Coming directly out of a highly politicized student environment in the United States, where city and state police in April 1969 had entered Harvard Yard to remove and arrest students occupying the main administration building to protest the Vietnam War, I felt a certain kinship with the Korean students. The situation of course only became worse, culminating in Park's declaration of the Yusin "revitalizing reforms" on October 17, 1972, a day I remember well. It was a crisp, sunny fall morning, and as I walked down main street of Sejongno, I passed the assembly of tanks and soldiers that had appeared overnight in front of the major government buildings, I remember thinking that a Rubicon had been crossed in South Korean political life and wondered where it would all lead.

Living under Yusin was in many ways like living in an armed camp, and Park Chung Hee himself liked to praise the system as being as secure as a " steel drum."[1] A strict curfew, which had predated Yusin, was in effect from midnight to 4:00AM. It was always amazing to see the busy streets and shops furiously emptying out in the last five minutes before midnight, as people scrambled to catch the last bus or taxi. At the stroke of the hour the whole scene became eerily still and quiet as a tomb, punctuated only by the conversations and crackling radio communications of the curfew police and the sounds of the young boys who were allowed to walk the streets from inn to inn selling seasoned seaweed rice rolls (kimbap) and barking out the name of their merchandise in a long, piercing, stylized "Kimmmmm-bap!" with an

Fig. 4.4 Riot police invading my university during student demonstrations against constitutional amendment allowing President Park Chung Hee to run for a third term, Spring 1969. Photo by Carter J. Eckert.

explosive accent on the second syllable. Surveillance was more subtle during the day, but one was always aware of a surrounding police or military presence; bus trips to the countryside were often interrupted by soldiers at various checkpoints who came on board and walked through the aisle stopping from time to time to check identifications, and sometimes forcibly removing passengers, especially students, from the bus for further interrogation.

Censorship and other forms of cultural intrusion were common, including in newspapers, books, magazines, and even music. Long-playing Korean pop song albums often included completely extraneous military songs on their tracks, and foreign magazines like *Time* and *Newsweek* always had pictures of Communist leaders like Mao Zedong blacked out. Huge banners stretched above streets and intersections exhorted citizens to "crush communism" (*myŏlgong*) and to report anyone or anything strange to the police. Regular daytime air-raid drills, which brought the city to a fifteen-minute halt, were designed to remind people of the dire state of emergency in which they all lived. For the most part I prided myself on being immune to such blatant indoctrination, chuckling at the idea that looking at an uncensored photograph of Mao might somehow inspire one to start reading Marx, but in 1976 I received my comeuppance. One evening that summer as I was reading in my seventh-floor apartment the whole building began to shake, and people started screaming and running down the stairs to get out. It turned out that we were experiencing aftershocks from the great Tangshan earthquake that had reached 8.2 on the Richter scale, an event that eventually killed hundreds of thousands of people in China. My first reaction, however, was that the North Koreans had invaded, and the first thing I grabbed as I ran out the building with everyone else was my passport. Later I learned that my panicked assumption had been more or less typical of most of the people in the complex. Foreigner or not, years of pervasive propaganda had left their mark, even on me.

If one eschewed confrontational politics, life went on more or less as usual, and foreigners were generally given special dispensations rarely enjoyed by Koreans. Student friends with books the government deemed subversive like Franz Fanon's *Wretched of the Earth*, a clandestine favorite among university students at the time, often left their suspect volumes with me on the assumption that my apartment would not be searched, and to my knowledge it never was.[2]

Even foreigners had to be prudent and careful, however. On one occasion returning from a party in the area of the presidential Blue House, I miscalculated the time to curfew and found myself shortly after midnight facing armed military police with their guns pointed directly at me. Even for a foreigner, the Blue House complex after curfew was dangerous territory. Fortunately, I was able to explain myself in Korean to the police, and one of them zipped me home through the empty streets of Seoul on the back of his motorcycle; the fastest ride I have ever experienced in the city.

On another occasion when I had misjudged the curfew, I was walking back home just after midnight when I saw a policeman harassing a young Korean student for being out on the street. I intervened, telling the policeman that we were together. Having ascertained I was a foreigner, the policeman told me to go home, but I foolishly persisted and wound up being taken to the police station with the student. I was quickly released, but it was a clear sign that there were limits to the dispensations granted to foreigners. This was especially the case if the offense was deemed a matter of national security. In the early 1970s, for example, I had become friends with a visiting Japanese reporter covering South Korean politics who was later arrested in 1974 for allegedly passing North Korean funds to anti-government South Korean students. The charge was completely bogus, but the Park Chung Hee government tried the reporter, and he was given a sentence of death, which in turn was later commuted to twenty years imprisonment. In the end he was eventually allowed to return to Japan. While he was in prison, I met with one of his friends whom I also knew, a fellow reporter, also Japanese, who had come to visit him and was staying in the Chosun Hotel in downtown Seoul. The timing of our meeting could not have been worse, as it came in the tense immediate aftermath of the assassination attempt on Park Chung Hee only weeks earlier by a Korean resident of Japan, Mun Segwang, which had taken the life of Park's respected wife, Yuk Yŏngsu. Within an hour after I had returned to my apartment, I received a visit from the head of my local police station, who questioned me for over an hour about my relationship with the reporter and with Japanese acquaintances in general. To this day I do not know how he identified me, though I presume either the hotel room where we met had been bugged, or I had been followed, or, most likely, both. For reasons such as these one also had to be careful discussing politics with Korean friends in public places such as tearooms or restaurants, especially at the height of the

Yusin period, when it became illegal to criticize the president in any way. One never knew who was listening. While the worst that was likely to happen to me was that I would be expelled from the country, my Korean friends were likely to face much more severe punishment for participating in those conversations, even if it had been I who had been the voicing the criticisms.

Given the poverty and political repression of the time, one might imagine that South Korea in the 1970s was a static, inert country, whose people had little energy or incentive to pursue their aspirations. The reality could not have been more different. If the poverty was tangible, so too were the innumerable and often remarkable escapes from it. One saw this at the macro level in the rise of the ROK's huge business complexes, then just beginning to find their niche in the international export markets. It was also present at the micro level in the countless numbers of smaller companies with only a handful of employees, including what were at the time called op'ŏsang, which often consisted of only a single person acting as a commercial agent for a foreign importer or exporter. One small entrepreneur from Kyŏngsang Province, whom I came to know well, began his career as a teenage laborer in his hometown delivering the charcoal briquettes that were used in those days to heat Korean-style ondol floors. He found his way to Seoul, and when I first met him, he had just started an op'ŏsang with a foreign client based in Chicago who was interested in purchasing metal pots and pans, as well as other goods, from South Korean companies. In time he was able to make enough money as an op'ŏsang to establish his own factory that produced all the items he had been purchasing on behalf of his client, and from there he continued to expand his manufacturing business many times over, eventually opening factories in China in the 1990s as well, where labor costs by then were more competitive than in South Korea.

The benefits of South Korea's impressive economic growth of the 1970s did not of course accrue equally, and workers at the smallest firms especially often suffered terribly from long hours and poor and often dangerous working conditions, not least of all the female garment workers whose industry in many respects led the early export drive of the period. Despite these hazards, tens of thousands of poor, young peasants, many female, flocked into the cities in the hopes of a better life for themselves and their families. By 1975, more than 50 percent of the South Korean population was living in urban areas, double the figure of other developing countries at the time, and more than two and a half times the number of Koreans living in cities at the end of the Colonial Period in 1945. For me one of the most iconic figures of the 1970s was the bus conductor or *ch'ajang*. Invariably a young teenage girl fresh from the countryside in what was probably her first job in the city, she often looked worn and haggard by the end of the morning rush hour, her black cap and uniform already coated with the early grime of the day. But somehow she persisted, politely and often with a shy smile, for the rest of her long day, and for the day after that and so on, collecting fares from often impatient and irritated passengers, and managing somehow to squeeze impossible numbers of people onto the bus as she yelled out "All right!" (*Orai!*) to the driver, letting him know he could move on to the next stop. I often think about those bus girls when I think about my Peace Corps time in South Korea and wonder what happened to them. Poverty brought them to the buses, but only hope and a fierce determination to improve their lives could have sustained them in such a wretched job.

The local cultural scene in Seoul in the 1970s was as vibrant and dynamic as the economy itself. Much of it, especially the music and theater, was centered in Myŏngdong, where all the well-known singers—the K-pop stars of the era before "K-pop" had become a term— including Song Ch'angsik, Yun Hyŏngju, Kim Pyŏnggŏl, Kim Min'gi, Yang Hŭiŭn, Kim Sehwan, and many others, performed regularly at a beer hall called OB's Cabin, named, appropriately, after South Korea's most popular beer at the time. When we had time on the weekends, my friends and I would often meet at the Café Theater, just a block away, to begin our evening, but we almost always ended up eventually at the OB listening to live new music. Some of the best songs of the era, like Kim Min'gi's "Morning Dew" (*Ach'im isŭl*) also subtly challenged the government's positive drumbeat of modernization and became important musical elements of a growing movement of protest and resistance that would explode with full force a decade later. As Paul Chang has pointed out in his recent book, *Protest Dialectics*, the protest movement was already well underway in the 1970s, in labor organizations, in Christian churches, and of course on the college campuses.[3] Even the curfew could not contain the vitality of 1970s Seoul, as many people disappeared at midnight into the technically illegal but largely tolerated after-hours drinking establishments, where, if you knew where to go, a friendly knock on the large sliding metal doors that had shuttered the shops would cause the garage-style door to roll up just enough for

you to duck quickly inside. Of course you were now effectively a captive cus-
tomer until 4:00AM, when the curfew ended, but some of the after-hours
places, such as the Silver Star (Ŭnsŏng) just down the street from Myŏngdong
Cathedral, were also the favorite haunts of the city's most outspoken writers
and artists, and the conversations were always lively, and not infrequently
interspersed with impromptu poetry recitations or songs.

As my experiences and relationships in South Korea grew, along with a
better understanding of the language, so too did my interest in the country as
a whole. As I like to tell my students at Harvard, in the full knowledge of what
I know today, the Peace Corps had unexpectedly parachuted me down into
one of the most exciting and transformative periods of modern world history,
not unlike, one might say, Japan's bustling early Meiji period. Even though at
that point I was still planning to return to the States to continue my study of
Western history, I decided to stay on a bit longer after my service with the
Peace Corps ended to see where life might take me. In retrospect, this was
one of the best decisions of my life, but at the time I think I was in no small
part reflecting the relaxed 1960s generational sensibility that encouraged
youth in their twenties to "drop out" from one's usual or routine existence for
serendipitous personal exploration. But clearly by this time South Korea, its
people, its language, its culture, and its history, were also starting to intrigue
me more and more. Through a friend I was able to secure a full-time job with
a maritime consulting company and later with one of the major South Korean
shipbuilding firms. At first I knew nothing about shipbuilding, one of the key
strategic industries on the peninsula at the time—or about business in general for that matter—but the company wanted my English skills not my business acumen, and the job turned out to be a unique on-site education, a
once-in-a-lifetime opportunity allowing me to see in real time, first-hand and
up-close, how the so-called Miracle on the Han was taking place in terms of
government-business interaction, management-labor relations, and corporate
office culture. Eventually I decided I wanted to return to the States and continue my historical studies, but this time with a focus on the modern transformation of South Korea—to make historical sense, if you will, of what I had
been observing and experiencing during the past eight years.

When I returned to the United States in 1977, Korean studies was still very
much in its infancy. Edward Wagner at Harvard and his former student James
Palais at the University of Washington (UW) in Seattle, both Chosŏn Dynasty

historians, were actively seeking to recruit graduate students to their programs and to develop the field, but there was little financial support available, and job prospects, after the required eight to nine years of study for a doctoral degree, were bleak to say the least. One had to be very committed, very optimistic, and a little "crazy," as some of my relatives pointedly put it at the time, to pursue such a career. I had met and talked with both Wagner and Palais at different times when I was still living in Seoul and had great respect for them both. In the end I chose to go to the UW because Palais, together with Bruce Cumings, then a newly minted PhD from Columbia, and fellow Peace Corps volunteer who had just been hired by the UW, were focusing on developing a modern history component of their program, something Harvard did not have at the time. In addition, Michael Robinson, a good friend from my own Peace Corps group, was already enrolled at UW studying modern Korean history and waxed eloquently about the program and Palais' extraordinary mentorship.[4] He was not exaggerating. The time I spent at UW was among the most intellectually rewarding of my life, and it also provided the basis for a lifelong network of colleagues and friends, from Palais and Cumings to a

Fig. 4.5 Educational conference at one of the universities, including a number of K7–K8 Peace Corps volunteers. I am in the front row, second from left, next to the Catholic sister. Mike Robinson (chapter 8) is in the top row, center, head slightly above everyone else. Seoul, South Korea, Spring 1969. Photo courtesy of Carter J. Eckert.

large circle of seniors and juniors in the program, many of whom went on to develop Korean studies programs at other universities.

One of the most intriguing and rewarding aspects of studying modern Korean history derives from its rich overlap with the histories of other countries, including China (both Qing and the People's Republic of China), Japan, Russia (both Tsarist and Soviet), and of course the United States. My interest in the historical context of the Korean peninsula's modern transformation took me down many fascinating and unforeseen paths that often wove their way through these other connected histories. Perhaps the most unexpected and controversial of these paths led me to Japan and the Japanese Colonial Period, which was little studied at the time, and which, indeed, I myself had largely ignored until I began looking at South Korean business history and the primary documents from the time. At the moment I am engaged in a project to study the historical origins and formation of the Park Chung Hee modernization state, which also has a significant colonial dimension, and I find myself in a kind of dialogue between my own experience and the deeper history I am trying to explore.[5] The gift of Korea, which the Peace Corps unexpectedly gave me more than fifty years ago, is truly a gift that has kept on giving in manifold ways and on multiple levels in both my professional and personal lives.

NOTES

1. Chŏng Chaegyŏng, ed., *Pak Chŏnghŭi silgi: haengjŏk ch'ŏrok* [The true record of Park Chung Hee: Selected excerpts] (Sŏul: Chimmundang, 1994), 481.

2. Frantz Fanon and Constance Farrington. *The Wretched of the Earth.* (New York: Grove Press, 1968).

3. Paul Y. Chang, *Protest Dialectics: State Repression and South Korea's Democracy Movement, 1970–1979* (Stanford, CA: Stanford University Press, 2015).

4. Mike Robinson has detailed his experiences in the Peace Corps in chapter 8 of this volume. See Michael Robinson, "Empathy, Politics, and Historical Imagination: A Peace Corps Experience and Its Aftermath," in *Peace Corps Volunteers and the Making of Korean Studies in the United States,* edited by Seung-kyung Kim and Michael Robinson, 141–58 (Seattle: University of Washington Center for Korea Studies, 2020).

5. Carter J. Eckert, *Park Chung Hee and Modern Korea: The Roots of Militarism 1866–1945* (Cambridge, Ma., Harvard University Press, 2016).

BIBLIOGRAPHY

Chang, Paul Y. *Protest Dialectics: State Repression and South Korea's Democracy Movement, 1970–1979*. Stanford, CA: Stanford University Press, 2015.

Chŏng Chaegyŏng, ed. *Pak Chŏnghŭi silgi: Haengjŏk ch'ŏrok* [The true record of Park Chung Hee: Selected excerpts]. Sŏul: Chimmundang, 1994.

Eckert, Carter J. *Park Chung Hee and Modern Korea: The Roots of Militarism 1866–1945*. Cambridge, MA: Harvard University Press, 2016.

Fanon, Frantz, and Constance Farrington. *The Wretched of the Earth*. New York: Grove Press, 1968.

Robinson, Michael. "Empathy, Politics, and Historical Imagination: A Peace Corps Experience and Its Aftermath." In *Peace Corps Volunteers and the Making of Korean Studies in the United States*, edited by Seung-kyung Kim and Michael Robinson, 141–58. Seattle: University of Washington Center for Korea Studies, 2020.

5

Serendipity, Uyŏn, and Inyŏn

BRUCE FULTON

Serendipity is defined as "the faculty for making desirable discoveries by accident."[1] Combine serendipity with uyŏn (chance, accident, fortuity) and inyŏn (prior connection) and you have the best possible explanation as to how I became involved with Korea and Korean studies. In the summer of 1977, I was living in Brunswick, Maine, the small town where I had graduated from college seven years earlier, and I had a decision to make. I could spend the rest of my life in that small corner of the world, or I could expand my horizons by venturing outside the United States. Having decided on the latter course and focusing on the Peace Corps as the means to that end, I ultimately entrusted myself to a language and culture that have claimed me for life. The combination of serendipity and uyŏn brought me to one desirable discovery after another: South Korea as a Peace Corps country (I had wanted to go to Nepal and was first offered Afghanistan); North Chŏlla Province (my assigned post in 1978 with Peace Corps–Korea group K-44); Yun Ju-Chan (whom I would marry in 1979, and with whom I began a career in literary translation that continues to this day); Seoul National University (my assigned post in 1979; I would return there in the 1990s to complete my PhD in Modern Korean Literature under the supervision of Professor Kwon Youngmin [Kwŏn Yŏngmin]); and Hwang Sunwŏn (whom I met through an SNU professor and whose short fiction would become the subject of my SNU dissertation). As for inyŏn, I discovered that my birthday, October 9, is Korean Alphabet Day, the day in 1446, when the admirably precise Hangŭl, invented by the great King Sejong, was officially announced to the people of Chosŏn. This series of fortuitous discoveries and events is the basis for my life with Korea and Korean literature.

Before leaving South Korea at the end of my Peace Corps term in late December 1979, I was told by a member of our group from the state of Washington, that a man named James Palais taught Korean history at the University of Washington (UW). Well, here was more inyŏn: my mother had grown up in a small city outside Seattle and had graduated from the UW, and I had lived in Seattle for a year and a half in the early 1950s during one of my father's several postings as an engineer working for General Electric. In the early 1980s, when I returned to the United States with Ju-Chan, the UW was one of a handful of institutions in North America with a Korean studies program, which was, and still is, housed in the Henry M. Jackson School of International Studies.

In the summer of 1981, Ju-Chan and I departed for Seattle. My first objective was not Korean studies; rather it was a Master of Arts in Teaching degree. As it turned out, that program was run by the UW Department of Linguistics, whose spokesperson advised me that my almost two years abroad teaching English as a foreign language counted for little; I would have to earn a background in linguistics as a foundation for the program. No thanks. Instead I gained admittance to the MA program in Korea Regional Studies, an interdisciplinary program whose faculty boasted three of the pioneers of Korean studies in the United States: the aforementioned James Palais, a historian of the Chosŏn period, who would train an entire generation of Korea historians; Bruce Cumings, a political scientist whose broad understanding of the political and socioeconomic development of Korea within the broader Northeast Asia region would lead him to focus more broadly on Korea's modern history; and Fred Lukoff, a linguist and the author of the first textbook on spoken Korean by a non-native Korean.[2]

That this MA program was housed in the UW Henry M. Jackson School lent it additional benefits. Both Ju-Chan and I took up the study of a second foreign language, Mandarin, and I availed myself of coursework offered by two engaging historians of traditional China, Jack Dull and Chan Hok Lam. (I had also hoped to study Japanese literature and history but found the instructors of those two areas to be singularly unaccommodating.) The resulting interdisciplinary thrust of my MA program has shaped my involvement in Korean studies to this day.

Uyŏn resurfaced in 1983 as Ju-Chan and I neared the end of our respective MA programs (hers was in special education). We had made plans to study

Mandarin abroad—at Beijing University in China, with funding from the Council on International Educational Exchange (CIEE). Such was the hold that the Chinese language exercised on us at the time. But then geopolitical realities entered. With only a few months remaining before our planned departure for Beijing, Ju-Chan received a letter from the Chinese consulate to which she had applied for a visa. As a Republic of Korea (ROK) national (she had not yet obtained US citizenship) she was not eligible for a visa from the People's Republic of China (PRC). Fortunately, we had arranged a plan B: I would study at the Korean Language Institute at Yonsei University in Seoul.

Study at Yonsei in the summer of 1983 was beneficial in two ways. First, I furthered my learning of *insa mal*, the short phrases that break the ice in situations where Koreans and foreigners are brought into contact. I found that *Sugo hasimnida* (literally, "You're hard at work" but more aptly "Good work") and *Sugo haseyo* ("Keep up the good work") were especially effective. The more practical benefit, which involved the *inyŏn* of having met Hwang Sunwŏn in 1979 while I was posted at Seoul National University, was that Ju-Chan and I were approached out of the blue by a representative of the ROK Ministry of Culture (as it was known then; it is now the Ministry of Culture, Sports, and Tourism). The ministry had received funding from a foundation called the International Communications Foundation (ICF; Kukche kyoryu chinhŭnghoe), to support the translation and publication of several contemporary (*hyŏndae*) novels. (*Hyŏndae* by definition in Korean literary history means post-1945.) Among the novels was none other than Hwang Sunwŏn's *Umjiginŭn sŏng*. We jumped at the opportunity, and our translation, *The Moving Castle*, was published by Si-sa-yŏng-ŏ-sa—now YBM Sisa, which turned out to be the parent company of the ICF—in 1985. In 2016, our revised translation, retitled *The Moving Fortress*, was issued by MerwinAsia.

The translation of this novel led in turn to the enrichment of my engagement with Korean culture and Korean studies, in that the text contains a strong element of traditional Korean religiosity, or *musok*. We met several times with Mr. Hwang, and on one such occasion he shared with us the works of Kim T'aegon, an anthropologist and pioneering researcher of *musok*. Thus began my encounter with one of the two central streams of the Korean literary tradition, oral literature (*kubi munhak*). Oral literature has long been eclipsed by the much more elite, conservative, and patriarchal stream of recorded literature (*kirok munhak*). For me, though, thanks in large part to the translations of Kevin O'Rourke, our finest all-around translator of Korean literature, oral literature is the heart and soul of the Korean literary tradition.

Ju-Chan and I now had a novel translation under our belt. What next? Hwang Sunwŏn, an inveterate reader of contemporary Korean literature as well as contemporary Japanese literature, had the answer. Actually, three answers: O Chŏnghŭi, Kang Sŏkkyŏng, and Kim Chiwŏn. O in the mid-1980s was reaching the high point of her career, having received the Tongin Literature Prize in 1982 for her story "Tonggyŏng" ("The Bronze Mirror"), to go along with the Yi Sang Literature Prize she had earned in 1979 for "Chŏnyŏk ŭi keim" ("Evening Game"); the Tongin and Yi Sang prizes are the two most prestigious South Korean awards for literary fiction. Kang for her part had just published a novella, "Sup sok ŭi pang" ("A Room in the Woods"), soon to be the title work of a story collection that would become the best-selling book-length work of fiction issued to that point by Minŭm sa, one of the elite publishers of literary fiction in South Korea. Hwang was interested in the coming-of-age element of this story, having published several classic works on that theme, such as "Sonagi" ("The Cloudburst"). As for Kim, she had been introduced to the South Korean literature power structure, or mundan, by Hwang back at a time when established authors could recommend newcomers for admittance to the establishment.

During my MA program at the University of Washington I met Mark Peterson, a PhD student under Edward Wagner at Harvard, who spoke at a Korea colloquium hosted by the Korean studies program at the Henry M. Jackson School. In the summer of 1985, Ju-Chan and I learned that Brigham Young University would host an international conference on Korean literature. One of the sessions would be a translation workshop attended by graduate students past and present who would each prepare a translation. We had the good fortune of receiving an invitation from Mark Peterson, who had begun teaching at BYU. We submitted "The Bronze Mirror," our translation of O Chŏnghŭi's "Tonggyŏng," and to our surprise were awarded a prize for our efforts.[3]

More important, among the scholars attending the conference were two who would have a crucial impact on my professional life—Marshall R. Pihl and Kwon Youngmin, who, it turned out, had their own uyŏn; they had met at Harvard in 1984, where Professor Kwon taught as a visiting scholar. In 1985, Professor Kwon published, through the aforementioned Minŭm sa, a four-volume literature anthology marking the fortieth anniversary of Korea's liberation from Japanese colonial rule.[4] How would Ju-Chan and I like to collaborate with them in producing a one-volume anthology of fiction in English translation deriving from the Minŭm sa anthology? Eight years later, in 1993, this project bore fruit as Land of Exile: Contemporary Korean Fiction, translated by Marshall R. Pihl and Ju-Chan and myself and published by M.E. Sharpe.

Kwon Youngmin was a professor of modern Korean literature at Seoul National University (where I had taught in 1979 in the Peace Corps). He was also the managing editor of the monthly Munhak sasang (Literature and thought), one of the premier journals of Korean literature, and whose parent company oversees the annual Yi Sang Literature Prize. Ju-Chan and I soon had in our possession the 1984 Yi Sang Literature Prize anthology containing the prize-winning story as well as the short list of nominated stories. The prize-winning story, the late Yi Kyunyŏng's "Ŏduun kiŏk ŭi chŏp'yŏn," captured our attention. We decided to give it a try, and submitted our translation, "Beyond the Dark Memories," to the 1989 Korea Times translation competition. We were pleasantly surprised to receive first prize in the short-fiction category.

Our confluence with Marshall Pihl and Kwon Youngmin and the forty-years-of-post-Liberation-fiction project led to another serendipitous meeting—with Cho Chŏngnae. In 1986, six of the translations that would go into Land of Exile were published, side by side with the Korean original and commentary by the author, the translator(s), and a scholar, as features in the monthly literary journal Han'guk munhak (Korean literature). Among those stories was the one, "Yuhyŏng ŭi ttang," that would become the title story of Land of Exile, and Cho was its author. At the time he was halfway through what would become a ten-volume historical novel, T'aebaek sanmaek (The T'aebaek Mountains), one of the most influential works of fiction in modern South Korea. He asked if we would be interested in translating this epic, but at the time we lacked the confidence to undertake a project of such magnitude.

Nevertheless, we continued to follow Cho's career as he completed T'aebaek sanmaek and two other epic novels, Arirang (Arirang; the name of Korea's best-loved folk song) and Han'gang (The Han River). At the same time, Land of Exile became a standard English-language anthology of post-1945 Korean fiction, and we have always believed that the title story is one of the most compelling works of modern Korean fiction. In the meantime I had begun teaching in the Department of Asian Studies at the University of British Columbia (UBC), and one of the courses I taught was KORN 410, an entry-level course in reading and translating Korean literary fiction, created by Ross King, professor of Korean and a historical linguist in our department. Among the stories assigned in this course, I discovered Cho's "Pinghagi" ("The Ice Age"). Later I learned that this story had been pronounced by none other than Korea University professor Yi Namho as the best Korean story of the 1970s (and the 1970s was a very good decade for Korean fiction indeed). When Cho returned to writing shorter novels after his three epics, Ju-Chan and I had the rare experience of coming across a work of fiction that utterly engaged us, a work we felt compelled to translate—Cho's *O hanŭnim* (*How in Heaven's Name*). That experience led us in turn to translate his three-volume novel *Chŏnggŭl malli* (*The Human Jungle*).

How do translations of Korean literature connect with Korean studies? First of all, in Cho Chŏngnae we have an author who is the son of a Colonial Period activist, a man who learned early on how his country has been influenced not only by two neighboring empires—those of China and Japan—but more recently by Western superpowers. He has always reminded his readers of the vicissitudes of modern Korean history within the larger context of geopolitical conflict, and to reach his audience he has developed superb storytelling skills. To sustain his prodigious output, he adopted a spartan lifestyle and a rigor that would put to shame writers who are decades his junior. As much as Ju-Chan and I in our translation work have come to believe in the viability of art-for-art's sake literature, it is translations of literature that embodies a historical consciousness (*yŏksa ŭisik*—a term that is practically a cliché in Korean literary criticism these days) that likely have proved more useful in the Korean studies classroom.

Perhaps there is a more salutary lesson for Korean studies that is offered in Cho's fiction, and that is the importance of narrative. In a recent interview Cho declared that present-day Korean fiction writers have lost the knack of telling a good story; they can no longer write in the third person. Cho's third-person narratives often give voice to the nameless millions who have played crucial roles in Korean history, most recently from the 1960s into the 1990s as South Korea transformed from a war-ravaged agrarian economy into one of the most high-tech nations in the world. For a narrative to be effective it must reach an audience, and as of 2015 Cho's three sagas had sold 17 million copies.

Our experiences in the mid-1980s prompted us to continue translating. We submitted Days and Dreams," our translation of Kang Sŏkkyŏng's story "Nat kwa kkum," to the 1987 Korea Times translation competition and again earned first prize in the short-fiction category. "Days and Dreams" is a military camp town story (kijich'on sosŏl), and was for me a first-of-a-kind portrayal of the cross-cultural contact I myself had experienced as a Peace Corps volunteer a decade earlier. And so it was that on our next occasion of serendipity—meeting Faith Conlon and Barbara Wilson of Seal Press in Seattle—we had already translated stories by both Kang Sŏkkyŏng and O Chŏnghŭi. Seal was a feminist press founded in 1976 (it is now an imprint of Hachette Book Group) and among its imprints was Women in Translation, devoted to international literature.

Words of Farewell: Stories by Korean Women Writers was published by Seal Press in 1989, the first and only Korean volume in the Women in Translation series. The centerpiece of this anthology was none other than the Kang Sŏkkyŏng novella "Room in the Woods," recommended to us by Hwang Sunwŏn a few years earlier. Kang's "Days and Dreams" along with three stories by O and two by Kim Chiwŏn (the third author recommended to us by Hwang), filled out the volume. We could not have imagined the reception accorded this book. Seal Press kept detailed records of college and university course adoptions of its books, and we were amazed to learn that within a few years of its publication Words of Farewell had been adopted by instructors at institutions as far afield as Bates College (Maine), Colorado Mountain College, Gustavus Adolphus College (Minnesota), Eastern Carolina University, and Northeast Missouri State University as well as flagship American universities such as the University of Georgia, Penn State University, Michigan State University, the University of Southern California, the University of Illinois, the University of Maryland, the University of Washington, Princeton University, and Purdue University.

It soon became apparent that Words of Farewell filled an enormous gap: as far as we could tell, there was no other anthology of Korean women's literature in English translation. Equally important, as professional writers, each with a career ranging over several decades, our three authors were living examples of the possibilities to which creative women in a patriarchal society could aspire. As Elaine Kim, a pioneering scholar of Asian American literature, once told us in conversation, the writers and stories in Words of Farewell proved immensely empowering to her female students and in particular to those of Korean ethnicity.

It was the appeal of *Words of Farewell* that perhaps more than any other factor shaped my approach to Korean literature, Korean-to-English literary translation, and indeed to Korean studies in general. I had become aware that we had an audience and that we needed to continually engage with that audience. What good would our translations do if they were never published, and what good would published translations do if we relied only on our publisher and its distributor to spread the word? Early on we learned that it behooved us, for example, to supply our publishers with a database of individuals who might adopt our translations for their courses (anecdotal evidence suggests that course adoptions continue to constitute the majority of sales of English translations of Korean literature); individuals and press outlets for potential reviews of our books; and individuals to whom direct mail publicity might be sent. We learned of the efficacy (and the enjoyment) of doing readings from our publications, at bookstores, colleges and universities, and public libraries. We learned in short that we had a public role to play, the end to which was greater visibility for the little-known but millennia-old Korean literary tradition.

The year 1989 was a most fortuitous year in another sense. Marshall Pihl, who had worked on behalf of Korean literature since the 1960s (he was the first foreigner to earn a graduate degree in Korean language and literature from Seoul National University), accepted an offer to teach Korean literature at the University of Hawai'i at Mānoa—a vacancy created by the departure of Peter Lee, another pioneer of Korean literature in the United States, for a position at the University of California Los Angeles. The University of Hawai'i at Mānoa featured one of the few Korean studies centers in the United States, and that center had a budget to support two visiting scholars a year. For six months in 1991, I occupied one of those positions and had an opportunity to work not only on the *Land of Exile* stories but also on an anthology of Colonial Period stories, *A Ready-Made Life: Early Masters of Modern Korean Fiction*, with Kim Chong-un (whom I had met at Seoul National University and the University of Washington, where Professor Kim taught while on sabbatical from SNU).

The partnership Ju-Chan and I enjoy as literary translators may be seen as a representation of the Peace Corps mission of mutual cultural exchange.

Indeed, Song Ki-jo (Sŏng Kijo) the publisher of our very first book of translations (stories the publisher himself had written) declared upon first meeting us that we comprised a partner whose first language was Korean and a partner whose first language was English—an ideal translation team! An additional dimension to this cultural exchange is offered by the opportunities we have had, both in South Korea and North America, to appear in public with our authors for bilingual readings and discussions. We have also had the experience of moderating dialogs between Korean and American authors, such as Kim Young-ha (Kim Yŏngha) and Susan Choi.

Our translation career has coincided, not always harmoniously, with efforts by South Korean foundations and government entities to promote Korean literature abroad. To the extent that the Peace Corps involves a rapprochement between Americans and a host culture—a relationship that yields a better understanding of that culture in the United States—literary translation may be understood as an essential form of the cultural transmission that has always been one of the primary objectives of the Peace Corps experience. The nature of that transmission is inextricably linked to the viability of that which is transmitted. An example of language learning as cultural transmission may be instructive. During K-44's ten-week, in-country training in the city of Ch'ŏngju, we studied the Korean language four hours a day, six days a week. We were told by our instructors that the best Korean speakers in the previous groups tended to be those who liked to drink (no surprise there!) and, more important, who had a genuine desire to communicate with native speakers of Korean. In contrast, Korean learners of English often offer a substantially different reason for seeking proficiency in a foreign language— *ch'ulse*, or getting ahead in the world.

Likewise, our approach to literary translation has always been primarily communicative. We find an author and/or work that engages us deeply and commit to communicating that author and his or her work to an English-language readership, hoping readers will engage with the translation as much as we engaged with the original work. The South Korean foundations and government entities, perhaps inevitably considering budgetary constraints, take more of a quasi-*ch'ulse* approach to their work. In their case, *ch'ulse* may be understood as international acknowledgment (*injŏng*) of Korean literature in the form of literary awards and book sales. *Please Look After Mom*, Chi-Young Kim's translation of Shin Kyung-sook (Shin Kyŏngsuk)'s novel *Ŏmma rŭl* put'akhae, and The Vegetarian, Deborah Smith's adaptation of Han Kang's linked-story novel Ch'aesikchuŭija, are instructive. Both were held up in the South Korean media as examples of a higher state of development of Korean literature, resulting in the long-overdue cachet of acknowledgment by English-language readers—Please Look After Mom on account of its being issued by a prominent American commercial publisher, Alfred A. Knopf, and The Vegetarian because it was awarded the prestigious Man Booker Prize, an award centered in the British Commonwealth. In comparison with the fanfare for Please Look After Mom and The Vegetarian in the South Korean press, there was little commentary by the mundan on the quality of the original Korean literary works. Rather than revisit Ch'aesikchuŭija, for example, South Korean critics and scholars have tended to focus on the shortcomings of The Vegetarian.

Specifically, how has the combination of serendipity, uyŏn, and inyŏn shaped my involvement with Korean literature? It was perhaps to be expected that the pioneers of the Korean literature field in North America—Peter Lee, Marshall Pihl, and David McCann—would be called upon to teach courses from all time periods and genres. I myself have followed that pattern at the University of British Columbia, teaching two survey courses on Korean literature, one on traditional literature and the other on modern literature. Since 1999, I have taught both courses annually. While at Seoul National University I had been trained in modern Korean fiction, and thanks to Words of Farewell, Land of Exile, Wayfarer: New Fiction by Korean Women (published by Women in Translation, first an imprint of Seal Press and then a separate publishing company), and A Ready-Made Life, I had a variety of anthologies on which to draw. With traditional literature, however, I was self-taught (a process that continues to this day). Fortunately, I had inherited from Marshall Pihl a reader in traditional Korean literature, and it remains the textual basis of the survey course I teach on that subject.[5]

My expertise as a generalist, my years of residence in South Korea beginning with my Peace Corps experience, and my training in Korean studies at the MA level have shaped my approach to classroom teaching, especially in the case of the two survey courses I teach at UBC. Uyŏn is a factor in the demographics of the students who enroll in these courses, in that the Faculty of Arts at UBC requires undergraduates to successfully complete coursework in literature. My two survey courses, averaging about fifty students each, consist overwhelmingly of ethnic Koreans, either immigrants or international students, and the great majority of those students, while perhaps curious as to how an older Caucasian man came to be teaching Korean literature, enroll primarily to satisfy a graduation requirement. An ever-increasing number of these students have completed middle school and even secondary school in the South Korean educational system, in which literature tends to be commodified for easier mastery in preparation for the all-important university entrance exam. Anecdotal evidence from my students from such backgrounds suggests that they have had limited experience with engaging critically with literature and are generally not encouraged to deviate from the standard critical evaluation of major authors and their "representative works." I thus find myself taking a Socratic approach to engaging my students with the assigned readings, asking a variety of questions that are neither susceptible to facile yes or no answers nor reliant primarily on factual knowledge. My overall goal, while focusing on textual analysis, is to position the assigned readings, and their authors, in the overall historical, political, societal, cultural, and spiritual tradition that Korea enjoys. Students can then better appreciate the connections within the Korean literary tradition, and increasingly the connections with foreign literatures and cultures, that are a signal characteristic of Korean literature.

Likewise, in the Korean-language courses I teach, in which students learn to read and translate literary Korean short fiction into English, and in the translation workshop to which select students from those courses progress, I encourage students to inhabit their translations, to mentally situate themselves in Korea (still the setting of almost every work of Korean fiction), in the rural or urban setting of the literary work, among the family, school, or workplace networks portrayed, and to participate in the dialogues that take place. In a way this approach to translation re-creates the experience of living in Korea and/or a Korean-language environment.

What I have learned from teaching the two Korean literature survey courses, as well as the four seminar courses I have created at UBC—Korean Women's Literature, the Modern Korean Novel, the Literature of the Korean Diaspora, and Topics in Korean Popular Culture (Hallyu)—is consistent with what I have learned from the serendipity, uyŏn, and inyŏn that characterize my engagement with Korea in general and Korean literature in particular: that the Korean literary tradition is most fruitfully understood as an interconnected whole. For proof of that, consider the abundant intertextuality of the Korean literary tradition and the wave of South Korean popular culture (*Hallyu*) that currently drives cultural production worldwide. The international popularity of South Korean television dramas, K-pop music, online gaming, and graphic novels (*manhwa*)—especially the online versions (webtoons) of the last of these—bear witness to the visual and performative elements of the oral tradition in Korean literature. The performance element is attested to in what is thought to be the earliest reference in the Chinese annals to the "people east of the sea" (that is, the inhabitants of the Korean peninsula, which lies east of the sea that separates the peninsula from China)—that they were fond of singing and dancing.

As for the extent of intertextuality, consider three of the iconic figures in the Korean literary tradition: Hwang Chini, Sim Ch'ŏng, and Ch'unhyang. Hwang Chini, to whom at least six *shijo* and four poems in Chinese are attributed, is the subject of fiction by Yi T'aejun, Pak Chonghwa, Chŏng Hansuk, Ch'oe Inho, Chŏn Kyŏngnin, Kim T'akhwan, and Hong Sŏkchung (Hong's novel earned him the distinction of being the first North Korean recipient, in 2004, of the prestigious Manhae Literature Prize in South Korea) as well as at least five films and two television series.[6] Sim Ch'ŏng, paragon of filial devotion, is the subject of one of Korea's best-known folk tales as well as a *p'ansori* work (*p'ansori* being a traditional oral narrative, partly sung and partly spoken by a single performer, usually in an outdoor space accessible to all social

Fig. 5.1 Bruce Fulton. Photo courtesy of Oliver Mann, University of British Columbia.

classes), a traditional fictional narrative, and in the modern period appears in fiction and drama by Ch'ae Mansik, novels by Hwang Sŏgyŏng and Pang Minho, a play by O T'aesŏk, and at least one film.[7] Ch'unhyang, exemplar of faithfulness to one's spouse, is also the focus of a *p'ansori* work and a traditional fictional narrative and, in the modern period, no less than nine works of fiction by writers such as Yi Haejo, Im Ch'ŏru, and Ch'oe Inhun, the first poetry collection by Pak Chaesam, a play by Yu Ch'ijin, a film by Im Kwŏnt'aek, and a music video featuring Lizzy, one of the members of the K-pop idol group After School.[8]

The notion of an interconnected whole also appears in two of the best-known stories of modern Korea, Yi Hyosŏk's "Memilkkot p'il muryŏp" ("When the Buckwheat Blooms") and Kim Tongni's "Yŏngma" ("The Post-Horse Curse"). Both stories involve itinerant peddlers and a seemingly fated connection between a pair of characters that remains unbeknownst to them until they have reached maturity.

We often speak of our lives and careers in terms of a calling, of answering a call. Perhaps the best way I can conceptualize my forty-plus years of involvement with Korea and Korean studies is to say that Korea happened to come calling, and I happened to hear the call. I consider myself fortunate to have been chosen. What is it, though, that distinguishes the few of us, among the fifty-one groups of Peace Corps–Korea volunteers, who pursued a Korea-related career, from the vast majority who moved on to more conventional careers? I can't help but think that we Koreanists were quick to internalize the Peace Corps mission of mutual cultural exchange and thereby develop an awareness of ourselves not so much as temporary denizens of a different cultural tradition but as a bridge between traditions that allowed us to appreciate the interconnectedness of those traditions.

NOTES

Bruce Fulton is indebted to Ju-Chan Fulton for assistance in preparing the bibliography for this chapter.

1. *The Random House Dictionary of the English Language*, ed. Jess Stein and Laurence Urdang (New York: Random House, 1966), s.v. "serendipity."

2. Fred Lukoff, *Spoken Korean, Basic Course*, 2 vols. (Ithaca, NY: United States Armed Forces by the Linguistic Society of America and the Intensive Language Program, American Council of Learned Societies, 1945, 1947).

3. Consul General's Award (top prize), Translation Workshop, "Korean Literature in Its Social Setting" (International Conference on Korean Literature), Brigham Young University, Provo, Utah, October 10–12, 1985.

4. Kwŏn Yŏngmin, *Haebanghu 40 nyŏn ŭi munhak* [Forty years of post-Liberation literature], 4 vols. (Sŏul: Minŭm sa, 1985).

5. Marshall R. Pihl, comp., "Reader in Premodern Korean Literature," manuscript photocopy (Honolulu: University of Hawai'i at Mānoa, 1989–95).

6. See Yi T'aejun, *Hwang Chini* (Sŏul: Tonggwangdang sŏjŏm, 1939); Pak Chonghwa, "Hwang Chini ŭi yŏkch'ŏn" [Hwang Chini's bucking of fate], *Saebyŏk* (November 1955); Chŏng Hansuk, *Hwang Chini* (Sŏul: Chŏng'ŭm sa, 1958); Ch'oe Inho, "Hwang Chini 1," *Hyŏndae munhak* no. 207 (March 1972); Ch'oe Inho, "Hwang Chini 1," trans. Benjamin Cheung, *Acta Koreana* 11, no. 3 (December 2008): 184–95; Ch'oe Inho, "Hwang Chini 2," *Munhak sasang* no. 1 (October 1972); Chŏn Kyŏngnin, *Hwang Chini*, 2 vols. (Sŏul: Irum ch'ulp'ansa, 2004); Kim T'akhwan, *Na, Hwang Chini: Yŏksa wa sosŏl ŭi p'oong* [I, Hwang Chini: Embracing history and fiction] (Sŏul: P'urŭn yŏksa, 2002); and Hong Sŏkchung, *Hwang Chini*, section 25 trans. Bruce and Ju-Chan Fulton, *Azalea* 2 (2008): 155–62. South Korean film versions of her life include Cho Kŭngha's *Hwang Chini* (1957); Yun Pongch'un's *Hwang Chini ŭi ilsaeng* [The life of Hwang Chini] (1961); Chŏng Chinu's *Hwang Chini ŭi ch'ŏt sarang* [Hwang Chini's first love] (1969); Pae Ch'angho's *Hwang Chini* (1986); and Chang Yunhyŏn's *Hwang Chini* (2007). At least two South Korean television dramas, each titled "Hwang Chini," have been devoted to her: the first was broadcast from November 4, 1982, through March 11, 1983, by the Munhwa Broadcasting Corporation (MBC), the second from October 11 through December 28, 2006, by the Korean Broadcasting System (KBS). On the film versions see Hyangsoon Yi, "The Unbearable Heaviness of Being: Hwang Chini in Korean Cinema" (Presentation to the Annual Conference of the Association for Asian Studies, Atlanta, April 5, 2008).

7. See "The Faithful Daughter Sim Ch'ŏng," in Suzanne Crowder Han, *Korean Folk & Fairy Tales* (Elizabeth, NJ: Hollym International, 1991), 134–40; "Song of Sim Ch'ŏng," trans. Marshall R. Pihl, in *The Korean Singer of Tales* (Cambridge, MA: Harvard University Asia Center, 1994), 123–234; "The Tale of Sim Ch'ŏng," trans. Marshall R. Pihl in "Reader in Premodern Korean Literature," Marshall R. Pihl, manuscript photocopy (Honolulu: University of Hawai'i at Mānoa, 1989–95), 139–74; Ch'ae Mansik, "Sim Pongsa" [Blind Man Shim], *Sinsidae* (November 1944–January 1945); Ch'ae Mansik, "Blind Man Shim" (three-act play), in *Sunset: A Ch'ae Mansik Reader*, ed. and trans. Bruce and Ju-Chan Fulton (New York: Columbia University Press, 2017), 182–205; Hwang Sŏgyŏng, *Sim Ch'ŏng, yŏnkkot ŭi kil* [Shim Ch'ŏng, the way of the lotus blossom] (Sŏul: Munhak tongne, 2003); Pang Minho, *Yŏnin Sim Ch'ŏng* [Shim Ch'ŏng, lotus of love] (Sŏul: Tasan ch'aekpang, 2015); Oh T'ae-sŏk [O T'aesŏk], "Why Did Shim Ch'ŏng Plunge into the Sea Twice?" in *The Multicultural Theater of Oh T'ae-sŏk: Five Plays from the*

Korean Avant-Garde, trans. Ah-jeong Kim and R.B. Graves (Honolulu: University of Hawai'i Press, 1999), 125–62; and Shin Sangok's film version, *Hyonyŏ Ch'ŏng'i* [Faithful daughter Ch'ŏng'i] (1972).

8. See "The Song of a Faithful Woman, Ch'un-hyang," in *Virtuous Women: Three Classic Korean Novels*, trans. Richard Rutt and Kim Chong-un (Seoul: Royal Asiatic Society, Korea Branch, 1974), 237–333; Yi Haejo, *Okchunghwa* [Flower in confinement], *Maeil shinbo*, January 1–March 16, 1912; Im Ch'ŏru, "Okchungga" [Song of confinement], *Wŏlgan haein* no. 98 (April 1990), http://www.haeinji.org/contents/?pgv=v&wno=57&cno=320, translated by Teresa Lee as "Jailhouse Blues," manuscript photocopy (University of British Columbia, 2005); Ch'oe Inhun, "Ch'unhyang tyŏn" [Tale of Ch'unhyang], *Ch'angjak kwa pip'yŏng* 2, no. 6 (summer 1967): 227–34; Pak Chaesam, *Ch'unhyangi maŭm* [Ch'unhyang, heart and soul] (Sŏul: Shin'gu munhwasa, 1962); Yu Ch'ijin, *Ch'unhyang chŏn* [Tale of Ch'unhyang], *Chosŏn ilbo*, February 1–April 15, 1936; and Im Kwŏnt'aek's film version, *Ch'unhyang tyŏn* [Tale of Ch'unhyang] (2000). The music video featuring Lizzy can be viewed on YouTube: Lizzy, "Shwiun yŏja anieyo" [Not an easy girl], YouTube.com, accessed August 20, 2019, https://www.youtube.com/watch?v=ipouIsX1phI.

BIBLIOGRAPHY

Ch'ae Mansik. "Sim Pongsa" [Blind Man Shim]. *Sinsidae* (November 1944–January 1945).

Cho Chŏngnae. *Arirang*. 12 vols. Sŏul: Haenaem ch'ulp'ansa, 1990–95.

Cho Chŏngnae. *Chŏnggŭl malli*. 3 vols. Sŏul: Haenaem ch'ulp'ansa, 2013. Translated by Bruce Fulton and Ju-Chan Fulton as *The Human Jungle*. Seattle: Chin Music Press, 2016.

Cho Chŏngnae. *Han'gang* [The Han River]. 10 vols. Sŏul: Haenaem ch'ulp'ansa, 2001.

Cho Chŏngnae. *O hanŭnim*. Sŏul: Munhak tongne, 2007. Translated by Bruce Fulton and Ju-Chan Fulton as *How in Heaven's Name: A Novel of World War Two*. Portland, ME: MerwinAsia, 2008.

Cho Chongnae. "Pinghagi." *Hyŏndae munhak* no. 237 (September 1974). Translated by Sally Foster as "The Ice Age." Manuscript photocopy. Vancouver: University of British Columbia, 2002.

Cho Chŏngnae. *T'aebaek sanmaek* [The T'aebaek Mountains]. 10 vols. Sŏul: Han'gilsa, 1986–89.

Ch'oe Inho. "Hwang Chini 1." *Hyŏndae munhak* no. 207 (March 1972). Translated by Benjamin Cheung as "Hwang Chini 1." *Acta Koreana* 11, no. 3 (December 2008): 184–95.

Ch'oe Inho. "Hwang Chini 2." *Munhak sasang* no. 1 (October 1972).

Ch'oe Inhun. "Ch'unhyang tyŏn" [Tale of Ch'unhyang]. *Ch'angjak kwa pip'yŏng* 2, no. 6 (Summer 1967): 227–34.

Chŏn Kyŏngnin. *Hwang Chini*. 2 vols. Sŏul: Irum ch'ulp'ansa, 2004.

Chŏng Hansuk. *Hwang Chini*. Sŏul: Chŏng'ŭm sa, 1958.

Ch'unhyang tyŏn. Directed by Im Kwŏnt'aek, produced by T'aehŭng yŏnghwa, South Korea, 2000.

Fulton, Bruce, and Ju-Chan Fulton, eds. and trans. *Sunset: A Ch'ae Mansik Reader*. New York: Columbia University Press, 2017.

Fulton, Bruce, and Ju-Chan Fulton, eds. and trans. *Wayfarer: New Fiction by Korean Women*. Seattle: Women in Translation, 1997.

Fulton, Bruce, and Ju-Chan Fulton, trans. *Words of Farewell: Stories by Korean Women Writers*. Seattle: Seal Press, 1989.

Han Kang. *Ch'aesikchuŭija*. Sŏul: Ch'angjak kwa pip'yŏng sa, 2007.

Han, Suzanne Crowder. *Korean Folk & Fairy Tales*. Elizabeth, NJ: Hollym International, 1991.

Hong Sŏkchung. *Hwang Chini*. P'yŏngyang: Munhak yesul ch'ulp'ansa, 2002.

Hwang Chini. Directed by Chang Yunhyŏn, produced by Cine 2000, South Korea, 2007.

Hwang Chini. Directed by Pae Ch'angho, produced by Tonga such'ul kongsa, South Korea, 1986.

Hwang Chini. Directed by Cho Kŭngha, produced by Yŏngnam yŏnghwa, South Korea, 1957.

"Hwang Chini." Korean Broadcasting System (KBS), October 11–December 28, 2006.

"Hwang Chini." Munhwa Broadcasting Corporation (MBC), November 4, 1982–March 11, 1983.

Hwang Chini ŭi ch'ŏt sarang [Hwang Chini's first love]. Directed by Chŏng Chinu, produced by Haptong yŏnghwa, South Korea, 1969.

Hwang Chini ŭi ilsaeng [The life of Hwang Chini]. Directed by Yun Pongch'un, produced by Yi T'aekkyun, South Korea, 1961.

Hwang Sŏgyŏng. *Sim Ch'ŏng, yŏnkkot ŭi kil* [Sim Ch'ŏng, lotus blossom]. Sŏul: Munhak tongne, 2003.

Hwang Sunwŏn. "Sonagi." *Hyŏptong* (1953). Translated by Edward W. Poitras as "The Cloudburst." In *The Stars and Other Korean Short Stories* by Hwang Sun-Won [Hwang Sunwŏn]. Translated with an introduction by Edward W. Poitras, 133–48. Hong Kong: Heinemann Asia, 1980.

Hwang Sunwŏn. *Umjiginŭn sŏng*. Sŏul: Samjungdang, 1973. Translated by Bruce Fulton and Ju-Chan Fulton as *The Moving Fortress*. Portland, ME: MerwinAsia, 2016.

Hyonyŏ Ch'ŏng'i [Faithful daughter Ch'ong'i]. Directed by Shin Sangok, produced by Annyŏng yŏnghwa, South Korea, 1972.

Im Ch'ŏru. "Okchungga." [Song of confinement]. *Wŏlgan haein* no. 98 (April 1990). http://www.haeinji.org/contents/?pgv=v&wno=57&cno=320. Translated by Teresa Lee as "Jailhouse Blues." Manuscript photocopy. University of British Columbia, 2005.

Kang Sŏkkyŏng. "Sup sok ŭi pang." In *Sup sok ŭi pang*, by Kang Sŏkkyŏng. Sŏul: Minŭm sa, 1985. Translated by Bruce Fulton and Ju-Chan Fulton as "A Room in the Woods." In *Words of Farewell: Stories by Korean Women Writers*. Translated by Bruce Fulton and Ju-Chan Fulton, 28–147. Seattle: Seal Press, 1989.

Kim, Ah-jeong, and R.B. Graves, trans. *The Multicultural Theater of Oh T'ae-sŏk: Five Plays from the Korean Avant-Garde*. Honolulu: University of Hawai'i Press, 1999.

Kim Chong-un, and Bruce Fulton, selected and ed. *A Ready-Made Life: Early Masters of Modern Korean Fiction*. Honolulu: University of Hawai'i Press, 1998.

Kim T'akhwan. *Na, Hwang Chini: Sosŏl wa yŏksa ŭi p'oong* [I, Hwang Chini: Embracing history and fiction]. Sŏul: P'urŭn yŏksa, 2002.

Kim Tongni. "Yŏngma." *Paengmin* (1947). Translated by Marshall R. Pihl as "The Post Horse Curse." In *Land of Exile: Contemporary Korean Fiction*, expanded edition. Translated and edited by Marshall R. Pihl, Bruce Fulton, and Ju-Chan Fulton, 13–28. Armonk, NY: M.E. Sharpe, 2007.

Kwŏn Yŏngmin. *Haebanghu 40 nyŏn ŭi munhak* [Forty years of post-Liberation literature]. 4 vols. Sŏul: Minŭm sa, 1985.

Lizzy. "Swiun yŏja anieyo." [Not an easy girl]. YouTube.com. Accessed August 20, 2019. https://www.youtube.com/watch?v=ipouIsX1phI.

Lukoff, Fred. *Spoken Korean, Basic Course*, 2 vols. Ithaca, NY: United States Armed Forces by the Linguistic Society of America and the Intensive Language Program, American Council of Learned Societies, 1945, 1947.

O Chŏnghŭi. "Chŏnyŏk ŭi keim." *Munhak sasang* (January 1979). Translated by Bruce Fulton and Ju-Chan Fulton as "Evening Game." In *Words of Farewell: Stories by Korean Women Writers*. Translated by Bruce Fulton and Ju-Chan Fulton, 181–201. Seattle: Seal Press, 1989.

O Chŏnghŭi. "Tonggyŏng." *Hyŏndae munhak* (April 1982). Translated by Bruce Fulton and Ju-Chan Fulton as "The Bronze Mirror." In *Land of Exile: Contemporary Korean Fiction*, expanded edition. Translated and edited by Marshall R. Pihl, Bruce Fulton, and Ju-Chan Fulton, 215–32. Armonk, NY: M.E. Sharpe, 2007.

O T'aesŏk. "Sim Ch'ŏng'i nŭn oe tu pŏn Indangsu e mom ŭl tŏnjyŏnnŭn'ga." Translated by Ah-jeong Kim and R.B. Graves as "Why Did Shim Ch'ŏng Plunge into the Sea Twice?" in *The Multicultural Theater of Oh T'ae-sŏk: Five Plays from the Korean*

Avant-Garde. Translated by Ah-jeong Kim and R.B. Graves, 125–62. Honolulu: University of Hawai'i Press, 1999.

O'Rourke, Kevin, ed. and trans. *The Book of Korean Poetry: Songs of Shilla and Koryŏ*. Iowa City: University of Iowa Press, 2006.

O'Rourke, Kevin, ed. and trans. *The Book of Korean Shijo*. Cambridge, MA: Harvard University Asia Center, 2002.

Pak Chaesam. *Ch'unhyangi maŭm* [Ch'unhyang, heart and soul]. Sŏul: Shin'gu munhwasa, 1962.

Pak Chonghwa. "Hwang Chini ŭi yŏkch'ŏn" [Hwang Chini's bucking of fate]. *Saebyŏk* no. 8 (November 1955).

Pang Minho. *Yŏnin Sim Ch'ŏng* [Sim Ch'ŏng, lotus of love]. Sŏul: Tasan ch'aekpang, 2015.

Pihl, Marshall R. "Reader in Premodern Korean Literature." Manuscript photocopy. Honolulu: University of Hawai'i at Mānoa, 1989–95.

Pihl, Marshall R. *The Korean Singer of Tales*. Cambridge, MA: Harvard University Asia Center, 1994.

Pihl, Marshall R., Bruce Fulton, and Ju-Chan Fulton, eds. and trans. *Land of Exile: Contemporary Korean Fiction*, expanded edition. Armonk, NY: M.E. Sharpe, 2007.

Rutt, Richard, and Kim Chong-un, trans. *Virtuous Women: Three Classic Korean Novels*. Seoul: Royal Asiatic Society, Korea Branch, 1974.

Shin, Kyung-sook [Shin Kyŏngsuk]. *Please Look After Mom*. Translated by Chi-Young Kim. New York: Knopf, 2011.

Yi Haejo. *Okchunghwa* [Flower in confinement]. *Maeil shinbo*, January 1–March 16, 1912.

Yi Hyosŏk. "Memilkkot p'il muryŏp." *Chogwang* no. 1 (October 1936). Translated by Kim Chong-un and Bruce Fulton as "When the Buckwheat Blooms." In *A Ready-Made Life: Early Masters of Modern Korean Fiction*, selected and edited by Kim Chong-un and Bruce Fulton, 133–42. Honolulu: University of Hawai'i Press, 1998.

Yi Kyunyŏng. "Ŏduun kiŏk ŭi chŏp'yŏn." (1983). Translated by Bruce Fulton and Ju-Chan Fulton as "Beyond the Dark Memories." *Korea Times*, November 1–16, 1985.

Yi T'aejun. *Hwang Chini*. Sŏul: Tonggwangdang sŏjŏm, 1939.

Yi, Hyangsoon." The Unbearable Heaviness of Being: Hwang Chini in Korean Cinema." Presentation to the Annual Conference of the Association for Asian Studies, Atlanta, April 5, 2008.

Yu Ch'ijin. *Ch'unhyang chŏn* [Tale of Ch'unhyang]. *Chosŏn ilbo*, February 1–April 15, 1936.

6

Did Women Have a Peace Corps–Korea Experience?

LAUREL KENDALL

I have told this story many times. As a Peace Corps volunteer in the early 1970s, I experienced a *kut* (an elaborate shaman ritual) and found women at the center of the action as shamans, as gods, and as ordinary interlocutors who felt empowered to shout back and banter with the gods themselves. This encounter shook my perceptions of a gendered South Korea and set the course of my future research. This is true, but a partial truth. I had already known some feisty Korean women as they tried, with great tolerance and much mirth, to teach me the Pongsan Masked Dance while I tried to teach them English, and it was in the company of these women that I went to that fateful *kut*. Were it not for the generous mentoring of theater scholar Du-hyon Lee, I would never have met these women, and I might not have chosen spirited women and shamans as a research path had I not entered graduate school in 1973 and found a community intent on inventing an anthropology of women. Even so, without the Peace Corps, there would have been no Pongsan T'alch'um lessons, no dancing women being feisty against the grain, no *kut*, no shamans.

The Peace Corps made me an anthropologist of Korea. The Peace Corps introduced me to a lifelong research path. The Peace Corps made me sterile. What's wrong with this series? This last statement is also a partial truth. In those years, one did not have to be a Peace Corps–Korea volunteer to have had the misfortune of being issued a Dalkon Shield, an ill-fated intrauterine device; I received mine *before* they were so wrongly approved for distribution in the United States. It is estimated that some 200,000 women were damaged by the Dalkon Shield.[1] I would eventually join nearly 100,000 women in filing claims that resulted, for those of us who lacked medical records, in each receiving $725 as compensation for the scar tissue in our fallopian tubes.[2] The masked dancers and shamans and so much else were positive gifts from generous Korean friends and mentors such that I could have written a predictable paper had I hewed strictly to the intentions of the conference call that ultimately culminated in this volume. But the damage done to my body was also part of this history as encountered by women, particularly single women who went to South Korea as Peace Corps volunteers. The "history" invoked here is most directly a US history transplanted to South Korea, during a time of intense social conflict and contested mores in the United States that was being mediated by the Peace Corps administration abroad. I can recall at least one country director who referred to volunteers as "the kids." Many of us who had graduated in the tumultuous years of 1968, 1969, and 1970 tended to regard the Peace Corps administration with the same wariness bestowed on other authority figures from campus administrators to the US government. South Korea is a part of the story I shall tell insofar as the United States' Cold War interests in South Korea were enmeshed not just in the Peace Corps–Korea program, but in the institutionalization of white male privilege that was a consequence of a highly visible US Military presence on the peninsula.

Fig. 6.1 Laurel Kendall (second from the left) after a performance of mask dance drama in Yangju, South Korea, 1972. Dr. Du-hyon Lee is at the center wearing a hat. Photo courtesy of Laurel Kendall.

In the 1990s, long after the Peace Corps had left South Korea, Andrew P. Killick wrote a personal essay—at least as personal as this one—on being "white, straight, and male in Korea." He confessed, "It is rare for a Western man to spend any length of time in Korea without marrying a Korean woman. I had done so [Killick says]. What was wrong with me?"[3] He had experienced the frustration of being pigeonholed in a place where whiteness carried an aura of masculine privilege regarding Korean women as the presumed sexual Other. He described an expatriate world of possible one-night stands with prostitutes and hostesses and his own stated necessity to be "on my guard" against the matrimonial machinations of respectable Korean women who had failed to make a match on the "Korean marriage market." However stereo-typical, his characterization of expat life is buttressed by a body of literature that describes institutionalized military prostitution in South Korea (and else-where) and its reverberations in civilian expat life as enabling an ethos of Western men on-the-make seeking their alter in a Western fantasy of docile, accommodating, and sexy Asian women.[4] I could sympathize with Killick's plea for an appreciation of a more complex and varied single, hetero, white male subject, one who might not invariably claim the sexual privileges offered him by virtue of his race, nationality, gender, and sexual preference. In the context of this volume, I need not remind my readership that Peace Corps men were diverse white male subjects; that many Peace Corps men saw the world as Killick did even as many others reveled in the world evoked by Killick's inscription. Bruce Cumings, who was a member of the Peace Corps–Korea Group 3 (K-3), has written of his own disgust at being "approached on the streets of Seoul time and again by pimps offering women. The average Korean surmised, since the evidence was so abundant, that American men seen out 'on the economy' (American argot for the opaque, mysterious, unknown native territory otherwise known as Korea) were interested in 'only one thing'—as usually they were."[5] Single American women were more immediately present in the Peace Corps community circa 1970, than in the US military or in the transient expat business community. The Peace Corps–Korea program would witness a variety of attachments and relationships, many of them white on white. It would have been easier to be a diverse white male subject in the 1970s Peace Corps than in the post–Peace Corps 1990s that Killick encountered as an ethnomusicologist doing fieldwork. What caused my bemusement on reading Killick's essay was his portrayal of South

Korea as a place where the majority of expats were "male, heterosexual, and transient" and female expats of any persuasion were nowhere visible in his text.[6] We were always an awkward category. This had also been true in the 1970s. What did it mean to be single, white, and female in a space of white male privilege?

At the end of 1969, the Peace Corps–Korea groups K-10 and K-11 trained together in a sugarcane camp called Pepeekeo on the Big Island of Hawai'i. One night, somewhere in the middle of this three-month span, after a day of intensive language training and role-play English-as-a-second-language teaching, single men, single women, and married couples were divided into three groups for separate briefings. The married couples had been learning the mantra, "Korea is hard on marriages"; and on that evening, their discussion emphasized the lack of privacy they would experience living with Korean families. Married trainees had already experienced a lack of privacy, living as they did in a series of plywood cubicles at the training site.[7] The single women sat with a recently returned volunteer who described her life in South Korea as a single woman. Her task, it seemed, was to prepare us for the expectation that we would live as the daughters of conservative families, that we would have virtually no social life, and that we should expect to gain a great deal of weight as single Peace Corps women stationed in South Korea tended to do. I remember that she giggled, a symptom of trying to speak affably about uncomfortable things. She told us the next day that a Korean member of the training staff who had been her boss in South Korea had coyly asked her if she had talked to us "about sex." I did not remember that she had, except perhaps eloquently by omission.

We learned soon afterward that sex education had been a significant part of the briefing given the single men, our fellow trainees. They had been advised to use condoms, to be "careful who you sleep with" (respectable women weren't a good idea), and above all, had been treated to a panoply of smoking room stories—grounded in personal experience—about the ubiquitous availability of cheap commercial sex in South Korea. The storytellers were returned Peace Corps men, members of the training program staff, and, in effect, "role models." This was the vision of life in South Korea that the training program offered us. Men and women would lead vastly different lives, and *this was what the Peace Corps expected.* It was "the culture," just as it was impossible, owing to "the culture," for Peace Corps women to receive plum assignments in government ministries or for Peace Corps men to wear beards, even when teaching on campuses where respected expat faculty sported full facial hair. "The culture" would be invoked with clockwork regularity by persons representing an organization that otherwise encouraged us to think of ourselves as "agents of change."[8]

Did women have a Renaissance?[9] Did Japanese women have a Meiji Restoration?[10] Did single women have a Peace Corps–Korea experience? After so many years, I can still bitterly remember that evening with its carefully orchestrated segregation by gender so that the men could be let in on a dirty secret. It felt like a betrayal. It still does. A few weeks later, I had my final meeting with the Peace Corps psychiatrist. I had been approved for service in South Korea and was to leave for Seoul with the remaining K-10 and K-11 volunteers the next day. We would be traveling to Seoul via Tokyo because there were no direct flights at that time. I had survived the shrink's initial impression of me as having an insincere smile and his feelings that my dress was provocative. ("I wonder what the Koreans think about that?" he had mused on an evaluation form, projecting disapprobation and maybe something else onto the Koreans as would be a common Peace Corps staff gambit.) I had survived a background check that had turned up, along with somewhat inaccurate details of my personal life, reports that I had smoked pot (as had most of the class of 1969). I had even survived the faux pas of bringing literature on North Korea with me from Berkeley to Hawai'i. Even given these transgressions, they still let me go. "The only reservation," the shrink remarked "is that as a single woman, you would even want to go to Korea." This was a Catch-22. The discouragements and warnings had been effective. Of the ten single women who had reported for training I was one of five who remained to board the plane for Seoul.

Trained in Hawai'i, and not in South Korea itself as later groups would be, groups K-10 and K-11 had been offered a highly selective view of South Korean society. Prior to leaving for Hawai'i, I found that it was not easy to find books about Korea. I had taken the Peace Corps suggested reading list to the local library in my hometown where I discovered a full card catalog drawer of sources on the Korean War and only a few volumes related to culture and travel. Having studied anthropology, I read Cornelius Osgood's The Koreans and their Culture (1951), which had very little to say about Korean women in the village that he had briefly studied on the eve of the Korean War.[11] Women got more mention in his overview of Korean culture cribbed from missionary and traveler accounts from the turn of the last century, most memorably Isabella Bird Bishop's description of *yangban* women who only went abroad at night in covered sedan chairs.[12] The closed sedan chairs made an impression. During training in Hawai'i, Paul Crane's *Korean Patterns*, the most popular explanatory text among the expats of the time, circulated among us, evoking a tradition of gender segregation while acknowledging that some form of "dating" and love marriage had been taking root among South Koreans in the cities since the 1960s.[13] The classroom facilitators, including our well-born Korean-language instructors, participated in the construction of a mytholo-gized Korea, a place of exquisite adherence to etiquette and form where women took pride in serving men. We heard Confucian aphorisms and sick jokes, "In Korea the women walk ahead of the men—the roads are mined!" All of this fit very well into a postwar American romance of East Asia, per-petuated in Hollywood constructions of doll-like war brides (*Sayonara*) and tales of swashbuckling Western heroes served by willing and sexually agile Eastern partners (*Tai-Pan, Shogun*).[14] All of this—the dated and over-general-ized information, the fantasies that had grown out of the US military occupa-tion of Japan and taken on a life of their own in other places—served to naturalize a gendered order among the Peace Corps administration. As Cumings recalled of 1967, "No sooner had our Peace Corps group (yes, the sexual fever is by no means limited to the military) arrived than lore began circulating about how many single male volunteers had frequented this whorehouse or that bathhouse, not once, but twice and thrice, sometimes on the same evening."[15] Male whoring was winked at while women were expected to sit home and get fat in the name of "Korean culture." American women's sexuality, particularly single American women's sexuality, was a conundrum. I recall the bemusement reported by one of the women in my group when, at a reunion marking the completion of our first six months, we recorded our experiences for the benefit of another crop of single women. She recalled how as a Peace Corps–Korea trainee she had learned that a *yŏgwan* was like a hotel, a *tabang* was a place to go for coffee or tea, and an *ibalso* was a barber shop. We had all learned the appropriate dialogue for navigating these spaces and securing these services. After her arrival in South Korea she had realized that the *yŏgwan*, the *tabang*, and the *ibalso* were all sites for the provision of commercial sex.

No, we did not live like the *yangban* women of the Chosŏn period. It was even possible for a Peace Corps woman to discreetly experience a relationship. Women based in Seoul, as I was, and in other large cities, had more opportunities to fraternize. We had more mobility, the possibility of living by ourselves in a rented room, and no expectation that we would do our laundry crouched over an icy stream with a rock in hand, the lot of some down-country female volunteers. The Peace Corps medical office, like most campus medical services of the day, provided birth control pills on demand, although as I recall, this knowledge was not as publicly available to single Peace Corps women as was the availability of condoms and penicillin to single Peace Corps men. As the child of a breast cancer survivor I chose to avoid the pill even though I had been told from several quarters that taking the pill would have made it so much easier for everyone. I was aware that other birth control methods existed, but this was not, apparently, the case in the Peace Corps office. When I asked about diaphragms the Peace Corps doctor blushed slightly, looked down, and mumbled something about "maritals." Then he showed me what he meant; an enormous device such as could only be accommodated by vaginal walls already stretched in childbirth. The army hospital provided an intrauterine device (commonly referred to as an IUD), but it was the same story, a device in a size not meant for a still upstretched nulliparous womb, the insertion of which caused me to writhe in pain on the examination table, begging for its removal. The word "maritals" persisted. The message was clear. The US military had not imagined the contraceptive needs of women who had not first been married and pregnant. This fact was even more surprising given that nearly all Peace Corps women, whether married or single, were nulliparous. In other words, while a great deal of attention had been devoted to accommodating the presumptive exercise of a robust, hetero-male sexuality, women's bodies were a troublesome and not-very-well-imagined category.

This area of ambiguity was not unique to the Peace Corps–Korea program. American society at large had been slowly digesting the implications of the so-called sexual revolution. Two decades into the new millennium, the post-war American past has become another country where they did things differently. In her review of the two biographies of *Cosmopolitan* editor Helen Gurley Brown, social commentator Moira Weigel observed that, "When Helen Gurley Brown published *Sex and the Single Girl* in 1962, her frankness about the fact that unmarried women had sex—and liked it —shocked reviewers and sold millions of copies."[16] But revolutions have ambiguous and inconsistent results. Unmarried middle-class American women of the 1960s experienced this reimagining of their sexuality as a confusing welter of emotion, politics, and social pressure in a world of boundary-breaching and revolutionary reimagining. In 1970, an articulate Women's movement and related initiatives in women's health were still a few years down the road. The practical consequences of the generation gap were keenly felt not just by the class of 1968 and 1969 and their parents but also by college administrators embroiled in volatile, fluid situations on campuses across the United States. Some of the Peace Corps–Korea K-10 and K-11 volunteers had recently arrived from university campuses that had not only been roiled by antiwar demonstrations but where "three-feet-on-the-floor" rules and other parietals had collapsed, seemingly overnight, in favor of co-ed dormitories. In 1970, the Peace Corps–Korea program had been insulated from much of this and was coping, as best it might, with volunteers tempered by campus experiences significantly different from those of the K-1 volunteers who had arrived only a few years before. During an improvisational moment—in what seemed to be an act of doing the right thing—the Peace Corps doctor was able to acquire a specially ordered Dalkon Shield to match my contraceptive needs. This was done with limited information and was, in retrospect, a mistake on both of our parts.

On the one hand, the problem of medical misinformation for women loomed much larger than the Peace Corps. On the other, the fear of unwanted pregnancy, the motive for seeking effective contraception, was governed by Peace Corps policies that were as dire as they seemed to be arbitrary. Abortion was illegal in the United States until 1973, although by the early 1970s a number of states had legalized the procedure. Abortion in South Korea was illegal but widely practiced and was generally acknowledged to have been the primary means of family planning during those years. Nevertheless, a pregnant Peace Corps volunteer would be terminated and sent home from South Korea, in effect, disgraced. This was Peace Corps DC policy. When Susan Cowell (Lauster) (Peace Corps–Korea K-10 volunteer) received assurances that in the eventuality the policy might be mediated in the case of married volunteers like her, she took up the cause for both married and unmarried women in correspondence with the Peace Corps–Korea country director (who will remain anonymous here). His response is enlightening with respect to how single women volunteers were regarded.

> It is my opinion that abortions for married girls should be treated differently from those of unmarried girls. When abortion occurs overseas in the case of a Peace Corps situation, the data may possibly show that the psychological strain is even greater, especially for unmarried girls.
>
> The Peace Corps is not prepared to handle psychological cases resulting from any circumstances. So, I would agree on our policy to return an unmarried person to the States for health and psychological purposes.[17]

In other words, not only pregnant but crazy, an echo of the ancient Greek idea that a wandering womb made women hysterical. The country director's presumptions of what the "data might *possibly* show" give further testimony to the instability of single Peace Corps women as an administrative category. The country director goes on, "Apparently the times are such to argue that an unmarried pregnancy is a case of promiscuity which many will not tolerate especially if the Government-supported program tolerates or even promotes it by permitting abortions without other sanction."[18] Promiscuity?!? Excuse me, but this was from the administrator of a program that, as noted above, had most explicitly accommodated the wide-ranging sexual adventures of single men. If one were to look for promiscuity in a "Government-supported program" all one would have to do is review the information and medical back-up that male volunteers received. That was the real deal. Do not get me wrong. I am very glad that Peace Corps men had access to condoms and penicillin; these amenities were rightly intended to avert a great deal of unnecessary suffering both for the young men who availed themselves and for their partners. It is the absolute hypocrisy of the country director's characterization of women's lives and health needs that rankles.

Susan next addressed her appeal to the regional director of the Peace Corps, noting that:

> For many girls, married and unmarried, giving birth is far more emotionally traumatic and more likely to interfere with job performance than abortion. Yet [the] Peace Corps has no policy of termination for married Volunteers

who plan to give birth. Moreover, Peace Corps' policy encourages Volunteers who become pregnant and want to remain in Peace Corps to get an abortion secretly without Peace Corps medical supervision. Needless to say, this could be very dangerous both physically and emotionally.[19]

In response, the regional director simply restated Peace Corps policy, albeit in a less flustered tone than the country director, and raised the possibility that a terminated volunteer who went home for an abortion "may be reinstated" but did not specify the conditions of under which reinstatement might occur.[20] There is, of course, no way of knowing how many Peace Corps women had secret abortions. I knew one volunteer, a friend in a slightly later cohort than my own, who took her annual leave in Japan where she worked as a bar hostess in order to finance a Japanese abortion. I know of two other single women volunteers who vanished, seemingly overnight, suddenly "went home," leaving speculation in their wake.

It was all a long time ago. The language of Peace Corps "girls" used uncritically by both the country director and Susan herself recalls how archaic these issues now seem. Why bring up painful, negative memories? This volume gives us the opportunity not only to reminisce and collectively remember our lives but to historicize them. We have been asked to share our recollections as scholars of Korea on how our time in the Peace Corps provided foundations for our careers. I could have written a very different story in an honestly joyful key about the pursuit of folklore and my fledgling anthropological encounters, starting with the story I told to introduce this piece. However, if the study of history and society over the last several decades has taught us anything, it has taught us that history happens differently as a consequence of gender, class, race, and sexual preference. When the history of Peace Corps–Korea is being witnessed, then the particular experiences of Peace Corps women (and not just women) must be part of that story. What was it like to be gay or lesbian and closeted in the Peace Corps at a time when the initial staging included psychological tests to screen out "homosexual tendencies?" What was it like for the limited number of Peace Corps volunteers who were not white? To assume an unproblematic white, male, and hetero-normal Peace Corps–Korea volunteer as being the one true subject of our history is to miss a great deal about the Peace Corps–Korea experiences, how different volunteers conceptualized their lives, and how Peace Corps–administered policies affected them day-to-day.

As per the conference assignment that culminated in this chapter, I have written about experiences that were indeed foundational to my career as a scholar of Korean studies. There was a passion in my early work to blast through existing stereotypes of Asian women and write about some tough-talking shamans who would muddle the picture. When I began graduate school in 1973, it was a very good moment for a young scholar who wanted to understand how women's culture might reshape an understanding of any culture. At Columbia, what we then called "the anthropology of women" — the precursor to the anthropology of gender—was slowly emerging, and the literature was sparse. We all read Margaret Mead of course and Rosaldo and Lamphere's *Women, Culture, and Society* as soon as it was published in 1974. Margery Wolf's *Women and the Family in Rural Taiwan* was important for those of us who would work in East Asia.[21] This work turned our understanding of the Chinese family inside out and showed us how some basic social practices looked different when observed through the perspectives, experiences, and aspirations of wives, daughters, daughters-in-law, and mothers-in-law.[22] If there is any one book that shaped my own approach to ethnography and helped me to craft the project that eventually became *Shamans, Housewives, and Other Restless Spirits*, it would be *Women and the Family in Rural Taiwan*.

Women in graduate school in anthropology in the 1970s felt that we were on the edge of an important trend. In retrospect, yes, we were on the edge of an important trend and so successful in what we would accomplish that no one really remembers how absent women were from most ethnographies before the 1970s. There were a few exceptions, and we read them voraciously.

Graduate school also introduced me to the work of the British anthropologist, I. M. Lewis, most notably his, *Ecstatic Religion: An Anthropological Study of Spirit Possession and Shamanism*, published in 1971, a book that made me angry, and this was a very good thing. I found the passion to pursue a dissertation project disputing Lewis' claim that the role of women in possession religions was necessarily passive or that women were spirit mediums but never shamans. What I had glimpsed as a Peace Corps volunteer suggested otherwise. My resulting book, *Shamans, Housewives, and Other Restless Spirits: Women in Korean Ritual Life* published in 1985, is still in print and still debated.

I myself have reservations about the meta-generalizations I offered in the concluding chapter. Fieldwork in South Korea and career encounters with Korean female colleagues introduced me to worlds of female experience unimagined when I began, and I have tried to bear witness to all of this over a long career. There was also my brief time studying medical anthropology that included field research with immigrant Korean women in a Honolulu clinic, a path that my own medical misadventures had paved for me.[23]

As a graduate student in the 1970s, I would need an abundance of passion, anger, and excitement to get through. When I finished my degree in 1979, the Columbia University anthropology department produced more PhDs that year than there were jobs in the country. One male classmate, also a returned Peace Corps–Korea volunteer, told me while giggling that it was simply "too bad" for me because by the time I finished "everyone will have hired their token woman." I did land safely, after years as a post-doc, then visiting assistant professor, and effectively ignoring a chorus of advice to find some other line of work—*What Color Is Your Parachute?* I doubt that I would have persisted had the Peace Corps not made me tough. And I would need to be tough and determined to have a career in Korean studies, a field far from welcoming to women. No one would necessarily be watching my back and it did not surprise me when male classmates and colleagues played by different rules. In the end, I would bear the consequences of my mistakes. The Peace Corps made me what I am today.

NOTES

1. Rainey Horwitz, "The Dalkon Shield," *The Embryo Project Encyclopedia*, January 1, 2010, https://embryo.asu.edu/pages/dalkon-shield.

2. Linda Williams, "$2.4-Billion Dalkon Shield Payout Options Disclosed," *The LA Times* March 18, 1990, https://www.latimes.com/archives/la-xpm-1990-03-18-mn-1045-story.html. The Peace Corps only retained medical records for five years after service. I verified with the Washington DC office that mine had been destroyed as per practice.

3. Andrew P. Killick, "The Penetrating Intellect: On Being White, Straight, and Male in Korea," In *Taboo: Sex, Identity, and Erotic Subjectivity in Anthropological Fieldwork*, edited by Don Kulick and Margaret Willson, 76–106 (London: Routledge, 1995), 78.

4. Bruce Cumings, "Silent but Deadly: Sexual Subordination in the US-Korea Relationship," in *Let the Good Times Roll: Prostitution and the US Military in Asia*, edited by Saundra Pollock Sturdevant and Brenda Stoltzfus, 169–75. (New York: New Press, 1992);

Katherine Moon, *Sex among Allies* (New York: Columbia University Press, 1997); Maria Höhn and Seungsook Moon, *Over There: Living with the US Military Empire from World War Two to the Present* (Durham, NC: Duke University Press, 2010); and Saundra Pollock Sturdevant and Brenda Stoltzfus, *Let the Good Times Roll: Prostitution and the US Military in Asia* (New York: The New Press, 1992).

5. Bruce Cumings, "Silent but Deadly," 170.

6. Andrew Killick, "The Penetrating Intellect," 90.

7. I am grateful to Charles Lauster and Susan Cowell (Lauster) for sharing their memories of this event and to Susan for generously allowing me to quote from her correspondence with Peace Corps staff cited in this chapter.

8. In fairness, single women did eventually hear from another former volunteer, a woman living in Hawai'i, who described a free spirited and romantic existence on an island off the South Korean coast (I still have trouble imagining the degree of self-confidence and independence of spirit that would have enabled her to get away with it).

9. Joan Kelly, *Women, History and Theory: The Essays of Joan Kelly* (Chicago: The University of Chicago Press, 1984).

10. Sharon H. Nolte and Sally Ann Hastings, "The Meiji State's Policy Toward Women, 1890–1910," in *Recreating Japanese Women, 1600–1945*, Edition 1, edited by Gail Lee Bernstein, 151–74 (Berkeley: University of California Press, 1991).

11. Cornelius Osgood, *The Koreans and Their Culture* (New York: The Ronald Press Company, 1951).

12. Isabella Bird Bishop, *Korea and Her Neighbors* (New York: Fleming H. Revell, 1897).

13. Paul Crane, *Korean Patterns* (Seoul: Hollym Corporation, 1967).

14. *Sayonara*, directed by Joshua Logan, Pennbaker Productions, United States, 1957; James Clavell, *Tai-Pan* (New York: Atheneum, 1966); and *Shogun*, directed by Jerry London (Asahi National Broadcasting Company, Japan, 1980).

15. Bruce Cumings, "Silent but Deadly," 170.

16. Helen Weigel, "Was She a Feminist? The Complicated Legacy of Helen Gurley Brown," *New York Times* Book Review, July 17, 2016: 12.

17. Peace Corps country director to Susan Cowell (Lauster), September 13, 1971, letter, private collection.

18. Peace Corps country director to Susan Cowell (Lauster), September 13, 1971, letter, private collection.

19. Susan Cowell (Lauster) to Peace Corps regional director, September 21, 1971, letter, private collection.

20. Peace Corps regional director to Susan Cowell (Lauster), October 8, 1971, letter, private collection.

21. Margaret Mead, *Sex and Temperament in Three Primitive Societies* (New York: William Morrow and Company, 1963 [1935]); Margaret Mead, *Male and Female: A Study of the Sexes*

in a Changing World (New York: Dell Publishing Co., 1973 [1949]); Michelle Zimbalist Rosaldo and Louise Lamphere, Women, Culture, and Society (Stanford, CA: Stanford University Press, 1974); and Margery Wolf, Women and the Family in Rural Taiwan (Stanford, CA: Stanford University Press, 1972).

22. "China," of course, was a generalization soon to be refined when anglophone studies were no longer restricted to Taiwan and the Hong Kong New Territories, but the fundamental lesson of Wolf's book still holds, that the operations of patrilineal, patrilocal kinship and much, much else look different through a female lens and when accounting for female agency. Margery Wolf, Women and Family in Rural Taiwan.

23. Laurel Kendall, Shamans, Housewives, and Other Restless Spirits: Women in Korean Ritual Life (Honolulu: University of Hawai'i Press, 1985); Laurel Kendall, "Cold Wombs in Balmy Honolulu: A Korean Illness Category in Translation," Social Science and Medicine 25, no. 4 (1987): 367–76.

BIBLIOGRAPHY

Bishop, Isabella Bird. Korea and Her Neighbors. New York: Fleming H. Revell, 1897.

Clavell, James. Tai-Pan. New York: Atheneum, 1966.

Crane, Paul. Korean Patterns. Seoul: Hollym Corporation, 1967.

Cumings, Bruce. "Silent but Deadly: Sexual Subordination in the US-Korea Relationship." In Let the Good Times Roll: Prostitution and the US Military in Asia, edited by Saundra Pollock Sturdevant and Brenda Stoltzfus, 169–75. New York: New Press, 1992.

Höhn, Maria, and Seungsook Moon. Over There: Living with the US Military Empire from World War Two to the Present. Durham, NC: Duke University Press, 2010.

Horwitz, Rainey. "The Dalkon Shield." The Embryo Project Encyclopedia. January 1, 2010. https://embryo.asu.edu/pages/dalkon-shield.

Kelly, Joan. Women, History and Theory: The Essays of Joan Kelly. Chicago: The University of Chicago Press, 1984.

Kendall, Laurel. Shamans, Housewives, and Other Restless Spirits: Women in Korean Ritual Life. Honolulu: University of Hawai'i Press, 1985.

Kendall, Laurel. "Cold Wombs in Balmy Honolulu: A Korean Illness Category in Translation." Social Science and Medicine 25, no. 4 (1987): 367–76. doi: 10.1016/0277-9536(87)90275-9.

Killick, Andrew P. "The Penetrating Intellect: On Being White, Straight, and Male in Korea." In Taboo: Sex, Identity, and Erotic Subjectivity in Anthropological Fieldwork, edited by Don Kulick and Margaret Willson, 76–106. London and New York: Routledge, 1995.

Lewis, I. M. *Ecstatic Religion: An Anthropological Study of Spirit Possession and Shamanism.* Harmondsworth, England: Penguin, 1971.

Mead, Margaret. *Male and Female: A Study of the Sexes in a Changing World.* New York: Dell Publishing Co., 1973 (1949).

Mead, Margaret. *Sex and Temperament in Three Primitive Societies.* New York: William Morrow and Company, 1963 (1935).

Moon, Katherine. *Sex among Allies.* New York: Columbia University Press, 1997.

Nolte, Sharon H., and Sally Ann Hastings. "The Meiji State's Policy Toward Women, 1890–1910." In *Recreating Japanese Women, 1600–1945,* Edition 1, edited by Gail Lee Bernstein, 151–74. Berkeley: University of California Press, 1991.

Osgood, Cornelius. *The Koreans and Their Culture.* New York: The Ronald Press Company, 1951.

Rosaldo, Michelle Zimbalist, and Louise Lamphere. *Women, Culture, and Society.* Stanford, CA: Stanford University Press, 1974.

Sayonara. Directed by Joshua Logan. Pennbaker Productions, United States, 1957.

Shogun. Directed by Jerry London. Asahi National Broadcasting Company. Japan/United States, 1980.

Sturdevant, Saundra Pollock, and Brenda Stoltzfus. *Let the Good Times Roll: Prostitution and the US Military in Asia.* New York: The New Press, 1992.

Weigel, Helen. "Was She a Feminist? The Complicated Legacy of Helen Gurley Brown." *New York Times* Book Review, July 17, 2016.

Williams, Linda. "$2.4-Billion Dalkon Shield Payout Options Disclosed," The *LA Times* March 18, 1990, https://www.latimes.com/archives/la-xpm-1990-03-18-mn-1045-story.html.

Wolf, Margery. *Women and the Family in Rural Taiwan.* Stanford, CA: Stanford University Press, 1972.

7

At the Border: Women, Anthropology, and North Korea

LINDA LEWIS

When I applied to the Peace Corps in 1970—at the height of the Vietnam War, with the men of my age cohort subject to the draft—one of my professors hesitated to give me a reference, saying "How can you go off and be an agent of US imperialism in Asia?" I thought at the time: "You really believe young American BA generalists with no practical skills can have so much impact?" He overestimated both my abilities and my ambitions. I joined the Peace Corps because I knew I would have much more to gain than to give—for good or ill—and that turned out to be the case.

The South Korea I experienced in the early 1970s was still predominately rural and poor. North Chŏlla Province, South Korea's rice bowl, was literally where the pavement ended; the new expressway extended south from Seoul, veered east at the provincial border, and headed toward Pusan. Where I lived, roads were unpaved, and buses crowded. The public bathhouse was forty-five minutes away, and rural electrification hadn't yet reached all of the towns where we were placed.

My Peace Corps–Korea group, K-14, was anomalous. Serving as the first and last volunteers assigned to a rural community development project, we were by Peace Corps standards, a failure. Conceived by a group of Peace Corps public health volunteers who assumed (erroneously) that if South Korean farmers didn't coop up their chickens, it was due to ignorance, our project was supposed to help the Republic of Korea (ROK) agriculture extension officials to improve farming and rural life in general, through support for 4-H clubs. To turn us into agriculture experts, our training in Hawai'i included learning to operate a rototiller, to pour cement for pigpens, and to construct bamboo chicken coops.

It didn't take long after our arrival in the country for us to discover that not only were there few 4-H clubs around, but needless to say, we also had little to offer the South Korean farmers. If there were no chicken coops in evidence, it was because in weighing concerns of land, labor, and resources, the farmers had calculated that free range was more cost beneficial. There wasn't much for us to do, which for most of our group was just fine.

K-14 volunteers were placed in three counties in North Chŏlla Province, assigned to work at the branch (myŏn), county (kun), and provincial (to) levels of the ROK National Office of Rural Development. As one of fourteen at a branch office, I was told I was placed in the smallest village where any volunteer had ever lived; true or not, it was small enough that I never encountered an English-speaker there, not even a local English teacher. I stayed in a prosperous farm household with seven children about a mile away from the Rural Development branch office located in the myŏn center, where my three Korean male co-workers struggled to figure out what to do with me. Eventually, we settled into a routine, with me tagging along as they biked through paddy fields to visit farmers, advised visitors to the office, or slept off the effects of makkŏlli at lunch in the office back room. It was a near-perfect culture and language immersion experience, one that for me not only provided invaluable training for a career in anthropology but also immeasurably enriched my own young life.

After one year, K-14 volunteers were given the option of retraining as English teachers and reassignment to new job sites. I was one of the ones who chose to move, in my case from the bottom level of the ROK's agricultural extension system to the top, to the National Office of Rural Development in Suwŏn. There, I spent my next two years as a volunteer preparing agriculture researchers to go overseas for training, as part of the worldwide "green revolution." Having participated in the introduction of "miracle rice" and the beginnings of the New Village Movement at the local level, I could now observe the same processes from a national perspective.

It was only years later, and in retrospect, that I came to appreciate what a remarkable time the early 1970s were in the transformation of rural south Korea and to understand the value of my own experience. Over the years I have stayed in touch with my rural Peace Corps family, as the children—my "siblings"—prospered, left the countryside, and moved far away to Seoul, or stayed closer to home, to make careers in nearby Kunsan. On a 2015 visit, I learned that some of the family members of my generation had return-migrated, retiring to a new house in the old village, right beside the former family compound.

I also count it as one of life's great ironies that forty-five years later, lessons learned in the Peace Corps about agriculture and rural community development are still useful in my current work in North Korea. The Democratic People's Republic of Korea (DPRK) farm managers I know are resourceful, innovative, excellent problem-solvers who shrewdly balance multiple factors in making complex production decisions, under considerable structural constraints.

Fig. 7.1 Linda Lewis and English class of agricultural researchers, National Office of Rural Development, Suwŏn, South Korea, 1973. Photo courtesy of Linda Lewis.

The South Korea I experienced as a Peace Corps volunteer was also a military dictatorship. Censors blacked out sections of the international edition of Time magazine, and friends were careful about what they said in public. It was a time of midnight curfews, monthly air raid drills, and in cinemas, red-tinged, anti-North, ROK propaganda films were shown before the main feature. In the name of national security, critics of the government were silenced. While from the mid-1960s, the military regime of Park Chung Hee (Pak Chŏnghŭi, 1961–79) brought remarkable economic prosperity to the ROK, by the early 1970s the benefits of rapid industrial development were unevenly distributed, and opposition to authoritarian rule was widespread. In the Chŏlla provinces, the farmers I worked with were openly critical of the Park regime and supported native son Kim Dae-jung (Kim Taejung, 1998–2003) in the 1971 presidential election. In Suwŏn in 1972, there were military tanks on the agriculture university campus after Park declared martial law and closed universities in the prelude to the Yusin ("revitalizing") reforms.

Living in South Korea during this era of oppression transformed my political consciousness and shaped my beliefs about the responsibilities of a scholar toward the people he or she studies. When I returned to South Korea in 1979 to begin my dissertation fieldwork on mediation and the ROK courts, I chose to work in Kwangju, because I felt most comfortable in the southwest region. I lived in Kwangju from November 1979 until October 1980, and so it was my bad luck or good fortune perhaps, depending on one's perspective, to be one of only a few foreign observers of the May 1980 Kwangju Uprising. This experience was a happenstance that largely determined the direction of the next two decades of my academic career and research agenda in Korean studies and subsequently turned me into a politically engaged scholar.

I could never pretend, as a Koreanist, that I was not an eyewitness to the 1980 Kwangju Uprising, nor could I ignore my responsibility to bear witness to that momentous event. Beginning in 1987, with a panel on the Kwangju Uprising at the Association for Asian Studies annual meetings in Boston—the first attempt by the scholarly community to discuss the issue openly—and concluding in 2002 with the publication of my own book on the May uprising, my work focused on Kwangju.[1] It was only with the realization of democracy in South Korea, which I personally mark from when Kim Dae-jung became president in 1998, that I could turn my attention elsewhere.

WOMEN: NOT INVITED TO THE PARTY

One day soon after I started work as a Peace Corps volunteer, I glanced out the office window and noticed a commotion going on at the makkŏlli chip across the road. The only drinking place in the village where I worked, it also had a large back room where food was occasionally served, in effect the de-facto village party space. It was almost lunchtime, and I watched about a dozen men, including my three co-workers, go in. I wondered what they were doing. After about thirty minutes, my office chief came back and got me and took me across the street. I followed him into the back room, where a party was in progress; he indicated I should sit down and eat. After about ten minutes, he told me to stand up and give the self-introduction I had learned during Peace Corps training, which I did. Everyone clapped, and then he told me to return to the office, and that he would be back soon. About an hour later, all the men came staggering out, including my co-workers, who promptly retreated to the back room for their afternoon naps.

When I next got together with the three other Peace Corps volunteers placed near Kunsan, the two males talked about the lunch party their co-workers had held to welcome them to their respective villages. They got introduced to all of the local notables—the village head, the middle school principal—and of course everyone got very drunk, had a great time, and became the best of friends. It was only then that I understood what had gone on—or perhaps I should say, not gone on—at my own site.

I have often thought of that day, and the dilemma my co-workers faced. What to do in rural South Korea, circa 1970, when the guest of honor is a woman? In retrospect, I believe they did their best, in what was for them an awkward situation. However, the real point of this story is that my male Peace Corps colleagues knew the village chief and the middle school principal in their villages, and I did not. Then the question becomes, how does one build a career in Korean studies, when you're never invited to the party?

In the 1970s in the United States, of course, attitudes were only marginally better. My own experiences as a graduate student include being told by my main advisor in Korean studies that women like me getting PhDs instead of having babies would mean the death of the American middle class. Needless to say, no one suggested I look for an academic position as a Koreanist when I finished my degree; my first job was at the New York City Department of Juvenile Justice as an analyst.

This was typical for the time. My college classmates were going through the same thing, and most of the women my age in academe have similar stories. That world is past now, and the experiences of young women undertaking graduate work today are very different from mine. I believe the deeper problem of exclusion for women in Korean studies now lies in the extent to which gendering practices in the field remain rooted in South Korean cultural norms and behaviors, rather than American ones. In thinking about the future of Korean studies, I would urge those of us in Korea studies to consider the persistence of male privilege and gender inequality in South Korea itself, the impact that this has had on women advancing their careers in the field, and what, as professionals in the field, we should be doing about it.

These days I still spend time attending international conferences in Seoul, not academic gatherings, but ones on humanitarian assistance to the DPRK. At the first such conference I attended in 2010, as the newly appointed director of the American Friends Service Committee (AFSC) agricultural assistance program in the DPRK, I went into the dining room for the opening dinner and was instructed that as the head of a major INGO program, I would be seated at one of the head tables. As I approached the front of the room, however, it was clear my place had been given to an American male colleague of mine, who had long since retired from AFSC but was still attending such meetings. When friends asked why he was sitting at the head table instead of me, they were told that the older male Korean leaders of the hosting organization were more comfortable with him, so had requested he be seated with them. As I went to find a place at the back of the room, I couldn't help thinking that even more than forty years later, there was still no place at the table for a woman.

According to the World Economic Forum Report's 2015 Global Gender Gap Index, which ranks over 140 countries on how well they leverage their female talent pool, overall the ROK ranks a dismal 115th, just ahead of Kuwait, the United Arab Emirates, and other Middle Eastern countries. It ranks just 125th (of 140) in economic opportunities for women, 102nd in education, 101st in political empowerment, and 79th in health. Of twenty-four countries ranked in Asia, South Korea stands at nineteenth, ahead of Bhutan, Fiji, Iran, and Pakistan. In contrast, the United States ranks 28th overall, and China, 71st.[2]

While I don't expect we can do much to change South Korean practice—and we probably shouldn't even try—we can, as those who shape the field of Korean studies in the United States, refuse to be complicit in discriminatory practices that serve to perpetuate male dominance in the field, long after such practices have been disallowed in the United States. At the conferences I have attended in Seoul, funded in part by Western foundations, among those presenting papers, typically none of the South Koreans—and only about 20 percent of the international participants—are women. Only American men—never a woman—have ever served as the Asia Foundation Country Representative in Seoul. And how can it be that in 2016 the US-based National Committee on

North Korea, a membership organization to which I belong, is less than 15 percent female?

When I point these issues out to American men, the replies tend to focus on South Korean culture. Left unexamined is the difficulty of giving up privilege. I can't change the fact that South Korean men feel more comfortable sitting with my male colleague, even though I'm the one with the job title, and he is not. That said, I can fault my male colleague, for not relinquishing his seat to me.

ANTHROPOLOGY: NOT HISTORY OR LANGUAGE

I used to say that an anthropologist of Korea is like an expensive foreign sports car in an automobile showroom: lots of people are interested in a test drive, but no one would actually buy one. When I was beginning my career, there was a small but growing demand for Korean studies classes at US colleges and universities, but job opportunities tended to be of the "visiting" or "temporary" variety. This was particularly the case outside of established Korea programs at a few of the foremost universities, and even at those few Korean studies centers, cultural anthropology wasn't at the front of the line in the disciplinary pecking order.

There are reasons why the building of academic departments, and particularly those which are area studies programs, tend to follow certain patterns, and I leave it to others to fill in the details of the development of the field of Korean studies in the United States over the last four decades. I have observed the impact of that development process on my own experiences as an anthropologist of Korea and through this lens can suggest possible outcomes for the growth of Korean studies in the future.

In the 1970s, while members of my cohort studying Korean history, or perhaps Korean language and literature, could work with a scholar expert in that field, there were no professors of Korean anthropology to be found at US universities. Columbia University, where I went, offered four years of Korean language and Korean history, and I have always appreciated the solid foundation I received in both of those areas. However, the skills required to do text-based historical research versus anthropological field work are quite different. I would have made a lousy historian, and a worse linguist, and so I was relegated to the margins of the Korean studies department.

As a Korean anthropologist there was only a moderate amount of scholarly research to build on. The literature on Korea in either Korean or English was sparse, the majority of which focused on family structure and social organization. Almost any research topic was destined to break new ground, and while that provided the opportunity to do interesting work, it also, at least for an anthropologist, meant a dissertation that would be more descriptive than theoretical. This exercise was good for the field perhaps, but was not the best choice for building one's career.

Columbia, however, offered (and why I chose to go there) two preeminent anthropologists of China, a strong program in Chinese anthropology, a sociologist of Japan and coursework in that field, and, through its law school, an East Asian law program that included a scholar at the forefront of the emergent field of contemporary Chinese law. By the 1970s, the literature on Chinese and Japanese culture and society was relatively well-developed compared to work in the social sciences on Korea, and research done by scholars looking at Korea's two closest neighbors provided theoretical models and frames of reference that could be applied to Korea. In this regard, Columbia was resource rich, and I was fortunate in finding supportive faculty to work with, within the larger context of East Asia studies.

In the case of my own dissertation research, for example, in the absence of any information on contemporary South Korean courts and with only a few sources on Korean traditional law and conflict resolution, seminal work done on reconciliation and Japanese law offered a useful starting point for comparison, as did the relatively well-developed literature on mediation and traditional law in China. I conducted fieldwork at the district court in Kwangju, focusing on the judicial process and the role of the judge as both mediator and adjudicator. The result was necessarily primarily descriptive, but as my thesis provided previously unknown material on the South Korean courts, it was used for many years in courses on Korean law at several universities, and I would hope was helpful to the next generation of Korean studies scholars in law and anthropology. Thus, in graduate school, as an anthropologist of Korea I was something of an academic "orphan," working by analogy and comparison and hovering at the periphery of the real scholarly interests of my primary academic advisors. From a different perspective, I became an anthropologist of East Asia, albeit one specializing in Korean culture and society.

I have often contended (usually in job interviews) that Koreanists are the true East Asianists, an argument that works well at small liberal arts colleges, which is where I made my teaching career. Today, there are still only a few Korea experts at undergraduate institutions. However, given the choice among social scientists with research interests in China, Japan, or Korea, it is the Koreanist who is most likely to know something about the other two countries, and thus can offer the broader range of comparative courses demanded of professors teaching outside the context of a large university.

After all, what is the purpose of Korean studies? Are we, as Korean studies professionals, responsible for the production of more academic specialists and professionals in the field, or are we to more generally inform and shape the perceptions of a less well-known but important part of the world? If it is the later, we should consider further developing the Korean studies curriculum more broadly, particularly at the undergraduate level, in liberal arts settings, and at community colleges. This may require moving beyond a traditional area studies approach, of history and language first, to more support for other disciplinary interests.

NORTH KOREA: THAT OTHER PLACE, BEYOND THE DMZ

At the time of my Peace Corps service, Korea had been divided for less than thirty years. There were constant reminders of the Cold War tensions on the Korean peninsula—beaches meticulously raked every night to reveal the footprints of intruders, co-workers absent for national guard training, and the ubiquitous presence of US soldiers. National division was still recent enough that older South Koreans still referred to the Korean language as Chosŏn mal (the term used in the North), and South Korean friends routinely cited Paektusan (in North Korea) as the number one "must see" tourist attraction in the country. When I asked how to get there, they replied in surprise that, of course, that was impossible at present.

Thus, when on July 4, 1972, the Seoul and P'yŏngyang governments issued the historic South-North Joint Communiqué, following the first-ever high-level political meetings between North and South officials, in Suwŏn, the South Koreans I knew were jubilant. Surely, reunification was just around the corner. I happened to be in Seoul seventeen years later, in 1989, when the

Berlin wall fell. Watching it on TV, tears running down their faces, my Korean friends were sure Korea would be next.

Twenty-seven more years have passed, and North Korea is not going to go away. Now, more than seventy years after national division, I would argue that it is time for the field of Korean studies in the United States to move past focusing only on South Korean studies, and for professionals in the field to realign their attention on the Korea north of the DMZ.

Much of what is written about North Korea today, especially in the popular media, is frequently described—with accuracy—as a Rorschach test, revealing more about the analyst, than about North Korea itself. A largely Cold War perspective and a lack of reliable data have resulted in a voluminous literature that is highly speculative, a canon largely without context or grounding in any real knowledge of Korean history, language, culture, or society. As Bruce Cumings pointed out in his brilliant book *North Korea, Another Country*, "North Korea is an American blank slate, and anything written upon it has currency—so long as the words are negative."[3]

In looking at the "inconsistency and misrepresentation" that characterizes most of the "received wisdom" about the DPRK, the British scholar Hazel Smith suggests this is due not so much to ideological bias as to the "often unconsciously adopted paradigmatic lens in which knowledge about North

Fig. 7.2 Linda Lewis at American Friends Service Committee (AFSC) partner farm, North Hwanghae Province, North Korea, 2017. Photo courtesy of Linda Lewis.

Korea is subordinated and filtered through the classic concerns of national security."[4] Furthermore, "This securitization of knowledge about North Korea is evident in scholarship, the policy world, and the media."[5]

How has it come to pass that the field of Korean studies—at least in the United States—has largely ceded the terrain north of the Demilitarized Zone (DMZ) to security studies? The DPRK is a difficult place to know, but it is not unknowable. Again, to quote Cumings, "North Korea has been around for a long time . . . and contrary to media punditry, we know a lot about it."[6] As some of those few scholars who attempt to understand North Korea point out, there are source materials to work with from newly released government and military documents and other archival sources, not only for historians and political scientists but also, for example, for social scientists, as well. As Hazel Smith notes, "A by-product of the work of the humanitarian agencies with the North Korean government was the production of increasingly sophisticated data sets on nutrition, health, and agriculture. Over four-and-a-half *thousand* reports on aspects of DPRK society are immediately accessible on the United Nations Office of Coordination of Humanitarian Assistance (UNOCHA) Reliefweb website."[7]

Data exists. What else makes studying North Korea difficult? Well, understanding the DPRK is often a matter of making informed guesses. Serious scholars find it uncomfortable to generalize from small amounts of material, and it is almost impossible to prove that any claim made about the North, no matter how outlandish, isn't true. Access is clearly a barrier, as well, particularly in certain disciplines. I am continually surprised at how many of those who profess North Korean expertise—and not only Americans, but also Chinese, South Korean, and European scholars—have never met an actual North Korean. It doesn't help that currently the Republic of Korea criminalizes unsanctioned contact between South Korean citizens and their northern cousins.

During the famine of the mid-1990s, the DPRK government made an unprecedented appeal for humanitarian assistance and opened its doors for the first time in 1995 to international relief agencies. A few years later, in 2001, ROK President Kim Dae-jung's "Sunshine Policy" of reconciliation and cooperation with the DPRK ushered in a decade of political, economic, and humanitarian engagement between the two Koreas. What if during that period of relative opening there had been US Peace Corps volunteers serving north of the DMZ? Sounds inconceivable, doesn't it? Yet, US government-sponsored and private exchange programs—from the Peace Corps and Fulbright, to the International Visitors Leadership program and other kinds of people-to-people exchanges—are time-tested foreign policy tools, an engagement strategy long used to build understanding and trust with American enemies, including the USSR, China, Myanmar, Cuba, and Iran.

Unfortunately, the DPRK remains one of the few countries where the US government does not sponsor people-to-people exchanges. Given the current sorry state of US-DPRK relations, this represents a lost opportunity. In celebrating the importance of our own time in the Peace Corps, we acknowledge the power of firsthand experience and interpersonal contact, in laying the foundation for life-long connections and a commitment to mutual understanding and knowledge building. At the very least, as US Korean studies professionals (and ex-Peace Corps volunteers), we should be urging our government to engage with North Korea and the North Koreans.

In the introduction to *The Kwangju Uprising: Shadows Over the Regime in South Korea*, Don Clark wrote that "As professionals in the field of Korean studies, we have an abiding interest in the lives of our Korean colleagues, and in the stance our government takes toward the Korean people."[8] At the time, it was a courageous (and controversial) statement. Almost thirty years later, how many among us have North Korean colleagues or speak out regarding US policy toward the DPRK? Let's make the Korean studies of the future inclusive of both Koreas and of all of the Korean people.

NOTES

1. Linda S. Lewis, *Laying Claim to the Memory of May: A Look Back at the 1980 Kwangju Uprising* (Honolulu: University of Hawai'i Press, 2002).

2. World Economic Forum, "The Global Gender Gap Report 2015," accessed July 29, 2019, http://reports.weforum.org/global-gender-gap-report-2015/.

3. Bruce Cumings, *North Korea: Another Country* (New York: The New Press, 2004), 50.

4. Hazel Smith, "Crimes Against Humanity?" *Critical Asian Studies* 46, no. 1 (2014): 127.

5. Hazel Smith, "Crimes Against Humanity?" 128.

6. Bruce Cumings, *North Korea*, xi.

7. Hazel Smith, "Crimes Against Humanity?" 133. The website Smith refers to is still operating. See Relief Web, Accessed July 26, 2019, https://reliefweb.int/organization/ocha.

8. Donald N. Clark ed., *The Kwangju Uprising: Shadows Over the Regime in South Korea* (London: Westview Press, 1988), 6.

BIBLIOGRAPHY

Clark, Donald N., ed. *The Kwangju Uprising: Shadows Over the Regime in South Korea.*
London: Westview Press, 1988.

Cumings, Bruce. *North Korea: Another Country.* New York: The New Press, 2004.

Lewis, Linda S. *Laying Claim to the Memory of May: A Look Back at the 1980 Kwangju
Uprising.* Honolulu: University of Hawai'i Press, 2002.

ReliefWeb. Accessed July 26, 2019. https://reliefweb.int/organization/ocha.

Smith, Hazel. "Crimes Against Humanity?" *Critical Asian Studies* 46, no. 1 (2014): 127–43.

World Economic Forum. "The Global Gender Gap Report 2015." Accessed July 29,
2019. http://reports.weforum.org/global-gender-gap-report-2015/.

8

Empathy, Politics, and Historical Imagination: A Peace Corps Experience and Its Aftermath

MICHAEL ROBINSON

My first memory of Korea was in 1952, the year our family bought its first TV. I remember the news, political reports, the Republican and Democratic conventions, and the advertisements—but cartoons and children's programs held most of my attention on that flickering screen. One set of images from that period haunted me for years; the starving, disheveled children begging in a place called South Korea behind bold letter graphics enjoining viewers to donate to CARE, a nonprofit relief organization active there during and after the Korean War (1950–53). Along with civil defense public service announcements ("drop and cover" and hide under your desk in case of nuclear attack), these images of South Korean children reinforced my understanding of the world as divided into warring camps of communist and democratic nations, as well as between developed societies and the so-called Third World. I further learned that the United States led the democratic nations (the "Free World") and fought to bring justice, democratic ideology, and capitalist prosperity to the entire globe. What I knew of Korea remained informed by these images, and it flowed into my growing understanding of the Cold War and America's fight to not only save other nations from Communism but to help them obtain the prosperity promised by capitalist development.

By college I had become more sophisticated politically and had chosen to major in history with a concentration in East Asia. A survey of East Asian civilization had piqued my interest, and I ended up taking a number of offerings on Chinese and Japanese history as well as Chinese-language courses. Throughout my study I seldom encountered Korea, and when I did it was represented as a variant, a lesser version of China. That old, faded image of war-torn Korea remained unchallenged, and it was further complicated by my understanding of the war in Vietnam and the rising political furor and critique in the United States about our actions in Asia and our role as the "leader of the Free World." In the end, it was the escalation of our military intervention in Vietnam that indirectly sent me to South Korea as a Peace Corps volunteer. The selective service system eliminated educational deferments to the draft in 1968, the year of my college graduation. Exposed to the certainty of call-up, I found myself contemplating a number of unacceptable alternatives to military service: flight to Canada like my brother, jail as a refusenik, or hiding underground. I did not have the conviction or guts for any of these alternatives, and I received orders to report to Fort Wayne in Detroit in October 1968. Only a belated invitation from the Peace Corps saved me from conscription, and I departed for Hilo, Hawai'i, for training during the last game of the World Series that year (Detroit beat St. Louis).

Just as the clichéd Peace Corps recruiting pitch promised, the Peace Corps changed my life forever. In addition, it was the hardest thing I have ever done in my life. Particularly difficult were those first nine months residence in South Korea when I felt completely isolated, could not communicate in any meaningful way, didn't understand a fraction of what was going on around me, could not eat the food offered, and confronted a completely different scheme of material life. Eventually these problems passed, and the reward was entry into a completely alien world. The process of understanding this new world provided me with invaluable life lessons, reshaped my entire worldview, and committed me (then unwittingly so) to a life-long commitment to trying to understand and teach about the Other—in my case about Korea and East Asia. Once adjusted, I became fascinated, not intimidated, by the world around me, and for the next two years I absorbed all the knowledge of the Korean quotidian I could. Later, I discovered that this new life challenged every core assumption that I had about who I was as a human being. These challenges became the basis for reshaping me as a man, a son, a sibling, a friend, an educated person, an American, and a global citizen.

At the most personal level, living and working in South Korea gave me a new appreciation for the power and value of empathy. Living in a different world based on foreign rules and assumptions about human conduct, I found myself having to think deeply about what motivated and animated the people around me. Often the actions of my Korean friends and co-workers at first glance seemed irrational or bizarre. Sometimes I felt they treated each other cruelly or with indifference. Gradually, however, I started to see the relationship between Koreans' different values and social structures and their individual and collective behaviors. I learned that my individualism needed to be informed by my inclusion within the natural groups around me (the family I lived with, work, and friendships). I had to think more intensely about how my actions would affect with whom I was with, and I could not automatically assume that my individual needs and desires were independent of others.

Rethinking my actions as an individual gave me a new appreciation for Americans' fierce individualism, and I began to see differently its benefits and liabilities. Indeed, as every Peace Corps member eventually discovers, learning about the Other was a mirror on ourselves; as our cross-cultural skills advanced, so did our self-knowledge. Navigating the dense Korean social matrixes, learning about generational hierarchy, trying to use complicated Korean honorific language, and discovering an entirely new set of assumptions about gender relations forced me to contemplate the teachings of my own culture. All of this was both exciting and daunting, and upon returning home I began a life of trying to explain to others, directly and indirectly, what had happened to me. This ultimately took the form of teaching about Korea and the broader East Asia region.

Interestingly, most people upon hearing I was in the Peace Corps assume that living in the relatively deprived South Korea, which in the early 1970s was still often called the Third World, was the hardest part of the experience. In fact, material deprivation and adjustment were relatively easy. In my mind I traveled back to an earlier time that lacked the modern conveniences of middle-class American life. Yes, there were pit toilets, open sewers, faulty communications, intermittent power and little refrigeration, no central heating nor air-conditioning, and a narrow range of choices for food, clothing, and most consumer goods, but it was during this time that I began to really understand the relativity of material conditions. Growing up male, white, and middle-class in post–WWII America had not prepared me to fully understand the wide range of conditions in which humans live. Certainly, I knew about poverty having seen it in inner city Detroit, but I had never lived without the comforts and conveniences of the American middle class. In the beginning, living in an eight-by-six-foot room, lit with a dim 25-watt florescent bulb, with a sleeping roll and scarcely room for my Peace Corps footlocker was reminiscent of camping. Later, I understood things could be much worse.

Fig. 8.1 Muddy streets. Chŏnju, provincial capital of North Chŏlla, South Korea, March 1969. Photo by Mike Robinson.

In fact, in time the various material conditions in which I lived over the next two years mattered less and less as I was swept up in my new life. Everything happened outside of my room anyway, and the vibrancy of my students, hosts, and new friends belied the sometimes-dreary backdrop of that tiny room, ramshackle noodle shops, and my unheated classroom with damp concrete floors, rickety wooden desks, and missing glass panes in the windows. Within my circle of friends—drawn from the faculty of the national university, my students, host family, neighbors, and their myriad of kin and friendship networks—everyone seemed to be in similar circumstances. There was no grinding poverty, after all I was living among South Korea's middle class in its provincial form, but there was also no obvious affluence. That is, while this would change with the great economic expansion of the next twenty-five years, at that time, in 1968, there seemed little difference in people's material circumstances. People shared what they had, and there were always resources for a student trip, mountain hiking, a modest night out drinking, or just sitting in a coffee shop listening to music. I found myself feeling comparatively well off on my Peace Corps stipend of eighty-five dollars a month, particularly as I understood that this stipend for a single person equaled many families' monthly income. So powerful were these experiences that I continue to draw on these memories when I feel "deprived." When I forget my own privileged circumstances, I have only to recall the dignity with which the Korean people lived in conditions of heart-breaking deprivation to make an attitude adjustment toward gratitude.

Fig. 8.2 Plowing. North Chŏlla Province, South Korea, March 1969. Photo courtesy of Mike Robinson.

Fig. 8.3 In the fields. North Chŏlla Province, South Korea, March 1969. Photo courtesy of Mike Robinson.

A second set of lessons I learned in the Peace Corps were about who I was as an American. I had never considered the issue of national identity before I went abroad. I had not thought through the discussions about how Peace Corps volunteers needed to represent the best of America in our behavior and attitudes, but I was prepared to do my best as a cultural ambassador. What I discovered was that Koreans had a variety of views about what the United States represented, and they were more than willing to express them. I rediscovered my national identity by reacting to the often-outlandish assumptions some Koreans held about my country. No, not all Americans were rich, nor did they all live in the mansions portrayed in Hollywood films. No, American streets were not all sites of gun fights and mayhem. Yes, there has been progress in the civil rights movement, and not all African Americans live in desperate poverty. No, college tuition was not free to all citizens. No, the demonstrations against US actions in Vietnam were not illegal, nor were the demonstrators all communists. It went on and on. I discovered that when I countered erroneous beliefs about my country, I had to ask myself "What is the real and true America?" Often the answers were disturbing. Koreans watched events in the United States with intense interest, and its actions were judged from an entirely different frame of reference. I found that my own attitudes were often naive and not carefully considered; this realization forced me to think more carefully about American values, politics, foreign policy, and issues of distributive justice.

More troubling was to have my patriotism called into question. College students of the mid-to-late 1960s often conceitedly viewed the emotion of patriotism as being shallow and a sop for the uneducated. I proudly stood above the "my country, right or wrong" patriotism of right-wing Republicans and those who blindly supported US foreign policy whatever its consequences. Therefore, the fierce anticommunism stance of my South Korean students surprised and troubled me as did the uniformity of their discourse. This was highlighted by the fact that the husband of the family with whom I lived taught the anticommunism course at one of the local middle schools. For the first time, I saw how public school education informs values and political thinking. I realized that I too had been taught the dominant national narrative in school, I saw my students as victims of systematic propaganda and a closed political system.

During my time in South Korea, my self-righteous attitude as an independent free thinker was under constant attack. At the university I was paradoxically labeled interchangeably as one or both of the political polar opposites. On the one hand, I was a tool of the US government, and the Peace Corps was no more than another US institution insinuated into the heart of the South Korean body politic to advance US neo-colonial interests. On the other hand, I was a draft-dodging, communist sympathizer who was unwilling to carry the righteous fight to the Viet Cong and was shirking my obligatory military service. There was no middle ground. This dilemma offered me insights into the intersection of politics and patriotism and the plasticity of various political and patriotic alignments. It showed me that different imaginings of our nation of birth coincided with a specific, learned narrative. Believing in the South Korean narrative, that of becoming a new nation and struggling to survive North Korean aggression was not optional for my students. It is a shame that I didn't see this at the time and write the book about imagining and national identity formation. For that, I refer to Benedict Anderson's seminal *Imagined Communities: Reflections on the Origin and Spread of Nationalism.*[1]

My students' attitudes toward the Vietnam War were, for me, initially surprising. Coming directly from a United States torn by dissent over the war and an expanding antiwar movement, my students' desire to serve in Korean units fighting in Vietnam was perplexing. I understood students' political motivation given their commitment to anticommunism. It became clear, however, that pecuniary motives also motivated my relatively poorly off students. Many students coveted the US standard combat pay, access to consumer goods in the US Military Post Exchange (PX), and, I suppose, the adventure of leaving South Korea was also important at a time when foreign travel was highly circumscribed in the ROK. These facts opened my eyes and were yet another reminder of my naive politics. In the United States, with the onset of the draft, the idea of profiting by enlisting in the military was laughable, but in the different context in South Korea it made sense. By the time I left South Korea I understood more clearly why the Republic of Korea was anxious to send troops, and there were many more reasons than anticommunist solidarity: the access to US foreign exchange in the form of servicemen's pay, grants of military equipment, procurement of labor and engineering services, as well as the shoring up of US commitment to South Korean defense on the peninsula were just a few. How a different society and politics in South Korea could engender a different set of assumptions for policy formation was the real lesson for me.

Perhaps the most significant and unexpected lesson of my Peace Corps experience lay in the realm of geo-politics. I left the United States still quite conservative politically. I had remained on the fringe of the antiwar demonstrations, and I still believed that the United States government's foreign policies were driven by good motives. I couldn't accept the more radical denunciations of the United States as an imperialist or neo-colonialist power, and the various conspiracy theories offered as the "real" reasons for US involvement in Asia seemed farfetched. Furthermore, I joined the Peace Corps believing in the positive motives and benign politics behind its idealistic mandate. Two years witness to the US presence in South Korea was more than enough to disabuse me of these beliefs. As a Peace Corps member, I arrived blind to the paternalism inherent in the message of assistance and friendship for the developing world. It was immediately obvious that I had very little to offer the Koreans except my friendship. Yes, I was a native English speaker, but for the first year I labored as nothing more than an elaborate, animated tape recorder. I suspected that anyone needing to learn English could and did do so without my help. However, friendship was a worthy goal as well, and I contrasted my willingness to live on the South Korean economy and my sincere effort to learn about South Korean culture and society to that of the US diplomats, businessmen, soldiers, and civilian employees in holed up their walled compounds and bases. The value of the Peace Corps mission should not be dismissed, it did encourage international friendship and provide an alternate example of the best the United States had to offer the world, but my Peace Corps experience also taught me how soft power worked to blunt the uglier realities of the global struggle between the United States and Soviet Union for hearts and minds in the developing world.

There was also a fact that I could not ignore—that in South Korea I existed on a plain of privilege and entitlement not accorded to my Korean friends. I found myself being treated with much more deference than my age or occupation deserved, and it seemed that merely being an American insulated me from reality and even gave me a certain cachet. I didn't recognize this at first, but I finally figured out that I was just not that interesting a person. Koreans saw in me their access to the outside world or some future benefit as part of their networks. Additionally, I knew that I could get away with transgressions that might get a South Korean citizen in trouble such as ignoring the midnight curfew or freely discussing political topics without fear when Koreans felt circumscribed by their government's boundaries of acceptable speech. In addition, US soldiers lived under a different set of rules than Korean citizens and were insulated by the modified extraterritorial rules of the 1966 Status of Forces Agreement between the United States and the Republic of Korea. Perhaps the most obnoxious feature of this power differential was the attitude of expatriated Americans and their contempt for Korean ways and manners—often mirrored by US diplomats and military personnel. Pervasive Orientalism informed discussions about life in South Korea, and I found myself, to my great regret in retrospect, joining in. The entire South Korean population, their society and beliefs as individuals were being judged through the filter of American standards of behavior and material development. Of course, I know now that from the beginning of the US presence on the Korean peninsula during the post–World War II occupation, its relationship to Korea had always been asymmetrical—South Korea subordinated to US political will and economic power. By the late 1960s, things were beginning to change as the ROK became more assertive in their relations with their gigantic ally. While I didn't see this at the time, the patriotic passion with which my students defended their country (uri nara) was clearly related to this history of American arrogance and an even longer memory of outside powers meddling in Korean affairs.

Speaking of power differentials, gender dynamics in late 1960s South Korea was another part of my education. My time in college in the mid-1960s coincided with the rise of the Women's movement in the United States. When I moved to South Korea, I had not yet had a full-time job, a relationship, or any other experience in the adult world beyond my time as a college student. Having become more progressive by this time, I assumed my attitudes toward women were correct and in line with the times, and I had not had any experience with how sexism was manifest in my home country. My experience in South Korea, however, belied my pretentions in this regard. I readily took advantage of the privileges offered young males in South Korean society. It took time to recognize how the severe patriarchy of South Korean society mirrored male prerogatives at home. The strictures for women in the United States were only masked more efficiently than the blatant gender discrimination present in

South Korea. Living with a Korean family provided an intimate view of how gender dynamics operated and how overtly unbalanced gender relations were. I am embarrassed looking back at how these mores constricted my female friends' Peace Corps experience, and how I did nothing to ameliorate their situation. Where I was able to participate in office parties and impromptu drinking sessions with my colleagues, the wife of a volunteer couple in our office was left alone and excluded. I remember listening to the frustrations of Peace Corps women about how Korean expectations for their roles as women limited them to subordinate status. This is not to mention their outrage at being abandoned by the Peace Corps men as they frolicked in the bars and flesh pots of the entertainment districts. Finally, the Peace Corps itself did not support nor encourage single women volunteers to break these strictures.[2]

Fig. 8.4 Mike Robinson (back row) with other Peace Corps volunteers. Left to Right Mike Robinson, Susan Phillips, unknown, Ruth Howell. Chŏnju City, South Korea, 1969. Photo courtesy of Mike Robinson.

I also learned how poverty drove South Korean women to work in the bars and brothels of the military camp towns attached to the many US army bases. Here the ugliness of neo-colonialism was overtly manifest. Where else could eighteen-year-old boys from Oklahoma maintain a "mistress" in waiting on his weekly leave from any of the large US military bases at Ŭijongbu, Yongsan, Osan, Kunsan, and may others. Drinking in the bars of the US military camp towns was reminiscent of home (pay as you drink, no tabs) but with an overlay of contact with prostitutes and pimps who filled the niche for easily available sex for the thousands of GIs with money and the freedom of a weekend leave. Here it was difficult to maintain that my Peace Corps status somehow differentiated myself from the GIs intent on getting drunk and laid on a Saturday night. I made my forays into the flesh pots, but after a few experiences, I decided to eschew contact with this side of South Korea. That said, one could not avoid the intersection of male demand for sex and the circumstances that continued to drive women into sex work in South Korea. I didn't have to go to the military camp towns to see the sex industry in action. Barber shops, bath houses, private rooms in bars, and hostess clubs all offered sexual services for money to the South Korean male population. This was an eye opener for me having never even contemplated buying sex in the United States, after all this was not only illegal but dangerous, wasn't it?

Fig. 8.5 Mike Robinson with the family of one of his students. Iksan County, North Chŏlla Province, South Korea, 1970. Photo courtesy of Mike Robinson.

I returned to the United States after a little over two years in South Korea completely changed by the experience. All Peace Corps volunteers experience re-entry shock, the period of readjustment to life in the United States. It was great to be home, but I was unprepared for the how differently I felt about the most mundane American realities. It was a shock to enter a supermarket and its overwhelming cornucopia of items—seemingly such excess! Additionally, it was painful to try to explain to my friends what I'd experienced and how it had changed my world view. People listened politely, but I could tell they were unable to understand what I was trying to communicate. It was in that first year at home that I decided to try to do what was necessary to teach at the university level. There I figured I could make a difference, jog students to try harder to understand the world outside our borders. Of course, this idea didn't come as a sudden epiphany; looking back I can see that during my first experience in South Korea I had started on an inexorable path to teaching about the developing non-Western world. I went to graduate school to study more about Korea, and by sheer luck I ultimately found a position where I could teach about Korean society, culture, and history for the next thirty-seven years.

That two years in South Korea, bridging the late 1960s and the beginning of the 1970s, opened my eyes in unique ways, and in hindsight I can see its impact on my teaching philosophy. By experiencing such dramatic cultural difference, I gained an enhanced sense of empathy. Understanding how my South Korean students thought and behaved gave me an appreciation for how political and social constraints affected individual actions, and by extension I had to think about how those larger forces shaped the way I thought and acted. A corollary to this insight was how my education had inhibited my understanding the Other; my American education had created a filter of values, attitudes, and assumptions through which I strained information about the world. Without understanding how this distorted my understanding of others, I was doomed to judge and dismiss foreign cultures as different and somehow lacking. I entered the halls of academia with these ideas burned into my consciousness.

The Peace Corps experience unwittingly laid the basis for my core interest in teaching. First, it drove me to seek graduate education that included further language study and intense concentration on Korea and East Asia. Second, this experience inspired me to accomplish my desire to communicate with others about what I had learned during this extraordinary interval living within another culture. When I consider carefully what I was doing during my teaching career, I see now that what I wanted to inspire in my students in the United States was exactly the mindset forced upon me during that early period in the Peace Corps when all of my assumptions about life were challenged. As I developed into a professional historian and then a teacher of history, I discovered that those early experiences set the framework for my historical imagination. What I wanted from delving into history was to place myself once again in a foreign country. As a researcher, I realized that I was immersing myself in the past just as I had been immersed in South Korean culture in those early months in the Peace Corps. History to me was a foreign country; people did things differently there.

So, for the past thirty-seven years I have been trying to find ways to immerse my students in an equivalent mindset. Over the years I've asked myself the following questions. How does one develop a sense of empathy? How can I, as a professor, share the experience of another time frame and another culture with my students? What do I need to know to help me accomplish this sleight of hand, without the students knowing what I am up to? Along the way I developed some ideas that helped my students and me in this endeavor. Fundamental to this quest was encouraging my students to be open to understanding themselves and what ideas and presuppositions have inhibited their attempts to understand the motivations and core desires of the Other. This led to a discussion of American culture, individual cultures, family values, education, and social experiences to explicitly identify, to use another metaphor, the refractive valance of individualized lenses through which each person views the material at hand. If my students could even vaguely appreciate how they were shaped, guided, and constrained by their own culture then they could begin to organize information about the ideas, mores, and structures of the Other and in turn develop some empathy for how and why people in other places and times might act. I tried to get students to engage the Other in this manner in numerous ways: lectures, roll playing, debates, group discussions, in-class writing and peer review, and discussions of audio, film, and art. All of these activities were useful, but only if students placed themselves in front of the mirror of another culture.

Interestingly, I found that my best outcomes were revealed when students admitted to me that learning about Korea (I think it could have been any non-Western society) had helped them see something that had troubled them in their lives from a different perspective. For others, it was the surge of excitement after finding a picture window looking out on to the world. These have been the most satisfying moments of my teaching career. It mattered little just how much of the actual class content they had absorbed, the breakthrough was the shift in their world view. I later began to feel that my role as a teacher was deeply subversive. I wonder if I could have accomplished what came to be my primary purpose if I'd been teaching Renaissance Art History, American History, or French Literature. This brings me back to those first nine months in South Korea in 1968–69. The profound discomfiture I endured had led to this simple goal as a teacher. Interestingly my desire to understand the Other led to a career teaching about cross-cultural understanding. What started as an exotic and rather marginal work ended up contributing to what I think is essential to the education of our children, namely, cross-cultural understanding in a rapidly globalizing world.

When I reflect upon my teaching about Korea as a historian and area studies specialist, I can also see the imprint of my Peace Corps experience. Generally, my cohort of college professors hired in the 1970s and early 1980s brought a cynical stance toward US government power and the Cold War in general. In the culture wars that ensued after 1975, the American professorate was suspected of being left leaning, even un-American, by the forces of the right. I suppose I fell into that camp of leftist bias, but I think my Peace Corps experience further politicized my teaching. Being in South Korea during the period of authoritarian rule under Park Chung Hee (Pak Chŏnghŭi, 1961–79) left many of us critical of the ROK government and of the general lack of free speech and expression in South Korea at that time. Moreover, I returned to South Korea to research my PhD dissertation for two years in the middle of the Yusin repression after 1972.[3] At this point the ROK government had closed almost all avenues of political opposition, had actively censored the press, and had confined all college students to their campuses. The experience of living within such a repressed society shaped my own rather critical view of the official ROK line about its democracy, Korean-style or otherwise. Moreover, my stance as an outsider, writing and teaching about Korea, left me free to consider and teach about North Korea. I found myself trying to counter the relentless propaganda of the ROK regime as well as the ignorance of the US press about the Democratic People's Republic of Korea (DPRK) by attempting to deal equally with both the North and the South, to the consternation of many of my South Korean friends.

Because of this, my research has been criticized as being overly critical of South Korea, sometimes even "pro–North Korea." I reject this criticism, but I must always be aware of how politicized the study and teaching about the Korean peninsula could be, particularly in its early incarnation in the United States. It was not just political study and discussion that drew controversy.

Historical studies, I discovered, were also fraught with political over and undertones. I had to understand that my historical work would be appropriated as either a confirmation or denial of established and approved narratives in South Korea. Indeed, the story of South Korea's becoming was skewed in favor of justifying the telos of a modern "democratic," capitalist, South Korea. North Korea's narrative focused on a peoples' struggle and the rise and implementation of a social revolution. To write counter to the accepted lines of inquiry was to court criticism and attacks of one's work. Because of the conflict between North and South, each government had significant motivation to police its history as well as the manner in which its society was represented abroad.

My career coincided with early struggles of South Korea to fund scholarship on Korea and to attempt to encourage a favorable view of itself. To the credit of the ROK funders of Korean studies around the world, they discovered early that to attempt to influence the outcomes of scholarship on Korea were counterproductive. As South Korea became more prosperous, it provided additional funds for professorships, graduate study, and in-country research support. Such funding expanded the field of Korean studies exponentially in the 1990s and early 2000s. Since the late 1980s, South Korean politics have democratized. Peaceful transition of power, an open press, and local autonomy are features of a more open and transparent society. My younger colleagues who trained after "democratization" and benefitted from the more generous South Korean funding of the field are less critical of the Republic of Korea generally.

Korean studies has gained a place in many college and university curricula, and East Asia cannot be easily studied without reference to Korea's important place in its history and civilization. Some progress is evident in the lesson plans of K-12 teachers who have incorporated material on Korean society and culture into their classroom curricula. The status of Korean studies has much improved since the 1960s, but we have much more to do to expand the study of Korea into its rightful place within the study of East Asia, which has long been dominated by Chinese and Japanese studies. Numerous universities across North America have well-established Korea studies programs and provide the means for training Koreanists. We must now solve the problem of how to find places for these increasingly well-trained scholars and teachers at the college and university level. The effort to increase those trained at this level should continue, but we must be mindful of the limits of university budgets, hostility to area studies in general, and core changes to the traditional disciplinary organization of American academies.

The scholarship of the new generation of researchers and teachers on Korea ensures that the basic materials, monographs, course development, and graduate training in Korean studies will continue. Nonetheless, the greatest challenge remains the insertion of the study of Korea into the mainstream curricula of colleges, universities, and K-12 programs on world history and global studies. The effort to research both South and North Korea's place, in the increasingly volatile and rapid global flows of popular culture, trade, tourism, and migration, is only beginning. Expanding the study of Korea into elementary and high school classrooms and mainstream history courses at the college level should be a requirement to secure future funding. Teacher training, course development, and interdepartmental workshops will encourage the development of additional courses both on Korea and including Korea content. Providing additional opportunities for students to reside in Korea—study abroad, service-learning courses, travel courses, and volunteer programs—is equally as important. As much as my early contact with South Korean society led me to study further and ultimately teach about Korea, direct engagement for students will also fuel their interests and provide context for well-examined, globally conscious future citizens.

NOTES

1. Benedict Anderson, *Imagined Communities: Reflections on the Origin and Spread of Nationalism* (New York, Verso, 1983).

2. See chapters 6 and 7 of this volume: Linda Lewis, "At the Border: Women, Anthropology, and North Korea" and Laurel Kendall, "Did Women Have a Peace Corps–Korea Experience?" in *Peace Corps Volunteers and the Making of Korean Studies in the United States*, edited by Seung-kyung Kim and Michael Robinson, 111–26, 127–40 (Seattle: University of Washington Center for Korea Studies, 2020).

3. In 1972, then president of the Republic of Korea (ROK), Park Chung Hee, revised the existing constitution in order to stabilize his power and guarantee his continuing role. The revised "Yusin" constitution severely restricted free speech and assembly.

BIBLIOGRAPHY

Anderson, Benedict. *Imagined Communities: Reflections on the Origin and Spread of Nationalism*. New York: Verso, 1983.

Lewis, Linda. "At the Border: Women, Anthropology, and North Korea." In *Peace Corps Volunteers and the Making of Korean Studies in the United States*, edited by Seung-kyung Kim and Michael Robinson, 127–40. Seattle: University of Washington Center for Korea Studies, 2020.

Kendall, Laurel. "Did Women Have a Peace Corps–Korea Experience?" In *Peace Corps Volunteers and the Making of Korean Studies in the United States*, edited by Seung-kyung Kim and Michael Robinson 111–26 Seattle: University of Washington Center for Korea Studies, 2020.

9

Peace Corps–Korea Group K-1: Empowering to Serve as New Voices in Korean Studies

EDWARD J. SHULTZ

> It is indeed striking that this important idea, the most powerful idea in recent times, of a Peace Corps . . . should come from this mightiest nation on earth, the United States. Many of us who did not know about the United States thought of this great nation as a wealthy nation, a powerful nation, endowed with a great material strength and many powerful weapons. But how many of us know that in the United States ideas and ideals are also powerful? This is the secret of your greatness.
>
> Thanat Khoman, Foreign Minister of Thailand
> Chulalongkorn University, Bangkok
> January 28, 1964[1]

Over fifty years ago, in 1966, the first Peace Corps–Korea program, "K-1," pulled up its stakes in Hilo, Hawai'i, and left for the Republic of Korea (ROK). How did I, a callow twenty-two-year-old and recent college graduate end up on that plane to South Korea? Ironically, my road to the Korean peninsula started six years earlier when I studied in Norway as a high school junior. I was living with my aunt who had married a Norwegian, thinking this would give me a sound international experience, and I savored the taste of an international life. During my sophomore year at Union College in Schenectady, New York, Union offered its first course in the Chinese language. As I already had French and Norwegian languages on my list, I figured I might as well expand my horizons and take Chinese, which I did for three years.

With just a limited East Coast/Euro-centric experience, I was smitten by the bug to learn more about Asia. When a return Peace Corps volunteer came to Union's campus to recruit for the Peace Corps, I was an immediate prospect, hoping to use my Chinese-language preparation somewhere in Asia. In 1966, the United States was still refusing to maintain diplomatic relations with the People's Republic of China. I am not certain if the Peace Corps headquarters knew that the Chinese and Korean languages did not share a direct relationship, but South Korean newspapers tended, at that time, to use many Chinese characters along with Hangul. When the offer to join the Peace Corps' first volunteer group to Korea (K-1) arrived, how could I refuse?

In the months before I set off for Hilo, Hawai'i, I tried to get a clearer picture of what Korea was all about. This is what I knew of the Korea peninsula in 1966: Syngman Rhee (Yi Sŭngman, 1948–60), former president of the Republic of Korea (ROK), had been in the news in 1960, and our milkman had fought in the Korean War (1950–53), as did a couple of guys I worked with during my 1965 summer job as part of a road construction crew. My high school principal, also a Korean War veteran, had few if any positive comments about Korea. In contrast to these rather dubious views, my parents had a friend who had been a missionary in Korea before World War II. He had a very positive experience with Koreans, despite the Japanese occupation. Furthermore, several of my professors at Union College, who had also been to the Korean peninsula in one capacity or another, spoke highly of the Korean culture and the people; in short, two images of Korea slowly emerged.

In mid-June, with this background, I headed for Hilo, joined by fellow volunteers including Edward and Diane Baker, David McCann, Charlie Goldberg, Ed Klein, John Middleton, Frank Concilus, and others who later made Korea a part of their career.[2] We probably all arrived in Hilo with similar conflicted images of Korea. Prior to our arrival, the Peace Corps had sent us two books, The Martyred by Richard Kim and Korean Works and Days by Richard Rutt.[3] These were two interesting selections with somewhat contrasting views of Korea. Richard Kim's novel told the tale of the consequences of the Korean War and was on the New York Times bestsellers list that year, whereas Rutt's work described the lives of everyday Koreans as witnessed by a missionary priest. We also met with Koreans for our language instruction, mostly South Korean graduate students studying at the East-West Center at the University of Hawai'i. In addition, we heard from Peace Corps volunteers returning with Peace Corps experiences from other countries. We were also introduced to a number of scholars and a strong presence of people affiliated with Yonsei University including the program director. One clearly indisputable and memorable scholar was Glenn Paige, then at Princeton University. His discussions inspired a number of us to see the excitement and potential in the relatively underdeveloped field of Korean studies.

The K-1 training in Hilo was idyllic. Our home base was the former hospital beside the beautiful Rainbow Falls, and we took advantage of the various sites that the Big Island of Hawai'i offered. We spent one week in Waipio Valley, just north of Hilo, where we were taught how to "rough it" by sleeping on hard floors, using squat toilets, and bathing in a cool mountain stream. To hone our teaching skills, the Peace Corps sent us over to the Kona (west) coast of the Hawai'i Island to practice teaching in the public schools and engage in cross-cultural learning, through teaching indigenous Hawaiian as well as third-generation immigrant children. Thus, in addition to learning about Korea, we learned about ourselves as we interacted with a new culture unique to Hawai'i. What I believe the Peace Corps was trying to do was to teach us how to respond to totally new situations, how to innovate and meet challenges, and how to ask the right questions. Needless to say, these are skills every person can use. This experience assisted me as I charted my way through the bureaucracy of higher education from teaching assistant to dean, to my teaching sabbaticals in South Korea, and especially during my brief stint as an interim chancellor at a Japanese university branch campus in Hawai'i. The Peace Corps empowered all of its volunteers in novel ways.

In 1966, Western academic circles largely overlooked Korea having set their focus instead on China and Japan. Cornelius Osgood's study on Kanghwa Island, Homer Hulbert's two volume History of Korea, a chapter or two in the Reischauer-Fairbank's texts, and some writing on Korean literature by Peter Lee rounded out the material available in 1966.[4] The first generation of US-based Korean studies scholars, mostly with missionary or GI backgrounds, those who had obtained their PhD's in the 1950s and early 1960s, were just beginning to publish, but the Korea studies field was largely uncultivated. A quick examination of the bibliography Studies on Korea, edited by Han-Kyo Kim shows that it wasn't until the early 1970s that publications on Korea began to increase.[5]

Many of us were struck during training by how Korea was an academic field waiting to be discovered. We believed this lack of knowledge about Korea's history and culture led the United States to make costly foreign policy errors in the 1940s and 1950s. If the United States of America was to be a great nation helping to make the world a better place, we had an obligation to learn and appreciate other cultures. The Peace Corps opened our eyes to the possibility that our experiences in and knowledge of Korea would be both productive and informative.

Meeting the Republic of Korea head on in the fall of 1966 dismayed some and inspired other volunteers. I was especially fortunate in that I was assigned to Kyŏngnam Boys' High School, one of South Korea's elite high schools in the southern city of Pusan. There, I met students and faculty who had a vision

Fig. 9.1 Ned Shultz and students outside Kyŏngnam High School, Pusan, South Korea, 1966. Photo courtesy of Ned Shultz.

for the newly emerging South Korea. Kyŏngnam's principal, a former archae-ologist, encouraged me to look into Korean history and talked with me about the Silla Dynasty. Many Koreans, feeling that most foreigners did not appreci-ate Korea and its culture, continually suggested that I study their country and make Korea's story more widely known. The Peace Corps provided me with a firm foundation to understand Korea and its history and culture, as I came into contact with many sectors of South Korean society.

Unfortunately, my stomach did not adjust as quickly to South Korea as it should have. After one year, I had to return to the United States to attend to protozoa running through me. What started as amoebic dysentery led to a serious case of colitis. I was devasted after learning that I would have to leave South Korea but was fortunate in that the Peace Corps asked me to help train the K-3 program in Pennsylvania and the K-5 volunteers in Bisbee, Arizona, where I could share my own experiences on living and working in South Korea. After returning to the States, I was able to read more widely about Korea and started working toward a graduate degree. For those of us who have worked as a professor, it is a great profession in that one learns even more by teaching. When I left the Republic of Korea in the summer of 1967, I was certain I wanted to study Korea in an academic environment and started to look into graduate schools at Columbia, Harvard, Berkeley, the University of Washington, and Hawai'i. With the exception of Hawai'i, the other universities said I had to wait until fall semester. Hawai'i allowed me to start in January, so I chose to apply to Hawai'i and started graduate study in January 1968.

The University of Hawai'i (UH) laid the formal foundation of my study of Korea. The UH was attractive for many reasons but foremost, UH had more scholars studying Korea than any other US campus at the time. Glenn Paige, whom I had met in Hilo in 1966, had relocated to Hawai'i in 1967. There was also a cohort of young South Korean scholars studying at the East-West Center who became future academic colleagues. Fundamental to this formal academic study was my Peace Corps experience. It was through the Peace Corps that I discovered the excitement of scholarship, and where I gained insights into Korea and its people, that many other scholars from other fields missed.

The Peace Corps led us to believe that what we were experiencing, and learning was special. I believed South Korea, despite its poverty, was a rich and spiritually powerful country. Most importantly the Peace Corps provided us with a basis in the Korean language and introduced us to people who would later become academic colleagues and friends for the rest of our lives. We must also not forget the Fulbright program which enabled many former Peace Corps volunteer students to return to South Korea for further research and study. As a Fulbright grantee, I reconnected with other K-1 volunteers, my Korean families and friends, and also met more recent Peace Corps volunteers. When I would meet other volunteers, there was a certain pride and status in being a K-1.

Subsequent tours to South Korea whether it was with the University of Hawai'i East-West Center, Fulbright, or other sponsored visits were all

Fig. 9.2 Ned Shultz (on right) with other Peace Corps volunteers Sharon and Larry Toulouse and Rosemary Kerwin (in middle). Aegwanwŏn Orphanage, Kŏje Island, South Korea, 1967. Photo courtesy of Ned Shultz.

enhanced because of my previous Peace Corps commitment. It was much easier for Koreans to categorize who I was because I had first lived in South Korea as a Peace Corps volunteer. Having lived in South Korea, I felt much more empowered to wander the streets, meet new people, and venture more readily into libraries and archives. People whom I had met as a volunteer were most welcoming on return visits and endeavored to open doors and facilitate my research quests. Even today, when people ask about my facility in Korean (not that it is good), I respond it all started when I lived in Pusan as a Peace Corps volunteer.

This sense of commitment to the study of Korea is best seen in a conference in January 1978. Organized by David McCann, John Middleton, and myself, we obtained funding and met in South Korea in Seoul, at a place called Academy House. Fulbright helped us with the location. Subsequently we published a small conference volume titled *Studies on Korea in Transition*. In the introduction, the former Peace Corps–Korea director, Kevin O'Donnell, in describing K-1 volunteers noted, "These were a different breed of Americans . . . who came prepared to spend two years in [South] Korea, not as foreigners, but to live as their Korean fellow workers in Korean fashion."[6] I believe the *Studies on Korea* and this current volume, *Peace Corps Volunteers and the Making of Korean Studies in the United States*, edited by Seung-kyung Kim and Michael Robinson sponsored by Indiana University and published by the University of Washington Center for Korea Studies, "reflect [the] continuing efforts to interpret our Korean experience from the perspectives of our various career paths."[7]

In the *Studies on Korea* we went on to note,

> What may not be as immediately apparent, but which informs these papers just as strongly, is the sense of mutual discovery that we share as members of the first Peace Corps group in Korea and of mutual regard for the ways in which we have sought to work out through various approaches our answers to the questions: What is Korea? How [should we] define it? . . . These are broad questions that we have asked ourselves since the inception of our Peace Corps experience. They began in Peace Corps training in 1966, intensified during the experience of living and working in Korea, and continued as many of us maintained our ties with that experience through academic and professional careers.[8]

Studies on Korea included ten articles presenting the research completed by former Peace Corps volunteers and examined various topics including Korean history, anthropology, literature, and education. The quest to answer these questions is a journey many Peace Corps K-1 volunteers continue to pursue.

Meeting volunteers from later groups was always exciting. I was able to validate my own impressions and learn things I had missed. The later training programs also inevitably became much broader than the first program, as the Peace Corps started to tap more scholars in the field, and more educational material became available. By the mid-1970s, graduate schools had started to expand their offerings to accommodate the growing number of return Peace Corps volunteers who wanted to study East Asia and especially Korea. In a story now familiar, many returnees, like myself, took academic positions and leadership roles in Korean studies and later became what is now referred to as the second generation of Korean scholars in the United States and Canada.

When we entered the Peace Corps, we were informed that we had three main goals as volunteers: (1) to provide technical knowledge to the host country; (2) To learn about the host country; and (3) to return to the United States and share our knowledge and experiences.

Fig. 9.3 Huimun Lee Family. Miryang, South Korea, 1967. Photo courtesy of Ned Shultz.

Most returnees maintain that they learned and received much more from their host country than they ever gave to South Korea. Moreover, we bonded as a group having shared our experiences of living and working in South Korea. Just as we were confident of our own experiences, we could better understand and be appreciative of the experiences enjoyed by others. Although many of us were dispersed to campuses across the country, contact was relatively easy through Fulbright study tours, the Association for Asian Studies (AAS) annual meetings, and of course later, in the 1990s, email.

Quite certainly, the Peace Corps laid the foundation for all of our subsequent research and many of our careers. It provided us with a basic grounding in the Korean language; afforded us valuable time in the Republic of Korea (living and working in a Korean community), and it provided us with a network of like-minded individuals trying to understand Korea in novel ways. In essence, the Peace Corps empowered us with the confidence necessary so that we could begin to understand Korea and inspired us to share that understanding with others.

My research over the years has focused on Koryŏ history. Obviously, my Peace Corps experience played a role in guiding me in this direction. From the start I had been interested in learning more about Korean history, and as I noted earlier the high school principal shared Korea's rich past with me as did other teachers and friends I made in Pusan. As a young student, I even read a Korean history text with the help of one of the high school teachers. Field trips with other volunteers and Korean teachers to Kyŏngju, Haeinsa and other sites whetted my imagination and desire to learn more. My experience training Peace Corps volunteers after I returned to the United States, provided me with even more opportunities to read and talk about Korea's past. Obviously, my focused academic training to become a practicing historian evolved in graduate school, but it was my Peace Corps experience that empowered me to take the first steps toward studying history.

Some ten years ago I noted,

Although the study of Korea has witnessed significant strides in the last fifty years, there remains tremendous work ahead. Exchange will continue to be an important component in maintaining the vitality of Korean studies, but scholars must incorporate new ideas and look for areas in which innovation can succeed. As the nature of the student body and public interest change within very short periods, methods to retain and sustain interest among them are imperative. However, only when scholars have been trained in a rigorous and complete manner, will they be able to provide competently the direction needed for Korean studies to prosper.[9]

In the fifty years since I embarked on the study of Korea, the field has enjoyed phenomenal growth, pretty much mirroring South Korea's own journey from poverty to plenty. Pusan, where I lived in 1966, has been a significant part of the "Korea miracle." In 1966, although Pusan was the Republic of Korea's second largest metropolis, it was a relatively calm port city. It had a few vessels sailing in from various parts of the globe and at times daily voyages to and from Japan. In addition, there was healthy domestic maritime travel along South Korea's coastline with most routes starting and ending in Pusan. The airport consisted of a small landing strip near Haeundae Beach, and trains from Seoul and other locations arrived randomly throughout the day.

Of course, all that has changed. Pusan is the ROK's leading port and has expanded exponentially. Large passenger ferries ply their way daily between Japan and South Korea, and there are daily trips as well to Cheju Island. Huge cargo ships fill the harbor queuing to moor to offload thousands of shipping containers. Local maritime travel has all but disappeared as buses can cover the trip much more efficiently and quickly. The small airport near Haeundae Beach has disappeared and been replaced with Kimhae International Airport which has flights arriving and departing for locations across Asia. Trains of course and especially the Korea Train Express (KTX) depart from Pusan Station every fifteen minutes.

The exponential expansion that has become so obvious in transportation can also be seen in the development of education. In Pusan in 1966, there were four elite high schools, two male and two female, and a few feeder middle schools. In the mid-1970s the ROK did away with the rigorous high school entrance examination and this began to breakdown elitism in secondary education. These formerly elite schools still exist in name and boast both beautiful campuses and long traditions, but now Pusan, and South Korea more generally, exhibits much greater equality in secondary education. Admission to a university has also eased as well although examinations remain the primary criterion of admission. However, the number and quality of universities in Pusan have expanded dramatically, affording greater opportunities for many.

Pusan has expanded outward and upward. Haeundae Beach used to be a distant spot which could be traversed by bicycle (as I once did) in about two hours. Today a subway can carry you there in a half an hour and a taxi, if traffic is light, will take about twenty-five minutes. Sŏngjong Beach which was a short train ride north of Haeundae in 1966 is now part of greater Pusan, and the rice paddies which had dotted the city have been replaced by soaring apartments of over thirty stories. In 1966, there were few personal cars, whereas nowadays the roads are clogged with the latest model Hyundais, Mercedes, and BMWs. On the "downside" good domestic help is hard to find. Once well-heeled families might have employed several servants, a cook, and a driver or two, however, that lifestyle has changed with perhaps a cleaning lady once or twice a week at best.

Even so, "old" Pusan can be found with a little searching. The Chagalch'i Fish Market provides some of the freshest and tastiest fish in South Korea and sanitation has improved to the point that my own delicate stomach devours the raw fish offerings without a second thought. Market vendors also have started to follow the global transparency trend and will inform their customers of their catches' origins: South Korea, Japan, Russia, the United States, for example. Taejongdae, a beautiful park located on the southern tip of Yŏngdo Island, offers stunning vistas, whereas in 1966 it was less traveled, now the majestic cliffs can be easily reached by bus or taxi, and minibuses transport crowds of sightseers around the park. Haeundae Beach still harbors a fine sandy beach, which in the past was surrounded by natural areas and rice paddies. Today, it is encircled by hotels and condominiums. In Pusan, I used to know a fair number of people, but now few friends remain. Nevertheless, each time I have the opportunity to travel back to Pusan I am filled with extraordinary memories and whenever I hear the sound of the thick Kyŏngsang dialect I become nostalgic.

What has happened to Pusan in the last fifty years has also happened to Korean studies both in Korea and in the United States. From the perspective of a scholar of the University of Hawai'i, even in the late 1960s UH had more professors teaching about Korea than any other campus in the United States. Hawai'i was the first university in the country to develop a Center for Korean Studies in 1972 and under the auspices of the Center for Korean Studies, the number professors engaged in teaching about Korea has expanded today to over sixteen fulltime faculty members. Areas of research include most of the major disciplines in the humanities and the social sciences. In the late 1960s and early 1970s a number of returned Peace Corps volunteers found their way to the University of Hawai'i and participated in the expansion of Korean studies.

The UH Center for Korean Studies has been a catalyst for change and growth. Building on its already sizeable number of faculty, it has been able to foster especially strong programs in linguistics, second-language studies, the humanities, and social sciences. With an ever-expanding endowment, the UH Center for Korea Studies has been able to offer scholarships to graduate students and research stipends to faculty. It also brings visiting scholars to campus to present colloquia and their presence further enriches the university's intellectual environment. Immediately adjacent to the Center for Korean Studies is the East-West Center (EWC) which complements the University of Hawai'i's Korea-focused programming. The EWC has taken a direct interest in expanding the study of Korea by fostering seminars both in South Korea and on other campuses across the mainland in which non-Korean teaching faculty are introduced to the Korean culture and thereby encouraged to bring Korea studies to their home campuses. The University of Hawai'i Center for Korea Studies has also designed specialized curriculum on Korea that can be used by high school teachers in their classrooms. The East-West Center yearly hosts students, visiting faculty, journalists, and government leaders from the Republic of Korea, which adds yet another a component to the intellectual life of the University of Hawai'i.

I would be remiss not to mention the tremendous support both the University of Hawai'i and the East-West Center have received from the Republic of Korea. The ROK initially provided one-third of the building costs for the UH Center for Korean Studies in the early 1980s. In addition, such organizations as the Korea Foundation (KF) and the Academy of Korean Studies (AKS) have been generous in both building endowments and programming support. These two units (both the KF and the AKS) have played leading roles in fostering the study of Korea not only in Hawai'i but throughout the United States and other parts of the globe.

Nevertheless, despite the spectacular growth of Korean studies in the last fifty years, there remain areas that would benefit from further cultivation, and I have enumerated six areas below.

(1) *Develop an advanced Korean-language facility.* This is finally becoming a reality through a consortium of universities across the United States. The advanced Korean-language facility is modeled on similar programs that are found both in China and Japan. Advanced language instruction in the United States has made significant strides over the years, but we must do more to assure that young scholars are given the opportunity to receive a near fluency level of competence. Intensive, in-country training is vital to achieving this goal. We expect Korean students who study in the United States to be fully capable of studying in English, why shouldn't we expect the same level of competence in US students studying in Korea?

(2) *Construct a consortium to provide undergraduate students with a flexible yet organized year-abroad experience in Korea.* Study abroad programs are beginning to pop up on many campuses in South Korea. Students who partake in these programs are potentially an important group upon which to draw future Korea specialists, but to date there are few organized programs that provide undergraduate students with a solid introduction to Korea. An ideal experience would provide students with courses in language, history, and culture as well as housing arrangements that would be shared with Korean students rather than placing visiting students in an international housing.

(3) *Encourage training that focuses on premodern studies and training in classical Chinese.* There is a woeful lack of students studying premodern Korea. Part of the problem is that a "passport" is needed, that of a solid grounding in literary Chinese, in order to gain access to early sources. Because this area is somewhat neglected, there are few courses offered in this area, and those that do exist are essentially only available at the established campuses. Most Western students, already overwhelmed with the difficulty of studying modern Korea and Hangul, rarely muster the courage to take on the study of literary Chinese on their own. Furthermore, because this area is somewhat neglected, there are few courses offered in this area and those essentially only at major campuses, further exasperating this problem. By affording special funding for students anxious to take up both the study of premodern society and the literary Chinese language, this now withering field can once again begin to grow.

(4) *Be mindful of the need for gender balance.* Korean studies has long been dominated by men. It is in part a result of the fact that higher education traditionally has been dominated by men, but also the higher education environ-

ment both in the West and in Asia continues to be more favorable to men. In South Korea this is especially glaring but certainly in the United States the equality of gender is still being sought. It does not need to be pointed out that women contribute different perspectives of analysis and fuller participation by them will greatly enrich the field. Every effort needs to be made first to acknowledge this imbalance and then strive to overcome institutions inherent in academia that perpetuate it.

(5) *Be mindful of the need for disciplinary diversity.* A quick glance at statistics shows that history attracts a high proportion of people in Korean studies and within the study of history the twentieth century emerges as the main attraction. Other disciplines are less well represented and particularly areas such as music, art, philosophy, and archaeology. This lack of breadth weakens the field.

(6) *Provide more dissertation research assistance.* Students often discover that once it is time to research and write a dissertation, funding dries up. For those who were fortunate enough to tap resources for much of their graduate preparation, when it comes to their final step, when they need to focus on research and writing, there is little support. A student who is ready to finish their dissertation frequently has to prolong this period and seek various forms of employment to cover expenses while finalizing their dissertation. Additionally, students are often burdened by seeking full-time employment while trying to finish their dissertations. Grants and stipends at this crucial time will facilitate quicker passage through this phase of the academic process.

Although many Peace Corps–Korea volunteers are now senior professors or have retired, we need to continue to work to foster an even deeper examination of Korea and collectively address many of these constraints.

NOTES

1. David R. McCann, John Middleton, and Edward J. Shultz, ed., *Studies on Korea in Transition* (Honolulu: University of Hawai'i Center for Korean Studies, 1979), ix.

2. Edward Baker discusses his experiences with the Peace Corps in chapter 2 of this volume, "How the Peace Corps Changed Our Lives" in *Peace Corps Volunteers and the Making of Korean Studies in the United States*, edited by Seung-kyung Kim and Michael Robinson, 31–52 (Seattle: Center for Korea Studies, 2020).

3. Richard E. Kim, *The Martyred: A Novel* (New York: G. Braziller, 1964); and Richard Rutt, *Korean Works and Days: Notes from the Diary of a Country Priest* (Rutland, VT: C.E. Tuttle, 1964),

4. Cornelius Osgood, *The Koreans and Their Culture* (New York: Ronald Press, 1951); Homer Hulbert, *The History of Korea* 2 vols. New York: Hilary House, 1962); Edwin O. Reischauer and John King Fairbank, *East Asia: The Great Tradition: A History of East Asian Civilization Vol 1* (Boston: Houghton Mifflin, 1960); and John King Fairbank, Edwin O. Reischauer, and Albert M. Craig, *East Asia : The Modern Transformation: History of East Asian Civilization Vol 2* (Boston: Houghton Mifflin, 1965).

5. Han-Kyo Kim and Hong Kyoo Park. *Studies on Korea: A Scholar's Guide* (Honolulu: University Press of Hawai'i, 1980).

6. David R. McCann, John Middleton, and Edward J. Shultz, ed., *Studies on Korea*, ix.

7. David R. McCann, John Middleton, and Edward J. Shultz, ed., *Studies on Korea*, i.

8. David R. McCann, John Middleton, and Edward J. Shultz, ed., *Studies on Korea*, 1–4.

9. Edward J Shultz, "The Current State of Support for Korean Studies Abroad and Strengthening Korean Studies Internationally." Paper presented at Seoul National University, May 2006.

BIBLIOGRAPHY

Baker, Edward. " How the Peace Corps Changed Our Lives." In *Peace Corps Volunteers and the Making of Korean Studies in the United States*, edited by Seung- kyung Kim and Michael Robinson, 31–52. Seattle: University of Washington Center for Korea Studies, 2020.

Hulbert, Homer. B. *The History of Korea*. 2 vols. New York: Hilary House, 1962.

Kim, Han-Kyo, and Hong Kyoo Park. *Studies on Korea: A Scholar's Guide*. Honolulu: University Press of Hawai'i, 1980.

Kim, Richard E. *The Martyred: A Novel*. New York: G. Braziller, 1964.

Lee, Peter H. *Korean Literature: Topics and Themes*. Tucson: University of Arizona Press, 1965.

McCann, David R., John Middleton, and Edward J. Shultz, ed. *Studies on Korea in Transition*. Honolulu: University of Hawai'i Center for Korean Studies, 1979.

Osgood, Cornelius. *The Koreans and Their Culture*. New York: Ronald Press, 1951.

Reischauer, Edwin O., and John King Fairbank. *East Asia: The Great Tradition. A History of East Asian Civilization Vol 1*. Boston: Houghton Mifflin, 1960.

Fairbank, John King, Edwin O. Reischauer, and Albert M. Craig. *East Asia : The Modern Transformation: History of East Asian Civilization Vol 2*. Boston: Houghton Mifflin, 1965.

Rutt, Richard. *Korean Works and Days: Notes from the Diary of a Country Priest*. Rutland, VT: C.E. Tuttle, 1964.

Shultz, Edward J. "The Current State of Support for Korean Studies Abroad and Strengthening Korean Studies Internationally." Paper presented at Seoul National University, May 2006.

10

A Korean Perspective: Peace Corps Volunteers, Europe, and the Study of Korea

OKPYO MOON

This chapter is intended to provide a Korean perspective regarding the contribution made by Peace Corps volunteers. My experiences are limited, as I only met a few of them in the early 1970s, but I can reflect upon what I believe to be the major significance of the arrival of scholars with Peace Corps background in terms of the development of Korean Studies in general and, in particular, my specialty, anthropology. Since my training after receiving a BA and MA at Seoul National University was in the United Kingdom, I will try to relate and compare Korean studies in Europe and in the United States as a way of illuminating the special contribution made by scholars with a Peace Corps background.

ORIENTAL STUDIES, AREA STUDIES, AND KOREAN STUDIES IN EUROPE

In the 1970s, there existed only a few Korean studies programs in either Europe or in the United States. When I started my graduate work at the University of Oxford in the mid-1970s, for instance, there was not a single scholar doing Korean studies research. The main hub of Asian studies at Oxford was the Oriental Institute, which offered both undergraduate and graduate courses related to various areas of Asia. The Oxford Institute was, however, filled with specialists on China, Japan, the Middle East, and India, among others. No one seemed to have much interest in Korea, and some scholars were even unable to distinguish South Korea from the North. I clearly remember being constantly asked the same question again and again

at numerous parties and receptions (there were many of them for some rea-
son). When I introduced myself as Korean, the most frequent reaction was,
"Where on earth is Korea?" it was, indeed, a rather annoying experience that
I had to reply to those silly questions with, "It's between China and Japan!"

If the conversation continued, it might develop into a little more discussion about Japanese colonialism, the Korean War, and the subsequent North-
South confrontation, none of which were appealing subjects of conversation
at light-hearted receptions. If there were some people who expressed a little
more curiosity about Korean culture, the talk usually ended up with my
explaining it as something "in-between" things Chinese and Japanese, again
not a very satisfactory description. These episodes may be hard to believe, but
such was the situation at Oxford University, one of the most prominent intellectual centers in Europe. After those experiences, I began to realize that
Korea had indeed failed to have made much of an impression upon mainstream Western thinking, especially in academia.

It was in April 1977, when the inaugural meeting of the Association for
Korean Studies in Europe (AKSE) was held at the School of Oriental and
African Studies (SOAS) in London, under the leadership of William Skillend
and other European scholars, including Frits Vos, who became the first president of the AKSE, Dieter Eikemeier, and Ogg Li. As I remember, about thirty
to forty people attended the meeting, including Kwang-ok Kim and me, who
participated as graduate students. Martina Deuchler, who had recently
received a doctorate, also attended. She had started teaching Korean history
at the University of Zurich, Switzerland, and later, in 1991, joined the
Department of Far Eastern Studies at SOAS, where she remained until 2001.

The scholars who frequented the AKSE conferences during these initial
years were mostly from the humanities fields, the so-called *mun-sa-ch'ŏl*—literature, language, history, philosophy and religion—reflecting the age-old
tradition of oriental studies in Europe. There were also some scholars from
the field of what may be understood as folklore studies such as Alex
Guillemoz and Tuhyŏn Yi, who came from South Korea to participate in the
inaugural meeting in 1977, but none of the major social sciences fields dealing with contemporary issues were represented, a feature that, to some extent,
still characterizes the AKSE conferences after more than forty years of its
history. (The AKSE celebrated its fortieth anniversary in 2017).

There were two distinctive features of AKSE and Korean studies in Europe around this time. One is the fact that the establishment of AKSE in 1977 occurred only four years after the establishment in 1973 of the European Association for Japanese Studies (EAJS). The EAJS's first international conference was held in 1976, also in London. The dominance of tradition of oriental studies and the humanities was also prominent at the earlier EAJS meetings, as well as with Japan studies as a whole. Unlike in the case of Korean studies, however, the establishment of the Nissan Institute of Japanese Studies at Oxford in 1982 was a major turning point.

A series of grants made by the Nissan Company to Oxford stipulated that the study of Japan be introduced into the mainstream curricula of the university. This opened up the field of Japan studies not only to students from the Faculty of Oriental Studies, but also to those in politics, economics, social anthropology, history, and other fields. Significantly, the first director of the Nissan Institute was a political scientist from Australia, Arthur Stockwin. I believe that the establishment of the Nissan Institute for Modern Japanese Studies in the early 1980s was instrumental in developing and expanding the scope of Japan studies in Europe as a field of "Area" studies, beyond that of traditional Oriental studies. The Nissan Institute of Japanese Studies at Oxford now offers independent Master's and Doctoral courses in Japan studies and is an important part of the newly created School of Interdisciplinary Area Studies (SIAS), together with the centers for African studies, contemporary China studies, South Asian studies, Latin American studies, Middle East studies, and Russian and East European studies.

Korean studies in Europe was, unfortunately, unable to follow a similar path, for various reasons. Neither Korea was affluent enough yet to offer such large donations to the academic institutions in the West to promote Korean studies, as Japan was able to do thanks to its tremendous postwar economic growth following the Korean War (1950–53) and having had the advantageous trade relations with the United States for several decades. Apart from economics, there was another critical factor that resulted in a continuing low profile for the social sciences in Korean Studies in Europe, which in turn created special restraints and obligations for those doing Korean studies in Europe. That Korea was then, and is still, a divided country.

I remember, for instance, a substantial demonstration at the SOAS campus, just outside the room where the inaugural meeting of the AKSE was being held in 1977. It was a protest against the fact that the establishment of the AKSE was partly supported by the South Korean government, and that it therefore must be politically tainted. Such suspicions have remained a continuous burden that is unique to those engaged in Korean studies in Europe. Thus, Daniel Bouchez recalled in his speech on the past thirty years of AKSE history in 2007, that, at least during the initial years of the AKSE, "Present-day politics has to be absolutely avoided, classical and historical studies remained predominant, membership had to be kept confidential."[1]

With the gradual opening of East-West relations, participation from East European countries and P'yŏngyang began to increase.[2] After the fall of the Berlin Wall in 1989, the AKSE conference became one of the few venues where scholars from both parts of Korea could meet and talk, albeit with constraints. The relationship has undergone fluctuations, but academic dialogues between South and North Koreas have never been very active or open even at the AKSE meetings.

KOREAN ANTHROPOLOGY IN THE 1970S AND IMPACT OF PEACE CORPS SCHOLARS

I have described the beginning and evolution of Korean studies in Europe at some length, as I believe it may provide some background for understanding the impact of Peace Corps volunteers in the development of Korean studies in South Korea and in the United States, especially with regard to the social sciences. In the quote above, Daniel Bouchez indicated that the division of Europe and of Korea was the main reason why classical and historical studies remained predominant at the AKSE conferences, resulting in the inevitable under-representation of social sciences. Although I am not very well informed of the situation of Korean studies in the United States prior to the 1970s, I have had the impression that it also was dominated by mun-sa-ch'ŏl (language, literature, history, philosophy, and religion), in the tradition of civilizational studies. The few Korean studies programs that existed at that time were the ones at Harvard (led by Dr. Edward Wagner), Columbia (Drs. Gari Ledyard and Frank Baldwin), the University of Hawai'i (Dr. Peter Lee), and the University of Washington (Dr. James Palais).

Under the circumstances, the arrival of Peace Corps volunteers in the Republic of Korea (ROK) in the 1960s had a special meaning. Many of them later returned to South Korea to pursue Korean studies. This new generation of Korean studies scholars was distinguished from most of their predecessors in that they had first-hand experience of South Korean society before they even embarked on studying it. I believe, it was the Peace Corps returnees who provided new momentum for the development of Korean studies in terms of the methodology, scope, and depth in their respective fields.

Although the exact nature of the experiences Peace Corps volunteers went through in Korea varied from person to person, the fact that they had lived among the Korean people for a relatively long period of time and came to know the society must have made a considerable difference whichever subject they chose. In the field of anthropology, I may say it was in many ways the ex-Peace Corps volunteers returning to South Korea to carry out their doctoral fieldwork who constructed the cornerstone for studying the Korean society and people through sociological and anthropological survey methods, a new approach that had not been utilized that much in Korean studies prior to the 1970s.

Charles Goldberg, one of the Peace Corps volunteers who returned to South Korea to do doctoral fieldwork in 1972, recalled to me that he could find very few books to read about Korean village life, either in Korean or in English, when he was a graduate student at Columbia preparing for his field-

Fig. 10.1 Charles Goldberg and Kwang-ok Kim on the porch of their house. Solgol, Ch'ungch'ŏngnamdo, 1973. Photo courtesy of Kwang-ok Kim.

work.[3] Books by Cornelius Osgood, Suzuki Eitaro (in Korean translation), and Kim T'aek-kyu were among those few.[4] There were also a few doctoral dissertations by William Biernatzki (St. Louis University), Eugene Knez (Syracuse), Hyesung Chun Koh (Boston University), and Vincent Brandt (Harvard).[5] The latter work, by Brandt, was published by Harvard University Press in 1971 as *A Korean Village, Between Farm and Sea*, making it the first book-

Fig. 10.2 Charles Goldberg and his wife Julie on the porch of their home. Solgol, Ch'ungch'ŏngnamdo, 1973. Photo by Kwang-ok Kim.

length publication in English by an anthropologist who had lived for an extended period of time in a single Korean community.[6]

Village ethnography had not yet been established as a familiar method of research in Korean Studies until the 1970s. The Korea studies situation could again be contrasted with Japan Studies, where we find the well-known village ethnography by John Embree in the 1930s, Ronald Dore's seminal work on land reform in Japan of the 1950s, and the extensive collaborative village study by the Michigan team Beardsley, Hall and Ward, which was also published in the late 1950s, to mention just a few.[7] So, foreign graduate students who arrived in South Korea for doctoral research in the 1970s were mostly responsible for the ethnographic fieldwork that began to be an important methodology for studying Korean society and culture.

This is not to say that the study of anthropology did not exist in South Korea before the arrival of Peace Corps graduates. The Korean Society for Cultural Anthropology emerged in 1958, and Seoul National University opened the first department of anthropology jointly with archaeology as the Department of Archeology and Anthropology in 1961. After nearly a decade, however, there were only two faculty members in the department, one archaeologist and one cultural anthropologist. When I enrolled as an undergraduate student in 1969, the only fulltime anthropology faculty member, Sang-bok

Fig. 10.3 Charles Goldberg and Kwang-ok Kim with the villagers. Solgol, Ch'ungch'ŏngnamdo, 1973. Photo courtesy of Kwang-ok Kim.

Han, had taken leave for three years, from the fall of 1969 until the summer of 1972, to complete his own doctorate at Michigan State University in the United States. That meant that anthropology courses were not properly taught even at SNU during those years. By the early 1980s, there were only four departments of anthropology in all of South Korea: SNU (1961), Yŏngnam (1972), Kyŏngbuk (1983, jointly with archaeology), and Hanyang (1983). In 1988 alone, three more anthropology departments were added at Kangwŏn, Chŏnbuk, and Mokp'o universities.

In the early 1970s, a number of foreign anthropologists came to South Korea to carry out their doctoral fieldwork. The list included Charles Goldberg from Columbia, Griffin Dix from the University of California–San Diego, Paul Dredge from Harvard, Roger Janelli and his wife Dawn Hee from the Department of Folklore Studies at the University of Pennsylvania, and Frederick Carriere from Cornell. There was also Itoh Abito from Tokyo University, Shima Mutsuhiko from the University of Toronto (originally from Tōdai, Japan), Boudewijn Walraven from Leiden University, Mark Cozin from the University of London, and Laurel Kendall a few years later from Columbia. Charles McBrian, a student of Ezra Vogel at Harvard, who was the first Peace Corps graduate to complete a doctoral dissertation on Korean society, arrived somewhat earlier in the 1970s. In addition, Soon-Young Yoon arrived on the scene in the mid-1970s to do fieldwork in South Korea after already having received her doctorate in anthropology from the University of Michigan. Although only four of these researchers—McBrian, Goldberg, Dix, and Kendall—had a Peace Corps background, the sudden influx of people around the same time was quite unprecedented and left an important mark upon the development of Korean anthropology, given that it was still in its incipient stage.[8]

For many anthropology students at SNU, which had established its MA program in anthropology in 1973, it was through serving as the local "native" assistants and interpreters to these fieldworkers from abroad that they learned how to do anthropological fieldwork. Working as a field assistant for these future anthropologists proved to be extremely beneficial, as the Korean student–assistants actually lived in the village with the fieldworkers whom they were helping for the duration of the study, which was often for more than one year. Since at the time there were very few proper methodology courses offered at SNU, there could not have been a better training opportunity than that of becoming a fieldwork assistant. The relationship can therefore be considered truly mutual as Korean assistants provided critical information regarding Korean society and culture that the fieldworkers needed while Korean students received much needed knowledge on how to conduct proper field study in the course of carrying out collaborative fieldwork.

The relative proliferation of village ethnography in the 1970s also added a new dimension to Korean studies, which up until that point had largely focused on studying texts produced by members of the elite class. Ethnographic methods turned attention instead to the ordinary people and their lives and their way of thinking and emphasized "participant observation"—living among the people they were studying for a long period of time. In this regard, those with Peace Corps backgrounds seemed to have had a particular advantage, since most of them had already lived in Korean communities and had some Korean-language proficiency as well as preliminary understanding of the society, the two most critical assets for any fieldworker. While American-style ethnography, which developed in the study of non-literate societies, had sometimes been criticized for paying too little attention to the historical dimensions of the societies being studied, those whom I had a chance to observe were impressively historical in their data collection, considering a vast range of land records, genealogies, and other documents.[9]

Fig. 10.4 Charles Goldberg at a grave site ancestor ritual of the villagers. Solgol, Ch'ungch'ŏngnamdo, 1973. Photo by Kwang-ok Kim.

With a combination of extensive prior knowledge and experience in the society they studied and the professional training in social sciences, often accompanied by genuine affection toward the people, this new generation of scholars opened a new era in Korean studies. Adding to their contributions to Korean anthropology, two of these early fieldworkers (Charles Goldberg and Soon-Young Yoon) taught graduate-level courses in anthropology at SNU at the invitation of Dr. Sang-bok Han.

Fig. 10.5 Charles Goldberg on a picnic at the river with the villagers. Solgol, Ch'ungch'ŏngnamdo, 1973. Photo by Kwang-ok Kim.

As another example of how Peace Corps volunteers influenced the study of Korea, I would like to mention Laurel Kendall's work on Korean shamanism, which also took the form of a village ethnography.[10] Shamanism had long been considered an important topic for understanding Korean culture and identity. In the tradition of Korean folkloric studies shamanism had been extensively dealt with.[11] Shamanic songs, ritual paraphernalia, and typology had been described in detail, often in disregard of its sociological context. Kendall's study, however, squarely positioned it in the context of family and gender relations, world views, and other forms of household rituals of the Korean peasants. One might say that Kendall's study rescued shamanism from being disconnected from people's everyday lives.

During the late 1970s and early 1980s, after most of these researchers had finished their fieldwork in South Korea, two conferences were held, resulting in published books containing the papers delivered at those conferences. The first, *Studies of Korea in Transition*, published by the University of Hawai'i Press in 1979, was a collection of papers delivered at a conference in Seoul in 1977 by members of the first group of Peace Corps–Korea volunteers who had chosen to pursue careers in Korean studies. Among the papers printed in that volume were papers by Griffin Dix, Charles Goldberg, and Charles McBrian.[12] The second volume, *Religion and Ritual in Korean Society*, was based on a conference held at Mackinac Island, Michigan, in 1980. Edited by Laurel Kendall and Griffin Dix, the book contained, among others, papers by Dix, Kendall, C. Paul Dredge, Lee Kwang-gyu, and Mark Cozin.[13]

To my limited knowledge, among the Peace Corps graduates who carried out anthropological fieldwork in South Korea in the 1970s, only Laurel Kendall and Linda Lewis have continued to pursue Korean studies.[14] Given their critical contributions, as outlined above, it is indeed a loss that many of the rest had to abandon Korean studies for one reason or another. As indicated above, Korean studies could have been greatly enriched in terms of methodology, scope, and depth if only all of the earlier ethnographers with Peace Corps backgrounds had remained in the field.

HOPING FOR MORE BALANCED PERSPECTIVES IN KOREAN STUDIES

One final aspect that I would like to add to this recollection concerns the political leanings of some Korean studies scholars of this period. Daniel Bouchez mentioned in his speech quoted above that those engaged in Korean studies in the United States may have been relatively free of the political sensitivity arising from the East-West division and consequent restraints and obligations faced by their counterparts in Europe. It is my personal impression, however, that the latter may have been differently affected by political atmosphere.

The scholars most active in the formative stage of Korean studies in the United States carried out their field research in South Korea in the 1970s and the 1980s when the Republic of Korea was under two of the most oppressive regimes of its modern history. It is perhaps for this reason that some of these scholars have maintained rather critical perspectives of the society they study, or to put it more specifically, against the South Korean government. I have found this tendency of some Korean studies scholars in the United

States curiously contrastive with those engaged in Japan studies who appear to be, relatively speaking at least, less openly critical of the Japanese government. The difference may have arisen from some of the unsubtle approaches of the financing bodies. Yet, given the fact that no funding agencies (Japanese or otherwise) could be completely free of some sort of political stance, and the fact that Korean society has undergone considerable transformation since the 1970s when the earlier Korean studies scholars with Peace Corps background first encountered it, it may be time to take the later developments into full account and reflect upon the political nature of area studies with due nuance.[15]

NOTES

1. Daniel Bouchez, "Thirty Years @ AKSE! 1977–2007," *Association for Korean Studies in Europe Newsletter* no. 31 (September 2007): 4–6. It might be of some interest to note that similar objections were raised when the Korean Trade-Investment Promotion Agency (KOTRA) donated a grant of one million dollars in 1975 to endow the Modern Korean Economy and Society chair at Harvard. Among the prominent dissenters to the university accepting this gift from the Park Chung Hee (Pak Chŏnghŭi, 1961–79) regime were Harvard professor and Nobel laureate George Wald and the renowned professor Dr. Noam Chomsky from MIT. See "Harvard and Korea," *The Harvard Crimson*, December 10, 1976; and "Harvard's Relation with South Korea," *The Harvard Crimson*, October 3, 1983. I am grateful to Charles Goldberg for drawing my attention to this comparable episode as well as to other useful details of Peace Corps volunteer–scholars' subsequent activities and contributions.

2. The DPRK delegation has participated AKSE conferences. In 1989, they attended the London conference. In 1995, a group of North Korean scholars from Pyŏngyang presented on the Tan'gun Mausoleum and the subsequent excavation of Tan'gun's grave site. Tan'gun is considered the legendary founder of the first Korean kingdom. They also attended the AKSE conferences held in London in 2001 and in Sheffield in 2005.

3. Charles Goldberg, personal communication with author, May 2019.

4. Cornelius Osgood. *The Koreans and Their Culture* (New York: Ronald Press, 1951); Suzuki Eitarō, *Han'guk nongch'on sahoe tapsagi* (Sŏul: Ehwa Womans University Press, 1943 [1961]); and Kim T'aek-kyu, *Tongjok burak ŭi saenghwal kujo yŏn'gu* [A study of life structure of a lineage village] (Chŏngudaehak: Shilla kaya munhwa yŏn'guso, 1964).

5. William Biernatzki, "Varieties of Korean Lineage Structure." (PhD diss., Louis University, 1967); Eugene Knez, "Sam Jong Dong: A South Korean Village" (PhD diss., Syracuse University, 1969); Hyesung Chun Koh, "Religion, Social Structure, and

Economic Development in Yi Dynasty, Korea" (PhD diss., Boston University, 1959); and Vincent Brandt, "A Structural Study of Solidarity in Uihang Ni" (PhD diss., Harvard University, 1968).

6. The University of Washington Center for Korea Studies published Vincent Brandt's memoir, *An Affair with Korea*, in which he reflected on his time in South Korea. Vincent Brandt, *An Affair with Korea: Memories of South Korea in the 1960s* (Seattle: Center for Korea Studies/University of Washington Press, 2014).

7. John Embree, *Suye Mura: A Japanese Village* (Chicago: Chicago University Press, 1939); Ronald P. Dore, *Land Reform in Japan* (London: Oxford University Press, 1959); and Richard K. Beardsley, John W. Hall, and Robert E. Ward, *Village Japan* (Chicago: University of Chicago Press, 1959).

8. Apparently, as can be noted in her contribution to this volume, Linda Lewis had also served as a Peace Corps volunteer in the 1970s and later returned to Korea for an anthropological fieldwork. Since I was already in the United Kingdom doing my own graduate work since 1975, I have not been able to follow her work. Linda Lewis, "At the Border: Women, Anthropology, and North Korea," in *Peace Corps Volunteers and the Making of Korean Studies in the United States*, edited by Seung-kyung Kim and Michael Robinson (Seattle: University of Washington Center for Korea Studies, 2020).

9. See the review of *Village Japan* by Iwao Ishino (1960) in *American Anthropologist*. It was through Kwang-ok Kim, who worked as an assistant for Charles Goldberg from 1973 to 1974, that I had an opportunity to observe very closely how anthropological fieldwork was carried out. Iwao Ishino, "Book Review of *Village Japan*," *American Anthropologist* 62, no. 4 (1960): 711–13.

10. Laurel Kendall, *Shamans, Housewives, and Other Restless Spirits: Women in Korean Ritual Life* (Honolulu: University of Hawai'i Press, 1985).

11. The KOSCA (Korean Society for Cultural Anthropology) despite its name, was dominated by folklorists up until 1970s. Okpyo Moon, "Korean Anthropology: A Search for a New Paradigm." In *Asian Anthropology*, edited by Jan Van Bremen, Eyal Ben-Ari, and Syed Farid Atlatas, 117–36 (London: Routledge, 2005).

12. David R. McCann, John, Middleton, and Edward J. Shultz, *Studies on Korea in Transition: Occasional Papers of the Center for Korean Studies no. 9* (Honolulu: Center for Korean Studies, University of Hawai'i, 1979).

13. Laurel Kendall and Griffin Dix, *Religion and Ritual in Korean Society*, Korea Research Monograph 12 (Berkeley: University of California, Institute of East Asian Studies, Center for Korean Studies, 1987).

14. Laurel Kendall and Linda Lewis describe their experiences with the Peace Corps in chapter 6 and 7 of this volume. Laurel Kendall, "Did Women Have a Peace Corps–Korea Experience?"; and Linda Lewis, "At the Border: Women, Anthropology, and North Korea," in *Peace Corps Volunteers and the Making of Korean Studies in the United States*, edited

by Seung-kyung Kim and Michael Robinson, 111–26, 127–40. Seattle: University of Washington Center for Korea Studies, 2020.

15. At the Association for Asian Studies in Asia meeting held in Kyoto in 2016, for instance, it was rumored that some of the speakers had to modify the contents of their presentations at the request of the Japan Foundation, one of the main financing bodies of the meeting.

BIBLIOGRAPHY

Beardsley, Richard K., John W. Hall, and Robert E. Ward. *Village Japan*. Chicago: University of Chicago Press, 1959.

Biernatzki, William. "Varieties of Korean Lineage Structure." PhD diss. Louis University, 1967.

Bouchez, Daniel. "Thirty Years @ AKSE! 1977–2007." *Association for Korean Studies in Europe Newsletter* no. 31 (September 2007): 4–6. http://koreanstudies.eu/wp-content/uploads/2015/01/AKSENewsletter31_2007.pdf

Brandt, Vincent. *An Affair with Korea: Memories of South Korea in the 1960s*. Seattle: Center for Korea Studies/University of Washington Press, 2014.

Brandt, Vincent. *A Korean Village, Between Farm and Sea*. Harvard University Press. 1971.

Brandt, Vincent. "A Structural Study of Solidarity in Uihang Ni." PhD diss., Harvard University, 1968.

Dore, Ronald P. *Land Reform in Japan*. London: Oxford University Press, 1959.

Embree, John F. *Suye Mura: A Japanese Village*. Chicago: Chicago University Press, 1939.

"Harvard and Korea." *The Harvard Crimson*, December 10, 1976. http://www.thecrimson.com/article/1976/12/10/harvard-and-korea-pbibn-1975-the/.

"Harvard's Relation with South Korea." *The Harvard Crimson*, October 3, 1983. http://www.thecrimson.com/article/1983/10/6/harvards-relations-with-south-korea-pthe/.

Ishino, Iwao. "Book Review of Village Japan." *American Anthropologist* 62, no. 4 (1960): 711–13.

Kendall, Laurel. "Did Women Have a Peace Corps–Korea Experience?" In *Peace Corps Volunteers and the Making of Korean Studies in the United States*, edited by Seung-kyung Kim and Michael Robinson, 111–26. Seattle: University of Washington Center for Korea Studies, 2020.

Kendall, Laurel. *Shamans, Housewives, and Other Restless Spirits: Women in Korean Ritual Life*. Honolulu: University of Hawai'i Press, 1985.

Kendall, Laurel, and Griffin Dix, eds. *Religion and Ritual in Korean Society, Korea Research Monograph* 12. Berkeley, CA: Center of East Asian Studies, University of California, Berkeley, Center for Korean Studies, 1987.

Kim T'aek-kyu. *Tongjok burak ŭi saenghwal kujo yŏn'gu* [A Study of life structure of a lineage village]. Chŏngudaehak: Shilla kaya munhwa yŏn'guso, 1964.

Knez, Eugene. "Sam Jong Dong: A South Korean Village." PhD diss., Syracuse University, 1969.

Koh, Hesung Chun. "Religion, Social Structure, and Economic Development in Yi Dynasty, Korea." PhD diss., Boston University, 1959.

Lewis, Linda. "At the Border: Women, Anthropology, and North Korea." In *Peace Corps Volunteers and the Making of Korean Studies in the United States*, edited by Seung-kyung Kim and Michael Robinson, 127–40. Seattle: University of Washington Center for Korea Studies, 2020.

McCann David R., John Middleton, and Edward J. Shultz, eds. *Studies on Korea in Transition*. Honolulu: Center for Korean Studies, University of Hawai'i, 1979.

Moon, Okpyo. "Korean Anthropology: A Search for a New Paradigm." In *Asian Anthropology*, edited by Jan Van Bremen, Eyal Ben-Ari, and Syed Farid Atlatas, 117–36. London: Routledge, 2005.

Osgood, Cornelius. *The Koreans and Their Culture*. New York: Ronald Press, 1951.

Suzuki Eitarō. *Han'guk nongch'on sahoe tapsagi*. Sŏul: Ehwa Womans University Press, 1943 [1961].

11

Cultural Immersion, Imperialism, and the Academy: An Outsider's Look at Peace Corps Volunteers' Contribution to Korean Studies

CLARK W. SORENSEN

Before World War II, Sinology and Japan studies had already become established in the US academy in such places as the University of California, Berkeley, the University of Washington, Columbia University, and Harvard University, whereas, Korean studies got a late start with isolated academic positions first established in the 1950s and 1960s at Harvard, Berkeley, Columbia, Hawai'i, and the University of Washington. This first wave of scholars who were able to do original research using the Korean language consisted largely of non-heritage scholars who had been introduced adventitiously to the Korean language during their military service in the 1940s and 1950s, and subsequently specialized in Korean history and culture. They were aided by Korean immigrant language teachers and supplemented by a handful of Korean American scholars and a larger contingent of Korean immigrant scholars who had received their graduate training in the United States. Then key graduate schools, most of which had a single Korean expert in the late 1960s and early 1970s, recruited young Americans who had experienced South Korea in the Peace Corps.

Of those who came into graduate school through the Peace Corps in the 1970s not all entered academia, but those that did formed the core of a second wave of Korean studies scholars who, in the 1980s, consolidated the Korean studies field in the United States and began to move it into new institutions across the United States and (to a degree) Canada. This group stamped Korean studies with a distinctive *engagé* character that was not typical for Japan or China studies in the post–World War II period. The distinctiveness of the Korean studies profile was partly because the US government began intimidating the correspondingly *engagé* "China hands" in the diplomatic corps during the McCarthy period (1949–54), before Korean studies had even become established.[1] Japan studies, that had initially, like Korean studies, been developed based on US military language officers entering academia, did not benefit from the leavening provided by Peace Corps volunteers and their critical reflections on their country of interest. In the Korea case, the only one of the three countries that had Peace Corps volunteers, financial support for area studies, including Korea, burgeoned in the United States in the 1960s and 1970s just as Peace Corps volunteers were aspiring to enter academia. This resulted in the Peace Corps–Korea volunteers becoming some of the chief beneficiaries of the student funding of comprehensive regional studies centers that grew during that era.

Of course, the 1960s and 1970s—when Peace Corps volunteers began entering Korean studies—were also fraught decades of rapid change in American culture and politics as the baby boomer generation confronted the Vietnam War and stagflation. This encounter may explain the combination of critical engagement combined with sympathetic orientation to Korean politics and culture that characterizes the second wave of Korea scholars, an orientation that has often frustrated those Koreans who have longed for a frankly uncritical admiration for Korean culture and history among Americans. While the times may explain some of this critical yet sympathetic orientation of Peace Corps alumnae scholars to Korea, the tone of Korean studies may *also* be attributed to the Peace Corps experience itself as bright, impressionable American youth sent to sink or swim in a still-impoverished South Korea confronted the hope and anguish of Koreans under the authoritarian Park Chung Hee (Pak Chŏnghŭi, 1961–79) developmental regime.

THE PEACE CORPS

In his inaugural address on January 20, 1961, President John F. Kennedy (1961–63) had sounded a call to action, "Now the trumpet summons us again . . . [in] a call to bear the burden . . . of a struggle against the common enemies of man: tyranny, poverty, disease, and war itself," and summoning the youth of the United States he declared, "Ask not what your country can do for you—ask what you can do for your country."[2] As part of this call to America's youth President Kennedy established the Peace Corps by executive order and announced it on television on March 2, 1961, as part of his first hundred days. This was followed on March 13 by the announcement of the Alliance for Progress, a comprehensive aid program for Latin America.

The Peace Corps Act of September 21, 1961, defined its purpose as below:

The Congress of the United States declares that it is the policy of the United States and the purpose of this chapter to promote world peace and friend-ship through a Peace Corps, which shall make available to interested coun-tries and areas men and women of the United States qualified for service abroad and willing to serve, under conditions of hardship if necessary, to help the peoples of such countries and areas in meeting their needs for trained manpower, particularly in meeting the basic needs of those living in the poorest areas of such countries, and to help promote a better under-standing of the American people on the part of the peoples served and a better understanding of other peoples on the part of the American people.[3]

While Peace Corps volunteers were sent abroad to help less developed countries meet their "needs for trained manpower," the main goal was to "promote world peace and friendship." Peace Corps volunteers were sup-posed to "help promote a better understanding of the American people on the part of the peoples served" and "a better understanding of other peoples on the part of the American people."

It was understood in the discourse of the time that sending fine examples of young American manhood and womanhood to serve selflessly "under con-ditions of hardship if necessary" would create good will. Peace Corps volun-teers would live among the people and by showing selfless sacrifice engender feelings of friendship and gratitude. Peace Corps volunteers by their very presence would be able to counter the vicious Communist disinformation about the United States, that every red-blooded American in those days just knew was nefariously being propagated everywhere, and provide a clear-eyed understanding to the Others of the rugged virtues of Americanism—freedom, democracy, and capitalism. The flip side of this was that the volunteers, in immersing themselves among the Others, would learn about them from the ground up. It would be like ethnographic fieldwork. Volunteers would come back with detailed knowledge about how other people lived and what made them tick. Thus, though not explicitly stated in the Peace Corps Act, volunteers would eventually provide the United States with the intellectual infra-structure necessary to act on the global scale that the post–World War II Pax Americana required.

The organization of the Peace Corps was not an isolated action. As the United States expanded into the vacuum left by the defeated or faltering impe-rial powers that had provided the world order for the two hundred years preceding 1945, the United States had a genuine need to create new intellec-tual infrastructure to generate knowledge about parts of the world in which the United States now had interests, but precious little knowledge. In the late 1940's George Kennan argued that the Soviet Union (and later China) believed in an inherent antagonism between capitalism and socialism, and could not give up repressive institutions concluding that, "the main element of any United States policy toward the Soviet Union must be that of a long-term, patient but firm and vigilant containment of Russian expansive tendencies."[4] This containment policy meant that the "Free World" led by the United States confronted and attempted to contain the Communist bloc on a worldwide basis. The Korean War of 1950–53 has long been understood as Exhibit A of Soviet expansionism. US Secretary of State Dean Acheson is reported to have convinced President Harry Truman (1945–53) of this in an emergency cabinet session after the outbreak of fighting in Korea saying, "Unless we make a firm stand in Korea the Russians will continue with the conquest of Indo-China, and then take over Japan internally."[5] Because of this and other expe-riences leading up to the Cold War the need to develop American expertise on "Third World" countries such as Korea increasingly came to be understood as a matter of national security.

The first federal program to develop foreign expertise in the United States was the Fulbright educational exchange program signed into law by President Truman on August 1, 1946, by which US educators could study abroad, and foreign educators could come to the United States. This program sought to humanize international relations by using war reparations and foreign debt repayment monies to finance person-to-person educational exchange. The expansion of area studies, however, was more explicitly a Cold War project motivated by the moral panic created by the Soviet Union's launch of Sputnik, the first artificial earth satellite, on September 2, 1958. In his special message to the US Congress on January 27, 1958, President Dwight D. Eisenhower (1953–61) noted that, "American education faces new responsibilities in the cause of Freedom," and that, "Because of the national security interest in the quality and scope of our education system . . . the Federal government must also undertake to play an emergency role."[6] This emergency role consisted largely of improving education in science and mathematics through the programs of the National Science Foundation. In addition, however, Eisenhower proposed additional programs for the US Department of Health, Education, and Welfare that included graduate fellowships to prepare more students for college teaching careers, federal grants to institutions of higher education to assist in expanding graduate school capacity, money to improve foreign language education especially in the languages of "emerging nations in Asia, Africa, and the Near East" and "support of special centers in colleges and universities to provide instruction in foreign languages which are important today but which are not now commonly taught in the United States."[7] All of this was justified in the name of national security.

Eisenhower's proposal came to fruition in the National Defense Education Act (NDEA) of September 2, 1958. The NDEA mostly concentrated on funding education in science and mathematics, but Title VI provided for funding language and area studies programs at US universities. Under Title VI nineteen language and area studies centers (now referred to as National Resource Centers) were initially funded. In addition, modern foreign language fellowships for graduate students (precursors to today's Foreign Language and Area Studies [FLAS] fellowships) were funded, as well as international research and studies and language institutes through the US Department of Education.

As a country in which the United States had fought an anticommunist war in 1950–53, and where the United States continued to confront North Korea, China, and the Soviet Union by continuously stationing tens of thousands of US troops there, Korea became an important focus of area studies. Korean language and area studies, thus, came to be considered one of the critically strategic, but less popular, languages and areas that would receive financial support from the US government.

The Peace Corps followed Fulbright and Title VI in 1961, and if the Peace Corps and Fulbright programs were premised on the notion that they would somehow contribute to the building of an infrastructure of knowledge about the world, they were also extraordinarily idealistic and indirect methods by which to do so by counting on the magic of person-to-person contacts. The area studies programs being created at universities across the United States supported by the National Defense Education Act (NDEA), on the other hand, were explicitly designed to supply regional experts capable of providing policy guidance to the US government and its agencies, on the model of the Office of War Information (OWI) during World War II. These three policy initiatives, Fulbright, the NDEA, and the Peace Corps, moreover, proceeded in tandem. The Peace Corps supplied a substantial number of the students recruited to the area studies programs that would train required area experts; NDEA provided graduate school funding for many of the students specializing in lesser taught, strategic, foreign languages like Korean; and Fulbright supported research and exchange opportunities for American students and professors to study and research abroad while also bringing substantial numbers of foreigners to the United States for study and academic exchange.

It is no accident, then, that the era in which the Peace Corps flourished corresponds with the era in which Korean studies became institutionalized in the United States. In my view it is hardly coincidental, moreover, that 1961, the year that the Peace Corps program was announced and enacted, was also precisely the year that the United States started escalating the number of US troops assigned to South Vietnam. The United States had "lost" China in 1949, it had fought to a stalemate in Korea 1950–53, and subsequently, throughout the 1960s the United States continued to maintain nearly sixty thousand troops in South Korea to deter North Korea. President Kennedy's foreign policy of "the best and the brightest" was proactive in projecting American power abroad. Thus, the Peace Corps in East Asia—and probably worldwide—cannot be divorced from the US desire to contain Communism and build up front line nations—Japan, South Korea, Taiwan, South Vietnam, Thailand, Cambodia, and Laos—as modern bulwarks against Communism, examples of the superiority of capitalist development, and democracy (though this latter, as it turns out, could be postponed, if necessary). The Peace Corps was, in other words, another Cold War project.

Peace Corps volunteers were sent to South Korea over a fifteen-year period between 1966 and 1981. Economically speaking this corresponded to the beginning of South Korea's Second Five-Year Plan through the end of its Fourth Five-Year Plan. Politically speaking it was from the middle of Park Chung Hee's Third Republic (1963–72) until the Kwangju Uprising (May 18, 1980) and the beginning of the Chun Doo Hwan dictatorship (Chŏn Tuhwan, 1980–88). These were the heroic years of South Korea's development under

Park Chung Hee: fifteen years in which the Republic of Korea (ROK) GDP per capita grew from $130 to almost $2,000, when Koreans moved from abject poverty, through Heavy and Chemical Industrialization, into, if not yet affluence, adequacy in food, clothing, and education (but not yet housing). The second, third, and fourth Five-Year Plans were all managed by the ROK Economic Planning Board and the Blue House during this period, so it can be assumed that the Peace Corps contribution was systematically incorporated into South Korea's development plans. Many early Peace Corps volunteers were, in fact, assigned to English-language teaching positions in high schools and colleges. Later volunteers moved into public health, forestry, and more specialized fields.

AN OUTSIDE PERSPECTIVE: PARACHUTING INTO KOREAN STUDIES AND MEETING PEACE CORPS VOLUNTEERS

If the Peace Corps was structurally a Cold War project, the motivations of individual Peace Corps recruits were not necessarily Cold War specific. Many recruits were young, unpolitical, and without well-formed views on international relations when they left for South Korea. I will leave to those who actually experienced life as a Peace Corps volunteer, to describe the culture shock of middle-class kids encountering the abject poverty of South Korea in the 1960s, and the agony and ecstasy of idealistically sacrificing oneself for the purpose of generating goodwill for the United States and building world peace by learning about others.

I came to Korean studies by a different path that gives me an outside rather than inside view of the Peace Corps contribution to Korean studies. I parachuted into the Korea field in 1972 by enrolling in the Korean studies MA program at the University of Washington. I say "parachuted in" because I had never been to Korea, did not know any Korean language, had never had a course on Korea, and had only once in my life even met a Korean person.[8] I had just found reports I had read of Korean folk religion to be interesting, and thought I would study Korea. I knew about the Peace Corps, of course, but I had never considered applying and had never met a Peace Corps volunteer until after I began my study.[9]

Arriving at the University of Washington I found my fellow graduate students to be of two types: the PhD students studying Korean history with

James Palais were the elites, and they had all been Peace Corps volunteers. The second type, my fellow MA students, had either been Peace Corps volunteers or US Army intelligence officers who had been trained by the US Army in Korean language before leaving the military service. At the UW I was the only MA student in Korean studies who had never been to Korea. So far as I know I am the only baby boomer Korean studies scholar (apart from the University of British Columbia's Ross King, who is a decade younger than me) who entered the field without previous Peace Corps, military, diplomatic, or missionary service in Korea.

At the University of Washington, I moved from a background in cultural geography at the University California–Berkeley to the anthropology PhD program at the University of Washington in 1974 at the suggestion of Professor James B. Palais, the head of the Korea Program where I received my MA. Like many of the Peace Corps volunteers, I had financed my education with FLAS Title VI grants, so my link with America's Cold War project was through area studies just as theirs was. It was only in September 1976—on Ch'usŏk (the Harvest Moon holiday in Korea) I believe—two years after receiving my MA, that I arrived in South Korea for the first time with my newly married wife to do anthropological fieldwork.

My UW Korean studies *sŏnbae* Mike Robinson, a member of the Peace Corps K-7 group, met me at the airport and helped my wife and I get settled. I depended upon him a lot at first because I had never been to South Korea, and he had lived there from 1968 to 1970 in Chŏnju.[10] He knew people, he knew the ropes, and he knew the essential Korean phrases for getting by in Korea (as opposed to my book-learned Korean that wasn't yet ready for prime time). This went on until December 1976 when Mike left for a year of dissertation research in Japan. (Each of Jim Palais' history students in those days was expected to do a year of dissertation research in South Korea, and a year in Japan). By then I could get around in South Korea on my own, and in January I moved to the countryside for a year of field research leaving my wife in Seoul.

THE PEACE CORPS NICHE IN 1970S SOUTH KOREA

I arrived in South Korea in 1976, only a couple of weeks after the ax murder of a US soldier in the Demilitarized Zone (DMZ) and just as Kim Dae-jung

(Kim Taejung, 1998–2003) was about to be put on trial for the Myŏngdong Cathedral Declaration, so tensions were high on the Korean peninsula.[11] The American imprint was everywhere in those days. There were some forty thousand US troops stationed on the Korean peninsula. President Jimmy Carter had just proposed the withdrawal of US troops during his re-election campaign of that year. Every time I stepped into a taxi, I had to explain to the taxi driver what I thought about the Migun ch'ŏlsu (American military withdrawal). Usually the conversation ended with the taxi driver remarking, "President Carter! Humph! Peanut farmer!" (K'at'ŏ Taet'ongnyŏng ŭn, hŭng! Ttangk'ong nongbu kŭrae!)

Peace Corps volunteers had been stationed in South Korea for ten years by this time, but I emphasize this context of the American influence on South Korea in the 1970s because the Peace Corps volunteers that were in South Korea when I arrived—and the Peace Corps volunteer–scholars like Mike Robinson—were not, could not, be separated from America's larger presence in South Korea. (Neither could I, but that's a different story.) I observed at that time that Peace Corps volunteers occupied a distinctive and important niche in the overall American imprint on South Korea. The forty thousand US troops that were stationed in the Republic of Korea in 1976 lived in their own world and tended to have only superficial contacts with Korean culture despite their having a massive social and economic impact on the country.[12] To visit the Yongsan base, for example, was to pass from a teeming Seoul to a quiet bit of Kansas with brick houses and lawns all in the space of only 100 feet. The United States diplomatic corps in the ROK was formidable and variable including a significant USAID footprint. A few political officers took an intensive interest in Korean affairs, but most of the diplomats (including some of those who had been Peace Corps Korea volunteers) were looking for career advancement by rotating to more significant locations, and thus seemed just to be biding their time in South Korea. They, like the military, lived in their own cocoon of walled diplomatic compounds and embassy buildings, with a select few venturesome individuals sallying out for Royal Asiatic Society tours on weekends.[13] The expatriate business community was small and exclusive; South Korea was considered a hardship post in those days, and the Park and Chun administrations allowed very little foreign direct investment. The missionaries, many of whom I got to know while attending the Franciscan-run Myŏngdo Institute language school in Chaedong, learned more Korean, got out more, and met more Koreans than the US soldiers, diplomats, and businessmen, but they also lived in their own socio-intellectual bubble of Christian believers and fellow missionaries.[14] Among all of the Americans living in South Korea, the Peace Corps volunteers, thus, were some of the very few who had learned Korean, gone out into the true Korean society relatively unmediated by special privilege, and met and talked with the Korean people on a relatively equal basis. They also came from more diverse backgrounds and a set of intellectual commitments different from any other group engaged with South Korea and as such came to understand the various social and political aspects of South Korean society and culture that many of the other American were blinded to by social isolation or religious commitment.

With their mission of "technical assistance, helping people outside the United States understand American culture, and helping Americans to understand the cultures of other cultures, Peace Corps volunteers seemed to have an impact in South Korea well beyond their numbers."[15] Their niche being person-to-person ambassadors meant, in the South Korean context, "sincere American visitors" living (almost) like Koreans, and above all showing an appreciation for Korean language and culture by taking the time to learn something about it. Going out to the countryside or teaching English at less-then-first-rate institutions put volunteers in contact with Koreans who were not necessarily cosmopolitan or intellectually sophisticated.

Many of the Koreans I met in 1976–77 seemed sincerely grateful for this assistance. In the post–Korean War world order, the United States was the big brother South Koreans looked up to for help and protection (left wing, anti-American thought was well hidden underground in South Korea until the 1980s). Most Americans living in South Korea seemed to think the opposite: they were structurally and conceptually at the top of the heap, and thus felt no compulsion to immerse themselves in Korean culture. The non–Peace Corps Americans I met in South Korea didn't really seem to think deeply about it, but rather appeared to take it for granted that Koreans' job was to emulate Americans, learn English, and thus *become civilized and enlightened*. It wasn't Americans' job to *descend to Koreans' level*. In this context, the niche of the Peace Corps volunteers was to prove that Americans really cared, that the American imperium—obvious from the US bases, immense embassy buildings, and the development and missionary bureaucracies that were going to teach Koreans how to be *advanced like us*—really was benevolent and only superficially imperialistic. To an amazing degree it worked. The limited number of Peace Corps volunteers seemed to generate an amazing amount of goodwill among Koreans.

How do I know this? There were the Korean-sponsored reunions and appreciation programs for Peace Corps–Korea volunteers held in South Korea, of course, but having never served in the Peace Corps, I was not privy to these. Two observations that I frequently made in South Korea in the 1970s, however, leads me to believe there was a considerable reservoir of gratitude reserved for Peace Corps volunteers. One was my personal experience that the mere fact of being a white person able to speak credible Korean made many people seemingly go out of their way to help me, and so I presume this had also been extended to Peace Corps volunteers. I also have more direct evidence. After about six months my spoken Korean became reasonably fluent, and I was frequently asked if I was a Peace Corps volunteer or a missionary. P'yŏnghwa Pongsadan (Peace Corps) and sŏn'gyosa, (missionary) were words I learned early on and when I sometimes overheard Koreans talking about the Peace Corps in those days they tended to emphasize the volunteer nature of the Corps, and would often express admiration and thanks. They seemed to take the Peace Corps (and US) altruism at face value.[16]

For me, in my own little niche, the effect of the Peace Corps volunteers was different than for the Koreans. For me they were intimidating. Here I was, a newly arrived graduate student in South Korea with my book-learned Korean and no knowledge of how to live among Koreans, and to top it off as an anthropologist I was supposed to be learning Korean deep culture and preparing to provide "thick" description of it. Yet, I found there were already on the ground a group of young Americans already immersed in Korean culture, who had lived in the countryside, witnessed the South Korea of the 1960s (!), and what is more, they all seemed to know each other. They had their own lingo, "Oh, are you K-6? I was K-5." I was living on the economy and when sizing me up some thought I had been a Peace Corps–Korea volunteer, too.[17] "What were you, K-9?" they might ask. "I've never been in the Peace Corps," I would have to reply, admitting I was a greenhorn.

FULBRIGHT HOUSE

Among those of us who were students of Korea, Fulbright House on Sŏsomun near P'yŏngan Kyohoe (across the street from Chungang Ilbosa) was an important social center. The Fulbright program was one of the major funding avenues by which scholars could come to South Korea for research. Quite a few Fulbrighters were dilettantes, artists, and the like who wanted a taste of the exotic in South Korea, but there were also a significant number of scholars writing on Korea, or graduate students working on dissertations. I was one of these, but having been forewarned by my language professor at the University of Washington, Dr. Doo Soo Suh, that Fulbright house was an insensitive institution that excluded Koreans, I avoided living there. I did have a Fulbright grant, but on the advice of Mike Robinson I instead received a grant from the US Department of Education that paid me a stipend directly in dollars. This soured my relationship with Ed Wright, commandant of Fulbright House, and complicated my attempts to get a research visa. Even so, I could still pick up my mail at Fulbright House and meet people there, and Fulbright included me in their activities. Peace Corps volunteers who were coming back for PhD work could also sometimes be found there, and this is where I met Peace Corps volunteers outside the few I knew from UW. Some had research grants and were working on PhDs with a Korea focus. Others had stayed on in the Republic of Korea and only dropped by Fulbright House for social purposes. Of those that had stayed in South Korea, some had developed native-like Korean-language facility and were also living on the economy. Another ex-Peace Corps–Korea group that I became acquainted with had Friday night dinners at Kamch'on Restaurant behind the US Embassy which included whatever English speakers happened to be in South Korea at the time.

It was there at the Fulbright House that I gradually became aware of the legendary leaders of the Peace Corps–Korea volunteers who had mastered Korean society completely and who were attending Ivy League universities to complete their PhDs. That was what was intimidating for me about the Peace Corps–Korea volunteers. I had parachuted into the field with no previous contact with Korea whatsoever, yet now that I was there, I was finding out that that professors at the leading universities such as Ed Wagner at Harvard and Gari Ledyard at Columbia had been in South Korea actively recruiting Peace Corps volunteers for graduate study and several of these were finishing their PhDs at these institutions.[18] Previously I had only known of the two

Peace Crops–Korea volunteers who were PhD students at the UW. Now I had to confront the fact that the two I knew were only the tip of a huge iceberg of potential Korea experts.

TWO HYPOTHESES

We can see the entry of large numbers of Peace Corps volunteers into Academia during the 1970s and 1980s as significant in two ways: in terms of numbers, and in terms of their intellectual orientation. The minimal hypothesis would be that of the Peace Corps Act itself: the Peace Corps volunteers who went into academia have provided "a better understanding of [Koreans] on the part of the American People."[19] This minimal hypothesis is largely due to the fact that a large number of idealistic young people who would not have gotten interested in Korea did so because of the Peace Corps introduced them that country, and the result that a significant number went into academia built up the Korea field so that their teaching and publications have helped Americans—or anyone who reads English for that matter—achieve a better understanding of Korea.

A maximal hypothesis might ask, however, whether the Peace Corps experience itself was in some way intellectually formative: if the fact that a large number of academics came into Korean studies through the Peace Corps experience affected the intellectual orientation of the field not just through numbers, but also in intellectual substance. Peace Corps volunteers were already college graduates when they arrived in South Korea, so they were to a degree already intellectually formed, but perhaps not fully. Their experience in the ROK therefore might have had the potential to profoundly influence their intellectual make-up. When some Peace Corps–Korea volunteers went into the academy they may have had the potential to approach Korea from different points of view than their immediate predecessors whose formative years had mostly been in the military or on missions.

Untangling the strands of intellectual formation is notoriously difficult. In evaluating the possibility of the Peace Corps experience being intellectually formative for the Korea field, for example, it is important to consider other formative experiences for the baby boom generation during the 1966–81 period. The 1960s were a tumultuous period for the Civil Rights Movement, with the Selma marches in 1965, the urban riots, the Civil Rights Acts of 1964–68, the US invasion of Cambodia in 1970, Nixon's visit to China, and the withdrawal of US troops from Vietnam in the mid-1970s. The timing of individuals' Peace Corps entry and exit in South Korea in relationship to the Vietnam War (1964–75), moreover, is critical. The Gulf of Tonkin Resolution on August 7, 1965 was the "declaration of war." The escalation of US involvement in the Vietnam conflict began in 1961 with the Kennedy administration who had as mentioned earlier created the Peace Corps, but it was in 1965, when it became apparent that the South Vietnamese regime was faltering, that large-scale US troop commitments to South Vietnam commenced. This was also when the US anti–Vietnam War movement began: the first teach-ins against the war were held at the University of Michigan and at Columbia University in 1965. Peace Corps–K-1 volunteers landed in South Korea the following year in 1966.

Interviews with several Peace Corps volunteers of my acquaintance leads me to believe that the initial volunteers headed for South Korea in the 1960s were motivated primarily by idealism and adventure in part because the radicalization caused by the Vietnam War had not yet touched them. For later male cohorts the question of the draft and the Vietnam War cannot be ignored, however. By the summer of 1968, with race riots throughout the United States following the assassination of Martin Luther King, anti–Vietnam War riots on a variety of campuses, and the chaos of the 1968 Democratic National Convention in Chicago in which a major issue was whether anti–Vietnam War candidates could be heard, pretty much any male knew that he was vulnerable to being drafted and sent to Vietnam, and that he had better make up his mind if this was OK, or whether he would resist. In this context the question became Vietnam, Canada, or the Peace Corps for those who, for whatever reason, lost their student deferments and faced possible deployment in the Vietnam War.

Changes in the draft law during the 1960s raise the possibility that different Peace Corps cohorts had different incentives with regard to the draft. Between 1963 and 1965, for example, married men between nineteen and twenty-six—the prime draft age—were exempted from the draft. Men with children were exempted until 1986. Until 1967, students (including graduate students) could be deferred from the draft until they "aged out" at twenty-six. As civil rights workers such as Martin Luther King came out against the Vietnam War, the issue of student deferments—that were more plentiful for middle-class white students than for the poor and minority men of student age—became a political issue of fairness. After 1967, the US government ended student deferments at the time of graduation, or the age of twenty-four, whichever came first. Then in 1969, President Nixon (1969–74) implemented the draft lottery. Each of these changes made different men vulnerable to the draft. The draft applied only to men, of course, so female Peace Corps volunteers clearly had other motivations. With the end of student deferments in 1967, educated middle-class men who had been protected from the draft were now vulnerable, so male Peace Corps cohorts after that time may have been affected. After 1969 with the draft lottery, about a third of draft-age men got low enough numbers to be vulnerable, while the rest were off the hook. With the winding down of the Vietnam War in the early 1970s these incentives disappeared.

The question of the draft and incentives to enter the Peace Corps in the late 1960s has to do with the possible politicization of the Korea field by Peace Corps volunteers who were already opposed to the Vietnam War. As everybody knows, young people in significant numbers turned to the political left in the 1960s and 1970s amidst the struggle against racism and against the Vietnam War. Could it have been this, rather than the Peace Corps experience, that was intellectually formative? Yet, among the Peace Corps volunteers that I have talked to only a few were politicized before they got to South Korea. On the contrary, it seems to have been that South Korea had politicized them. In the Republic of Korea the poverty, the repression of the Yusin Period, and the obviousness of the United States imprint seems to have made many of them aware in a very visceral way of the reality of power differentials, and of the role of the United States in upholding the status quo of the Cold War world order. If this is the case, then the possibility of the Peace Corps experience being intellectually formative in a way that may have influenced the Korea field remains on the table.

ACADEMIC WINNOWING

All of the Peace Corps volunteers who aspired to contribute to Korean studies, however, did not make it to the Promised Land of the senior core of Korean studies professionals. The US academy has its own standards and structures that are designed to turn out scholars intellectually formed to fit into discrete academic fields. Budding Korean studies scholars, regardless of what they experienced in Korea, had to lie in the Procrustean bed of academic disciplines: not Korean studies scholars, per se, but anthropologists working on Korea, literature specialists working on Korea, historians, political scientists, or sociologists working on Korea. Here we have to address the academic winnowing process: admission to graduate school, completion of graduate school, getting a job as a professional, and keeping a job as a professional. At each stage of this process only some of the Peace Corps volunteers made it through. In entering the ranks of professional scholarship did academic specialization wring out any common formative experience Peace Corps volunteers may have had?

At the entry to graduate school Peace Corps experience may well have given potential entrants a lift in at least three different ways. Most obviously the Peace Corps introduced most of their volunteers to Korea in the first place, sparking interest in a country that few had taken an interest in before. Second, a Peace Corps experience would, I believe, have made candidates more attractive to admissions committees than they otherwise might have been. After all experience in and a working knowledge of the language necessary for one's studies would make Peace Corps volunteers seem serious and seasoned compared to those who didn't have that experience. Finally, having experience in Korea may well have allowed former Peace Corps volunteers to craft relatively interesting proposals based on what they saw in South Korea.

A Peace Corps experience, however, seems to have provided less of an advantage in the next three winnowing phases: dissertation completion, job-hunting, and tenure acquisition. In each of these cases potential Korean studies scholars had to fit their South Korea experiences and study into packages acceptable to their disciplinary peers. In this endeavor the intellectual capital Peace Corps volunteers brought with them to South Korea may be more important than their Peace Corps experience in conditioning their success in academia.

Some Peace Corps volunteers who made it into good graduate schools got writer's block during their dissertation writing, and never finished—often, I think, because the demands of their disciplinary field seemed so abstract and remote from their person-to-person Korean experience.[20] Others didn't get writer's block exactly, but instead became distracted by other projects with more immediate remuneration and political excitement than dissertation writing—such as entry into US intelligence or the diplomatic corps.

Immersion in South Korean culture and linguistic competence by itself, thus, does not seem to have guaranteed success in academia. The ability to frame an interesting question, collect data to answer it, and write it up seems to be a talent related to but distinct from the ability to immerse oneself in Korean language and culture. Here my best guess (and it is only a guess) is that prior academic preparation and at least some planning during the Peace Corps experience itself played a role. Of the Peace Corps volunteers I know who succeeded in academia, most had a prior interest in Asia, if not specifically in Korea, and had already thought about possible graduate work before entering the Peace Corps. They thus used their time in the Peace Corps wisely, looking around with intellectually open eyes and framing questions about Korea that they might want to answer. These are most probably the ones that finished their doctorates.

Quite a number of Peace Corps volunteers completed their dissertations on Korea at good universities, and yet were never able to acquire an academic job. By the late 1970s and early 1980s when Peace Corps volunteers began to receive their doctorates the big postwar expansion of US universities to accommodate the baby boomers was over. Stagflation had set in, making university financing precarious. Only a trickle of publications on Korea was available in English, so many academic administrators were disinclined to open positions about a country which they assumed there was little interest.[21] The initial Peace Corps volunteers who emerged with their PhDs in the 1970s and 1980s thus faced a very difficult job market. While Korea specialists were, mostly trained to be able to teach about China and Japan as well as Korea, moreover, those who wrote dissertations on Korea tended to be passed over in favor of China or Japan specialists for general Asia studies positions. This meant Korea specialists were, for the most part, limited to positions specifically defined for Korea specialists and these simply didn't exist in the 1970s when the first of the Peace Corps volunteers finished their doctorates. The senior-most generation of Korean studies specialists at the major centers were still active and nothing new was opening up.

A positive trend began when some of the senior scholars began publishing monographs that interested people outside the Korea field, and the few Peace Corps volunteers who early on became positioned to address issues of general interest began publishing, making the field more visible than it had been. Still the bulk of the early Peace Corps PhDs who survived eked a living at first from post-docs, temporary positions, and positions outside the ranks of tenured researcher teachers. A few who lacked teaching jobs yet nevertheless managed to publish, after a few years in the wilderness managed to land tenure track positions after years in contingent faculty status.

The process by which junior Peace Corps volunteer scholars eventually managed to get a toehold in academic tenure track positions seems to have been partly a matter of being in the right place at the right time, though coming from a major university and having written a substantive dissertation obviously was important. As more and more of these scholars managed to get established in academia in the 1970s and 1980s, they slowly began to produce interesting academic work and to present their findings at academic conferences where they generated additional interest in Korea, making the Korea field more visible than it had been.

A second positive trend, a rise in demand for Korea-related courses in the early 1980s, may also have been related to surging Korean immigration to the United States after 1965 when the immigration ethnic quota system was abolished.[22] With a large Korean immigrant population in the United States, non-Koreans began to meet Korean Americans, learn Taekwondo, eat Korean food, and develop curiosity about Korea. Demand for Korea courses also began to come from 1.5 generation Koreans who begin attending US universities in significant numbers in the 1980s and 1990s.

A third positive trend was that the Korea Foundation began endowing positions in Korean studies at US universities. This significantly changed the field. When I entered the Korean studies MA program at the University of Washington in 1972, the UW was the only mainland North American university to have more than one Korea specialist (the UW had three: linguist Fred Lukoff, literature specialist Doo Soo Suh, and historian Jim Palais). As the 1980s rolled around Harvard, Columbia, the University of California–Los Angeles, and other schools in the United States added additional Korea faculty, and UBC and University of Toronto in Canada made similar progress. Today I can easily think of a half dozen schools with several Korea faculty, and more than two dozen more in the United States and Canada that have a least one Korea scholar. Of the Korea specialists who managed to get academic jobs during this period, about a dozen were Peace Corps volunteers making them the majority of the cohort of Korean studies scholars who entered academia in the 1970s and 1980s.

INFLUENCE OF PEACE CORPS VOLUNTEERS ON KOREAN STUDIES

The confluence of the Peace Corps in South Korea with the growth of area studies in academia does seem to have conspired to introduce young and impressionable men and women at a critical time in their lives to Korea, many of whom would not otherwise have encountered Korea, and thereby made it possible for a significant number of them to enter academia and pursue Korean studies. The contributors in this volume are evidence of this, the minimal hypothesis that augmenting the supply of young scholars interested in Korea at a critical time in America's expansion into the world post–World War II is the most important influence the Peace Corps program had on Korean studies.

But can one say more? Can one argue a more robust hypothesis that despite the disciplinary framing imposed on Peace Corps volunteers, the orientation of the field was changed intellectually as a result of Peace Corps volunteers' experience? I think the answer to this question is, "yes," and I make the case below relying heavily on personal conversations with Peace Corps volunteers, and on what participants of this conference revealed in their comments during the conference held on September 9, 2016 in Bloomington, Indiana.[23]

For some the transformative power of the Korea experience lay in experiencing Korean culture and meeting Korean people. David McCann discovered the camaraderie of reciting poetry, a common practice among educated Koreans of the 1960s and 1970s, and Edward Shultz discovered Korean history in the ruins of Kyŏngju.[24] Both were inspired by the example of Richard Rutt, the Anglican cleric who appreciated and translated Korean poetry, but neither McCann nor Shultz reported a radical political transformation.

However, other Peace Corps volunteers who experienced South Korea in the 1960s and 1970s have related that their experience was far more transformative than simply being introduced to an exotic, enticing new culture. Several mentioned that observing the poverty, beggars, and street urchins of South Korea in those days and the contrasting American power induced in them critical reflections on American plenty and created empathy for the

South Korean underdogs, as well as an appreciation of their entrepreneurial drive. This took on a political dimension as some Peace Corps volunteers witnessed President Park Chung Hee changing the ROK constitution in 1969, enforcing strict curfews, and conducting monthly air raid drills of the Yusin Period. This experience for some combined with the excitement of finding forbidden political speech in nooks and crannies of South Korean intellectual life. Others reflected on the traces of the past Japanese Empire that still could be found in Seoul and the only-too-obvious present American imperium, both of which awakened in these volunteers questions about cultural imperialism and colonialism. Most traumatic were the experiences of those who witnessed or investigated the Kwangju Uprising and its suppression.[25]

These political awakenings had specific influence on the subsequent historical writings of many of the Peace Corps volunteers. Bruce Cumings has famously written revisionist interpretations of the Korean War influenced by disillusion about US policy engendered by the Vietnam War.[26] Michael Robinson responded to his experience in Korea by contemplating construction of national identity under colonialism, while for Carter Eckert it was the ambiguous interplay of class and national identity under colonialism that sparked his interest.[27] Donald Baker related that the competing claims he came across in investigating the Kwangju Uprising engendered in him a distrust of documentary sources, while for Linda Lewis experiencing the Uprising left her feeling a responsibility to bear witness to the events she saw.[28] All of these concerns are reflected in well-known publications by Peace Corps volunteer scholars.[29]

The female Peace Corps volunteers clearly had a distinctive experience in South Korea compared to that of their male counterparts. One commented in the conference on Peace Corps–Korea complicity with American males' availing themselves of commercial sex trafficking opportunities, while not knowing what to do with single female volunteers.[30] The female Peace Corps volunteers at the conference mentioned the strong impression American military prostitution made on them in Korea. Korean males' exclusion of her from some activities in Korea motivated one female Peace Corps volunteer to refuse complicity in sexually discriminatory practices at home or abroad. For Kendall her observation of Korean shamans "shook her perception of a gendered Korean possible" and inspired her to investigate the intersection of gender, shamanism, and Korean society—a topic that has proved to be relevant in anthropology for many forms of shamanism worldwide.[31]

These anecdotes all point to a strong hypothesis: it was not simply being immersed in a foreign culture that Peace Corps volunteers later studied in academia that makes the Peace Corps experience formative for Korean studies, but the specific *content* of their Korean experience that awakened many of them to colonialism, inequality, political struggle at the risk of beatings and jailing, national identity formation, and the complexity of strongly gendered social relations, and this *experience* is reflected in the works that they have produced after entering academia. The Korean studies that they produced is *engagé* precisely because what they experienced in South Korea during their formative Peace Corps years induced reflection that required their scholarship to be socio-politically engaged.

CONCLUSION

If, as I wrote at the beginning of this chapter, the Peace Corps, along with the Fulbright program, the National Defense of Education Act Title VI, and the growth of area studies programs at American universities were systematic attempts to create scholars able to advise American government agencies, one might ask if the scholarship produced by Peace Corps volunteers must not then be Cold War scholarship. In the sense that the Cold War institutions facilitated Peace Corps volunteers visiting South Korea and encouraged entry into academia there can be no doubt of their connection to the Cold War, but what about the content of Peace Corps volunteers' scholarship? Here I think it is precisely because the Peace Corps experience in South Korea tended to induce reflection and introspection in volunteers—about their national identity, America's role in the world, imperialism, power dynamics, gender, and the need to bear witness to the political struggles that they observed in South Korea—that the content of their work transcends any simple Cold War academic model.

Thus, the introduction of young Americans from a variety of backgrounds to South Korea surely expanded the range and variety of ways scholars have addressed Korea. While the older literature focused mostly on the diplomacy, politics, and government that interested the military veterans and diplomats,

or the missionology that interested the missionaries, the newer literature—
much of which was pioneered by Peace Corps volunteers—ranges into diplomacy, politics, and government for sure but also anthropology, cultural and
social history, literature, religion, musicology, cinema, and popular culture.
This expansion of the range of interest on Korea, both among producers and
consumers of written material on Korea, surely is to a great degree a byprod-
uct of the hundreds of young Americans who toured South Korea as Peace
Corps volunteers between 1966 and 1981.

Fig. 11.1 Clark Sorensen in front of the Maitreya Pavilion in the Gold Mountain Temple
near Chŏnju, North Chŏlla Province, South Korea, November 9, 2018. Photo courtesy of
Clark W. Sorensen.

Over time, of the two goals of the Peace Corps "to help promote a *better understanding of the American people* on the part of the peoples served and *a better understanding of other peoples on the part of the American people*," the first part seems to have faded as those Koreans who personally remember young Peace Corps volunteers living like Koreans in the community have aged and been replaced by youngsters without such memories. Conversely, the contribution of Peace Corps scholars to American understanding of Korea has only increased with time as Peace Corps volunteers have published more material and have themselves trained more Korea specialists. Does this make the Peace Corps program complicit with imperialism regardless of the individual motives of volunteers and the specific content of their academic work?

Here, as with other strands of argumentation in this chapter, the verdict seems mixed. On the one hand, it is safe to say that a significant proportion of the students trained in Korean studies programs at the MA level—including those staffed by Peace Corps volunteers—have gone into intelligence agencies, continued with military work, entered the diplomatic corps, or engaged in other activities associated with the United States' expansion abroad—and thus directly aided the maintenance of America's footprint in South Korea (and confrontation with North Korea). On the other hand, it is equally safe to say that Peace Corps volunteers' writings on Korea have often been quite critical of US policies in Korea including US support for military dictators, US demonization of North Korea, and US activities regarding the Kwangju Uprising. Here it seems that Peace Corps volunteers seeing the huge impact of US military and diplomatic bases had on South Korea from the vantage point of having lived on the economy were induced to see and subsequently analyze the disparities in power between dominant and subordinate countries, the rhetoric of domination, and the ambiguities of national, class, and gender positioning. To that extent the strong hypotheses that the Peace Corps experience induced reflection and shaped volunteers' consciousness in ways unanticipated by Washington DC policymakers still holds, and this is reflected in their publications.

NOTES

1. E. J. Kahn, *The China Hands: America's Foreign Service Officers and What Befell Them* (New York: Viking, 1975).

2. *First Book Edition of John F. Kennedy's Inaugural Address* (New York: Franklin Watts, 1964): 33–35.

3. Government Publishing Office, Public Law 87–293. Title 1—*The Peace Corps,* "Declaration of Purpose," September 22, 1961, Washington DC, https://www.govinfo.gov/content/pkg/STATUTE-75/pdf/STATUTE-75-Pg612.pdf.

4. George F. Kennan, "The Sources of Soviet Conduct," *Foreign Affairs* 65, no. 4 (Spring 1987): 852–68.

5. Drew Pearson, "Cabinet Provided Real Drama," *Washington Post,* June 30, 1950. Pearson describes Truman as being convinced by Acheson's argument and concluding that Russian expansionism was behind the outbreak of fighting in Korea. More recent research has debunked the theory of Soviet expansionism through the Korean War pointing out that Kim Il Sung was the main proponent of the invasion of the south, that Stalin withdrew all Soviet troops before the war broke out, and that China rather than the Soviet Union came to North Korea's aid after the UN intervention. See for example Bruce Cumings, *Korea's Place in the Sun* (New York: W. W. Norton & Company, 1997), 263.

6. Dwight D. Eisenhower, "Special Message to the Congress on Education," January 27, 1958.

7. Dwight D. Eisenhower "Special Message."

8. The only Korean person I can remember meeting before entering the UW's Korean studies program was a Korean graduate student returning from the United States whom I met at breakfast in my hotel in Tokyo's Haneda Airport where I had spent the night before transferring to a flight to Taiwan where I had a job for the summer of 1972. He was in the hotel for purposes of transferring to a flight to Seoul. By then I had already applied to the University of Washington's Korea program.

9. Perhaps this is because I was classified as 1-Y by my draft board because of asthma. Later, I received a high draft lottery number, so I was never seriously in danger of being drafted and sent to Vietnam.

10. See chapter 8 of this volume. Michael E. Robinson, "Empathy, Politics, and Historical Imagination: A Peace Corps Experience and Its Aftermath," in *Peace Corps Volunteers and the Making of Korean Studies in the United States,* edited by Seung-kyung Kim and Michael Robinson, 141–58. (Seattle: University of Washington Center for Korea Studies, 2020).

11. On March 1, 1976, Yun Posŏn, Kim Taejung, Mun Ikhwan, Ham Sŏkhŏn, and sixteen others published their "Declaration of Democratic National Salvation" (Minju kuguk sŏnŏn) in Seoul's Myŏngdong Cathedral. The declaration demanded rescission of the emergency measures under which South Korea was being governed, release of democratic prisoners, restoration of freedom of speech and the press, restoration of government through the National Assembly, restoration of independent courts, and

resignation of Park Chung Hee. Kim Taejung and Father Ham Se-ung were arrested and later tried for violating Presidential Emergency Decree Number 9. See "Ilbu chaeya insa chŏngbu chŏnbok sŏndong" [A group of opposition figures instigate overthrow of the government], *Chosŏn ilbo* March 11, 1976: 12.

12. Fraternization with Korean women among the US military and diplomats, of course, was common. This often led to marriages, but the wife's role in these cases tended to be as cultural and linguistic interpreter. The women became bilingual and bicultural while the men tended to remain monolingual and monocultural.

13. For a time, the United States Information Agency (USIA) personnel had better linguistic skill and more personal contact with Koreans, since those assigned to East Asia in the 1980s were required to learn two of the three languages (Chinese, Japanese, or Korean) and were rotated through those three countries. Alas, the USIA was abolished in 1999.

14. At the Myŏndo Institute I found the Catholic and Protestant missionaries quite distinct. The Catholics I met were often Columban or Maryknoll fathers who had been sent out alone to remote rural parishes (one I got to know well had been sent to Hŭksando). The nuns were often medical or educational missionaries. As unmarried priests and nuns, the Catholic missionaries depended on meeting Korean parishioners for much of their social life. Much of the Catholic missionization in those days, moreover, focused on workers, farmers, and fishermen who did not have command of foreign languages. The Protestants I met, on the other hand, were usually married couples (often from the southern United States), had cars that both husbands and wives drove, and they tended to live in Western-style houses on missionary compounds. Rather than interacting intensively with Koreans, the Protestant missionaries I met in the 1970s often struggled with Korean and seemed to serve primarily as exemplars of modern, American, Christian family life. Their core constituency seemed to be middle-class modernizers who often could meet Americans halfway on the language issue. Of course, there were also long-term American, Canadian, and Australian Protestant missionaries who lived in rural areas and mingled with the local population, but I didn't meet them while I was in Seoul.

15. "Peace Corps," Wikipedia: The Free Encyclopedia, Wikimedia Foundation, Inc., accessed August 11, 2016, https://en.wikipedia.org/wiki/Peace_Corps.

16. Actual Peace Corps volunteers whom I have talked with, however, often see the Korean reaction to them as much, much more complex than this. My only defense here is that I am writing as an outsider looking in. Not being a Peace Corps volunteer myself, I did not have to grapple directly with the ambiguities of the experience or Koreans' reaction to them.

17. The expression "living on the economy" in South Korea reflects the fact that most Americans living in South Korea were associated with institutions such as the

military, the diplomatic corps, or the church, that provided them with living accommodations and access to foreign goods unavailable to ordinary Koreans.

18. This was mentioned by Donald Clark during his oral presentation on September 9, 2016, at the conference that made this volume possible, "Peace Corps Volunteers: The Making of Korean Studies in the United States" at Indiana State University–Bloomington, though I have also heard this fact from other sources in the past. Donald Clark has relayed his experience as a Peace Corps–Korea volunteer during the 1960s in chapter 3 of this volume. Donald N. Clark, "On Being Part of the Peace Corps Generation in Korean Studies," in *Peace Corps Volunteers and the Making of Korean Studies in the United States*, edited by Seung-kyung Kim and Michael Robinson, 53–76. (Seattle: University of Washington Center for Korea Studies, 2020).

19. Government Publishing Office, Public Law 87–293. *Title 1—The Peace Corps*, "Declaration of Purpose,"

20. Okp'yo Moon in comments during the conference on September 9, 2016, quoted one American Peace Corps volunteer who failed to finish his dissertation as saying "too much chŏng inhibited his ability to write about research subjects" in an academic way, illustrating the danger of going "too native." Okp'yo Moon goes into detail regarding her impression of the Peace Corps and Peace Corps volunteers in chapter 10 of this volume. Okp'yo Moon, "A Korean Perspective: Peace Corps Volunteers, Europe, and the Study of Korea" in *Peace Corps Volunteers and the Making of Korean Studies in the United States*, edited by Seung-kyung Kim and Michael Robinson, 175–90. (Seattle: University of Washington Center for Korea Studies, 2020).

21. Even at the UW, I had battles with the deans over a Korean literature position because even the China and Japan literature specialists in the 1980s assumed there wasn't much of interest in Korean literature.

22. The Immigration and Naturalization Act of 1965 (Hart-Celler Act) abolished immigration quotas by ethnic origin that had been in place since 1921.

23. Based on twenty-eight pages of personal notes handwritten while attending the "Peace Corps Volunteers: The Making of Korean Studies in the United States" conference at Indiana State University–Bloomington, on September 9, 2019.

24. Edward Shultz relates his experiences with the Peace Corps in chapter 9 of this volume. Edward J. Shultz, "Peace Corps–Korea Group K-1: Empowering to Serve as New Voices in Korean Studies," in *Peace Corps Volunteers and the Making of Korean Studies in the United States*, edited by Seung-kyung Kim and Michael Robinson, 159–74. (Seattle: University of Washington Center for Korea Studies, 2020).

25. See chapters 1 and 7 of this volume by Don Baker and Linda Lewis respectively. Don Baker, "Kwangju, Trauma, and the Problem of Objectivity in History-Writing"; and Linda Lewis, "At the Border: Women, Anthropology, and North Korea" in *Peace Corps Volunteers and the Making of Korean Studies in the United States*, edited by Seung-kyung Kim

and Michael Robinson, 9–30, 127–40. (Seattle: University of Washington Center for Korea Studies, 2020).

26. Bruce Cumings, *The Origins of the Korean War: Liberation and the Emergence of Separate Regimes 1945–1947* (Princeton, NJ: Princeton University Press, 1981);

27. Michael Robinson, "Empathy, Politics, and Historical Imagination: A Peace Corps Experience and Its Aftermath" and Carter J. Eckert, "A Road Less Traveled: From Rome to Seoul," in *Peace Corps Volunteers and the Making of Korean Studies in the United States*, edited by Seung-kyung Kim and Michael Robinson, 77–92, 141–58. (Seattle: University of Washington Center for Korea Studies, 2020).

28. Linda Lewis, "At the Border: Women, Anthropology, and North Korea."

29. See Bruce Cumings, *The Origins of the Korean War*; Donald N. Clark, *The Kwangju Uprising: Shadows over the Regime in South Korea* (Boulder, CO: Westview, 1988) with contributions by Linda Lewis and David R. McCann; Michael E. Robinson, *Cultural Nationalism in Colonial Korea* (Seattle: University of Washington Press, 1988); Carter J. Eckert, *Offspring of Empire: The Koch'ang Kim's and the Colonial Origins of Korean Capitalism 1876–1945* (Seattle: University of Washington Press, 1991); and Linda Lewis, *Laying Claim to the Memory of May: A Look Back at the 1980 Kwangju Uprising* (Honolulu: University of Hawai'i Press, 2002).

30. Laurel Kendall, "Did Women Have a Peace Corps Korea Experience?" in *Peace Corps Volunteers and the Making of Korean Studies in the United States*, edited by Seung-kyung Kim and Michael Robinson, 111–26. (Seattle: University of Washington Center for Korea Studies, 2020).

31. Laurel Kendall, *Shamans, Housewives, and Other Restless Spirits: Women in Korean Ritual Life* (Honolulu: University of Hawai'i Press, 1987).

BIBLIOGRAPHY

Baker, Don. "Kwangju, Trauma, and the Problem of Objectivity in History-Writing." In *Peace Corps Volunteers and the Making of Korean Studies in the United States*, edited by Seung-kyung Kim and Michael Robinson, 9–30. Seattle: University of Washington Center for Korea Studies, 2020.

Clark, Donald N. *The Kwangju Uprising: Shadows over the Regime in South Korea.* Boulder, CO: Westview, 1988.

Clark, Donald. "On Being Part of the Peace Corps Generation in Korean Studies." In *Peace Corps Volunteers and the Making of Korean Studies in the United States*, edited by Seung-kyung Kim and Michael Robinson, 53–76. Seattle: University of Washington Center for Korea Studies, 2020.

Cumings, Bruce. *Korea's Place in the Sun.* New York: W. W. Norton & Company, 1997.

Cumings, Bruce. *The Origins of the Korean War: Liberation and the Emergence of Separate Times* 1945–1947. Princeton, NJ: Princeton University Press, 1981.

Eisenhower, Dwight D. "Special Message to the Congress on Education," January 27, 1958. *The American Presidency Project.* Accessed May 18, 2017. http://www.presidency. ucsb.edu/ws/?pid=11207. (site discontinued).

Eckert, Carter J. *Offspring of Empire: The Koch'ang Kim's and the Colonial Origins of Korean Capitalism 1876–1945.* Seattle: University of Washington Press, 1991.

Eckert, Carter J. "A Road Less Traveled: From Rome to Seoul via the Peace Corps." In *Peace Corps Volunteers and the Making of Korean Studies in the United States*, edited by Seung-kyung Kim and Michael Robinson, 77–92. Seattle: University of Washington Center for Korea Studies, 2020.

First Book Edition of John F. Kennedy's Inaugural Address. New York: Franklin Watts, 1964.

"Ilbu chaeya insa chŏngbu chŏnbok sŏndong" [A group of opposition figures instigate overthrow of the government]. *Chosŏn ilbo*, March 11, 1976:12.

Kahn, Ely Jacques. *The China Hands.* New York: Viking, 1975.

Kendall, Laurel. "Did Women Have a Peace Corps–Korea Experience?" In K*Peace Corps Volunteers and the Making of Korean Studies in the United States*, edited by Seung-kyung Kim and Michael Robinson, 111–26. Seattle: University of Washington Center for Korea Studies, 2020.

Kendall, Laurel. *Shamans, Housewives, and Other Restless Spirits: Women in Korean Ritual Life.* Honolulu: University of Hawai'i Press, 1987.

Kennan, George F. "The Sources of Soviet Conduct." *Foreign Affairs* 65, no. 4 (Spring 1987): 852–68.

Lewis, Linda. "At the Border: Women, Anthropology, and North Korea." In *Peace Corps Volunteers and the Making of Korean Studies in the United States*, edited by Seung-kyung Kim and Michael Robinson, 127–40. Seattle: University of Washington Center for Korea Studies, 2020.

Lewis, Linda. *Laying Claim to the Memory of May: A Look Back at the 1980 Kwangju Uprising.* Honolulu: University of Hawai'i Press, 2002.

Moon, Okpyo. "A Korean Perspective: Peace Corps Volunteers, Europe, and the Study of Korea." In *Peace Corps Volunteers and the Making of Korean Studies in the United States*, edited by Seung-kyung Kim and Michael Robinson, 175–90. Seattle: University of Washington Center for Korea Studies, 2020.

Pearson, Drew. "Cabinet Provided Real Drama." *Washington Post*, June 30, 1950.

Robinson, Michael E. *Cultural Nationalism in Colonial Korea.* Seattle: University of Washington Press, 1988.

Robinson, Michael E. "Empathy, Politics, and Historical Imagination: A Peace Corps Experience and Its Aftermath." In *Peace Corps Volunteers and the Making of Korean Studies in the United States*, edited by Seung-kyung Kim and Michael Robinson, 141–58. Seattle: University of Washington Center for Korea Studies, 2020.

Shultz, Edward J. "Peace Corps–Korea Group K-1: Empowering to Serve as New Voices in Korean Studies." In *Peace Corps Volunteers and the Making of Korean Studies in the United States*, edited by Seung-kyung Kim and Michael Robinson, 159–74. Seattle: University of Washington Center for Korea Studies, 2020.

US Department of Education. "The History of Title VI and Fulbright-Hays: An Impressive International Timeline." Accessed May 18, 2017. https://www2.ed.gov/about/offices/list/ope/iegps/history.html.

Afterword

KATHLEEN STEPHENS
November 2019

I am not and have never been a Korean studies scholar. I was what the academy calls a "practitioner": A career diplomat in the US Foreign Service for over thirty years, including nine cumulative years of diplomatic service in South Korea, and another three years in Washington working on issues related to US–Korean relations, South and North.

My link to this extraordinary collection of essays is not an academic one. It is that I, too, was a Peace Corps volunteer in South Korea, from 1975 to 1977. Perhaps more importantly, I have derived insights and lessons from each of the scholars included in this collection.

Many of them are my *sŏnbae*, having slightly preceded my service in South Korea. Most of the authors I do not know well. Of those I have met, it was in later, post–Peace Corps years. Over the decades I steadily acquired and read works by many of them—Donald Clark, *Christianity in Modern Korea*, Laurel Kendall, *Shamans, Housewives, and Other Restless Spirits*, Carter J. Eckert, *Park Chung Hee and Modern Korea*, Bruce Fulton and Yun Ju-Chan's transcendent translations of Korean novelists and poets, and many more.[1] These are the authors I have held onto and returned to again and again over the years, accessing a depth of expertise essential to counterbalancing the risks of diplomacy as a peripatetic dilettante. They write vividly, often critically, from diverse perspectives and with differing views, but always with insight and empathy. Because they were once Peace Corps–Korea volunteers, I feel I know something of how Korea got under their skin, into their bones, and stayed there.

I appreciate the attention the Institute for Korean Studies at Indiana University has brought to how former Peace Corps volunteers played a role in the development of Korean studies in the United States, both through organizing the 2016 conference and now in the publication of this book of essays in cooperation with the University of Washington Center for Korea Studies.

The intellectual contributions of the scholars stand on their own impressive merits. What strikes me in the sometimes deeply personal essays in this volume is the nature of memory and the extraordinary times we witnessed and participated in.

As Carter Eckert writes, those of us who were in South Korea in the late 1960s and through the 1970s were parachuted down into "one of the most exciting and transformative periods of modern world history," a period of "the greatest socioeconomic transformation in (Korea's) recorded history, and one of the most remarkable and rapid in the history of the world."[2]

I confess I did not perceive this so grandly when I left South Korea in 1977 at the end of my Peace Corps service in rural South Chungch'ong Province, though the changes in the short two-year period I lived in the countryside were astonishing, both at that time as well as in retrospect.

But then I returned to South Korea in 1983 as a young diplomat, covering the burgeoning political scene from Seoul. During the next six years I wit-

Fig. 12.1 Kathleen Stephens with students at Yesan Middle School as a Peace Corps volunteer 1975–77. Photo courtesy of Kathleen Stephens.

nessed a political transformation—as South Korea turned decisively toward democracy—that was every bit as dramatic, unpredicted, and profound as the economic and social changes we witnessed as Peace Corps volunteers in earlier years. Professor Eckert got it right.

That is a different, much bigger story, for another time, as is a full account of the yet-again-transformed Republic of Korea I experienced almost twenty years later when I returned to Seoul in 2008 as the new US ambassador.

But one part of my ambassadorial story that is perhaps relevant to the essays in this collection is the unexpectedly intense interest Koreans had in my Peace Corps experience and that of other volunteers, and in what Korea was like "back in the day." This surprised me. The Peace Corps had closed its program in South Korea in 1981. Living in South Korea in the 1980s as an embassy political officer, there was little such curiosity for those still-recent days. By 2008, though, Koreans couldn't get enough of the old photographs we had taken of everyday scenes of rural and urban South Korea, a world now long gone, and with the softening of time, looked back upon with considerable nostalgia. We former Peace Corps volunteers were recruited (with most of us delighted to oblige) in bearing witness to that bygone era.

Korean newspapers reporting my nomination as the new US envoy invariably spoke of my *inyŏn* (as Bruce Fulton tells us in his essay, meaning "prior connection," but also with a connotation of destiny or fate) with Korea; I

Fig. 12.2 Ambassador to South Korea Kathleen Stephens with students at Yesan Middle School in 2008. Photo courtesy of Kathleen Stephens.

usually responded (like Dr. Fulton) that it was uyŏn (fortuity, chance) as well as a heap of oyŏn (luck) that went into my finding my way back to Korea after a decade and a half working on the problems of post-Cold War Europe.[3] There were those in Washington who voiced doubts about whether Korea was "ready" for a woman as the top American diplomat in Seoul (the same doubts

Fig. 12.3 Ambassador Kathleen Stephens at the US Embassy in Seoul, the photo in the background was taken by Ambassador Stephens in 1976. Photo reproduced by permission from photographer Bongsub Kim.

expressed in the 1980s when there were no women in the embassy's political section), but for Koreans, the fact that I had been in Korea "when life was hard," as they put it, and that I spoke Korean, opened doors and contacts far beyond what I had dared to hope.

As George Orwell noted, our memories do not remain virgin.[4] Even those that seem most vivid have been refracted, overlaid, or colored by the experiences that follow. My Peace Corps memories are the same, compounded by the professional habit of thinking in terms of broader US policy goals. So, I especially admire and benefit from the rigor and honesty with which the contributors in this book have approached the task of sifting and interpreting their memories, and their subsequent engagement with Korea, throughout their lives.

Throughout my tenure in Seoul as ambassador from 2008 to 2011, I had the privilege of hosting former Peace Corps—Korea volunteers returning to Korea, most for the first time since their service, at the invitation of The Korea Foundation. Some hundreds returned on trips that included visits back to the villages, towns, and cities to see again the people and places among whom they had lived and worked. While few became Koreanists, their stories struck notes similar to those in this book, that of how Korea reshaped the way they saw the world and themselves, of how they learned and benefitted

Fig. 12.4 President Barack Obama and Ambassador Kathleen Stephens studying the Peace Corps–Korea and South Korea's volunteer program (KOICA) exhibit, 2009. Photo reprinted with permission from the US Embassy, Seoul.

so much more from living in and learning about Korea than they gave through their service.

In 2016, I was back in Seoul for the gathering Donald Clark describes in his chapter, an exhibition at the National Museum of Korean Contemporary History that marked fifty years since K-1, the first group of volunteers, arrived in South Korea. The exhibit's title, "Beautiful Journey, Endless Friendship" (*Arŭmdaun yujŏng, yŏngwŏnhan ujŏng*) moved us all, especially the loveliness of the Korean phrasing. But equally apt, I've concluded, thinking about my own journey and about the hundreds of other Peace Corps–Korea journeys I now know, is "Endless Journey, Beautiful Friendship" (*Yŏngwŏnhan yujŏng, arŭmdaun ujŏng*).

For all of us, the journey we began in Korea over fifty years ago remains ongoing.

NOTES

1. Donald N. Clark, *Christianity in Modern Korea* (Lanham, MD: University Press of America, 1986); Laurel Kendall, *Shamans, Housewives, and Other Restless Spirits: Women in Korean Ritual Life*. (Honolulu: University of Hawai'i Press, 1985); and Carter J. Eckert, *Park Chung Hee and Modern Korea: The Roots of Militarism 1866–1945*. (Cambridge, MA: Belknap Press of Harvard University Press, 2016).

2. Carter J. Eckert, "A Road Less Traveled: From Rome to Seoul." In *Peace Corps Volunteers and the Making of Korean Studies in the United States*, edited by Seung-kyung Kim and Michael Robinson, 77–92. (Seattle, WA: University of Washington Center for Korea Studies, 2020).

3. Bruce Fulton, "Serendipity, Uyŏn, and Inyŏn." In *Peace Corps Volunteers and the Making of Korean Studies in the United States*, edited by Seung-kyung Kim and Michael Robinson, 93–110. (Seattle, WA: University of Washington Center for Korea Studies, 2020).

4. George Orwell, "My Country Right or Left," Orwell Foundation, accessed December 4, 2019. https://www.orwellfoundation.com/the-orwell-foundation/orwell/essays-and-other-works/my-country-right-or-left/.

BIBLIOGRAPHY

Clark, Donald N. *Christianity in Modern Korea*. Lanham, MD: University Press of America, 1986.

Kendall, Laurel. *Shamans, Housewives, and Other Restless Spirits: Women in Korean Ritual Life*. Studies of the East Asian Institute. Honolulu: University of Hawai'i Press, 1985.

Eckert, Carter J. *Park Chung Hee and Modern Korea: The Roots of Militarism 1866–1945*. Cambridge, MA: Belknap Press of Harvard University Press, 2016.

Eckert, Carter J. "A Road Less Traveled: From Rome to Seoul." In *Peace Corps Volunteers and the Making of Korean Studies in the United States*, edited by Seung-kyung Kim and Michael Robinson, 77–92. Seattle, WA: University of Washington Center for Korea Studies, 2020.

Fulton, Bruce. "Serendipity, *Uyŏn*, and *Inyŏn*." In *Peace Corps Volunteers and the Making of Korean Studies in the United States*, edited by Seung-kyung Kim and Michael Robinson, 93–110. Seattle, WA: University of Washington Center for Korea Studies, 2020.

Orwell, George. "My Country Right or Left." Orwell Foundation. Accessed December 3, 2019. https://www.orwellfoundation.com/the-orwell-foundation/orwell/essays-and-other-works/my-country-right-or-left/.

Contributors

DON BAKER (K-19) served as a Peace Corps volunteer in Kwangju, South Chŏlla Province, from 1971 to 1974. He went on to earn a PhD In Korean History at the University of Washington and is now a professor of Korean Civilization in the Department of Asian Studies at the University of British Columbia.

ED BAKER (K-1, 1971–73) lived in Korea for about ten years and has traveled widely in Asia. He has a BA from Colby, a JD from Yale Law School, and an MA in Regional Studies–East Asia from Harvard. He was a staff member of the Subcommittee on International Organizations of the US House of Representatives during its Investigation of Korean American Relations in 1977–78. He was the associate director of the Harvard-Yenching Institute for twenty-five years and taught East Asian and Korean history at Hanyang University and Seoul National University 2007–10. He was a founding member of the board of Asia Watch in 1985 and was Amnesty International's US–South Korea coordinator from 1979–91. He frequently writes and speaks on Korean affairs and in recent years has taken a strong interest in promoting a peaceful solution to the confrontation between North Korea and South Korea.

DONALD N. CLARK (K-6, 1967–69) is retired after thirty-eight years on the history faculty at Trinity University in San Antonio where he also served as director of International Programs and founder of the East Asian Studies at Trinity program. He served multiple terms on the Association for Asian Studies Korea Committee on the board of the ASIANetwork consortium, and as Texas director for the National Consortium for Teaching about Asia (NCTA). During breaks he taught several semesters as a Fulbright professor at Yonsei University in Seoul and three round-the-world voyages of the Semester at Sea program.

CARTER J. ECKERT (K-7/8, 1968–71) is Yoon Se Young Professor of Korean History at Harvard University. His most recent book is *Park Chung Hee and Modern Korea: The Roots of Militarism 1866–1945* (Belknap Press of Harvard University Press, 2016).

BRUCE FULTON was a member of K-44 (1978–79). He taught English at Changgye Middle School in North Chŏlla Province in 1978 and at Seoul National University in 1979. He is the inaugural holder of the Young-Bin Min Chair in Korean Literature and Literary Translation, Department of Asian Studies, University of British Columbia, Vancouver, BC, Canada. With Ju-Chan Fulton he has translated numerous volumes of modern Korean fiction, most recently *The Future of Silence: Fiction by Korean Women* (Zephyr Press, 2016), *Sunset: A Ch'ae Manshik Reader* (Columbia University Press, 2017), *Mina*, a novel by Kim Sagwa (Two Lines Press, 2018), and *The Catcher in the Loft*, a novel by Ch'ŏn Un-yŏng (Codhill Press, 2019).

LAUREL KENDALL (K-11, 1970–72) is chair of Anthropology at the American Museum of Natural History and Curator of Asian Ethnographic Collections. The author and editor of many books on popular religion, ritual, gender, and modernity, Kendall's *Shamans, Nostalgias, and the IMF: South Korean Popular Religion in Motion* was the first recipient of the Korean Society for Cultural Anthropology's Yim Sok-Jay prize for the best work about Korea by a foreign anthropologist. Kendall is a former president of the Association for Asian Studies (2016–17).

SEUNG-KYUNG KIM is the Korea Foundation Professor in the Department of East Asian Languages and Cultures and director of the Institute for Korean Studies at Indiana University. She is the author of *The Korean Women's Movement and the State: Bargaining for Change* (Routledge, 2014), and *Class Struggle or Family Struggle?: Lives of Women Factory Workers in South Korea* (Cambridge University Press, 1997).

LINDA S. LEWIS (K-14, 1970–72) is the American Friends Service Committee (AFSC) Country Representative for the DPRK, managing AFSC's agriculture development program in North Korea. Before joining the AFSC in 2010, she served as vice-president for Academic Affairs at the Institute for Study Abroad and as director of Asian and Pacific Studies at the School for International Training. She also taught for many years at Wittenberg University, where she was Professor of Anthropology and director of the East Asian Studies program. Her publications include *Laying Claim to the Memory of May: A Look Back at the 1980 Kwangju Uprising* (University of Hawai'i, 2002).

OKPYO MOON is professor emerita of the Academy of Korean Studies, South Korea and currently works as a Distinguished Chair Professor at Shandong University, China. She has carried out extensive research both in Japan and Korea focusing on family and gender, urban and rural community making, ethnic minorities, tourism, and heritage policies. Her latest publications include "Challenges Surrounding the Survival of the Nishijin Silk Weaving Industry in Kyoto, Japan" (*International Journal of Intangible Heritage*, 2013) and the Korean translation of Martina Deuchler's *Under the Ancestor's Eyes: Kinship, Status and Locality in Premodern Korea* (2018).

MICHAEL ROBINSON (K-7/8, 1968–71) is a native of Michigan and a graduate of the University of Michigan (BA, 1968) and the University of Washington (PhD, 1979). His Peace Corps experience in Korea led him into a career of teaching about Korea and East Asia. He taught at both the University of Southern California and Indiana University between 1980–2015. He has published widely on issues of Korean nationalism and colonial history. Currently, he is retired and living in Kalamazoo, Michigan.

EDWARD J. SHULTZ (K-1, 1966–67) is professor emeritus at the University of Hawai'i at Mānoa. He first came to Korea as a Peace Corps volunteer in 1966, after graduating from Union College in New York, and lived in Pusan, South Korea. On receiving his PhD in 1976 from the University of Hawai'i, he taught at the University of Hawai'i until he retired in August 2013. His major area of research is Koryŏ history (918–1392) with a special interest in social, institutional, and political history.

CLARK W. SORENSEN is professor of International Studies at the University of Washington and director of the Center for Korea Studies in the Henry M. Jackson School of International Studies. An anthropologist, he did his initial fieldwork in South Korea in 1976–77 in a mountain village in western Kangwŏn Province. Since then he has done fieldwork in several other sites in South Korea, as well as revisiting his original field site several times.

AMBASSADOR (RET.) KATHLEEN STEPHENS (K-35, 1975–77) is a former American diplomat. She was US Ambassador to the Republic of Korea 2008–11. Other overseas assignments included postings to China, former Yugoslavia, Portugal, Northern Ireland, where she was US Consul General in Belfast during the negotiations culminating in the 1998 Good Friday Agreement, and India, where she was US charge d'affaires (2014). Ambassador Stephens also served in a number of policy positions in Washington at the Department of State and the White House. These included acting Under Secretary of State for Public Diplomacy and Public Affairs (2012), Principal Deputy Assistant Secretary of State for East Asian and Pacific Affairs (2005–7), Deputy Assistant Secretary of State for European and Eurasian Affairs (2003–5), and National Security Council director for European Affairs at the Clinton White House. Stephens was William J. Perry Fellow for Korea at Stanford University 2015–18. She is vice-chair of the board of trustees for the Asia Foundation and chair of the Korea Society. She has been president and CEO of the Korea Economic Institute of America since September 2018, based in Washington, DC.

Index

Gregg, Donald, 50n3
"The Group of 50," petition to US
    Embassy and, 37, 39
Guillemoz, Alex, 176

Habib, Philip, 50n3
Haeundae Beach, Pusan, South Korea, 169
Hall, John W., 181
Ham Se-ung, 215n11
Ham Sŏkhŏn, 214n11
Han, Sang-bok, 181–82, 184
Han King, 19
Han Seung-joo, 44–45
Han'gang (The Han River) (Cho
    Chŏngnae), 97
Han'guk munhak (Korean literature)
    (monthly journal), 97
Hangŭl, announced by King Sejong to
    Chosŏn people, 93
Hankuk University of Foreign Studies,
    Seoul, 36
Hanyang University, Seoul, 49–50, 182
Harvard Law School, EALS at, 38, 39, 42
Harvard University: graduate study
    recruiting among Peace Corps–Korea
    volunteers by, 203–4, 216n18; History
    and East Asian Languages program
    at, 39; Korea faculty at, 208; Korean
    studies program at, 178; Korean
    Trade-Investment Promotion Agency
    (KOTRA) grant to, 186n1; Regional
    Studies East Asia program, 66
Harvard-Yenching Institute (HYI), 44–45,
    49
Hawai'i, Peace Corps training in: Ed and
    Diane Baker's, 31–32; Eckert's,
    77–78, 78f; Kendall's, 114–15;
    Lewis's, 127–28; Robinson's, 142;
    Shultz's, 160–61
Hee, Dawn, 182
Henthorn, William, 65

historians: Don Baker on coherent narra-
    tive of, 18; on fictional portrayals vs.
    portrayals by, 19. See also Baker, Don;
    eyewitness accounts; objectivity
historical consciousness (yŏksa ŭisik),
    translations of Korean literature and,
    98
history: Don Baker on writing plausible
    vs. probable accounts of, 20; Ed
    Baker's discussions with Koreans
    about, 35; as confirmation or denial
    of established and approved narra-
    tives, 154–55; as constructed not
    found, 27n17; Sorensen on academic
    winnowing and, 205–9
"History, Language, and Reading:
    Waiting for Crillon" (LaCapra), 20
History of Korea (Hulbert), 161
Holbrooke, Richard, 46
Hollywood constructions of East Asia,
    Western heroes and, 116
Hong Samyŏng, 70
Hong Sŏkchung, 104
Howell, Ruth, 150f
Hulbert, Homer, 161
human rights in Korea, 42, 47
humanities, AKSE conferences and, 176
Hwang Chini, 104
Hwang Sŏgyŏng, 105
Hwang Sunwŏn, 93, 95, 96, 99
Hyundai, 82–83

Im Ch'ŏru, 105
Im Kwŏnt'aek, 105
Imagined Communities: Reflections on the
    Origin and Spread of Nationalism
    (Anderson), 147
Immigration and Naturalization Act of
    1965 (Hart-Celler Act), 216n22
Indiana University, Institute for Korean
    Studies, 222

history career of, 209; at Kyŏngnam Boys' High School, 162–63; with other Peace Corps volunteers, 164f; on Peace Corps' goals for volunteers, 166–67; as Peace Corps trainer, 163, 165; Peace Corps training, 160–62; on Pusan growth and development, 168–69; at University of Hawai'i, 163
Silla Dynasty, Shultz study of, 163
Silver Star (Ŭnsŏng), 89
Sim Ch'ŏng, 104–5
Sinology, in the US before World War II, 191
Si-sa-yŏng-ŏ-sa (publisher), 95
Skillend, William, 176
Smith, Deborah, 102
Smith, Hazel, 136–37
Social Science Research Council (SSRC), 66–67
soft power, 3–4, 148
Sŏl Sŏnsaengnim, 78f
"Sonagi" ("The Cloudburst") (Kang Sŏkkyŏng), 96
Song June-ho, 65
Song Ki-jo (Sŏng Kijo), 101
Sonyŏni onda (Human Acts: A Novel) (Han King), 19
Sorensen, Clark W.: on academic winnowing, 205–9; on Fulbright House, Seoul, 201–3; on his entry into Korean studies, 197–98, 214nn8–9; at Maitreya Pavilion, Gold Mountain Temple, North Chŏlla Province, 212f; on Peace Corps and Korean studies programs, 191–92; on Peace Corps establishment, 192–97; on Peace Corps influence on Korean studies, 209–11; on Peace Corps niche in 1970s Korea, 198–201, 215n16
South Chŏlla Province, Korea. See Baker, Don; Kwangju

South Korea (Republic of Korea [ROK]): academic dialogues at AKSE conferences with North Koreans and, 178; academic freedom issues in, 69; assumptions about Americans in, 146–47; Ed Baker not admitted to, 44–45; Clark's childhood in and negative views of, 53–55; cold winters in, 10–11, 31, 34, 78; development of large business complexes in, 87; economic growth and income inequality in, 87–88; Eisenhower and regime change in, 56; exclusion of women and cultural norms of, 131–33; farming and rural life in, 127–28; Five-Year Plans and development in, 196–97; foundations and government entities, Korean literature abroad and, 101–2; Global Gender Gap Index (2015) and, 132; gratitude for Peace Corps volunteers in, 201; Peace Corps as US history transplanted to, 112; Peace Corps niche in 1970s in, 198–201, 215n16; reunification hopes of, 135–36; Shultz's praise for, 163–64; South-North Joint Communique and, 39, 135; Status of Forces Agreement between US and, 149; student leaders, Chun harassment of, 22; television dramas, oral Korean literature and, 104; Tokyo Embassy, 44; University of Hawai'i and East-West Center support by, 170; on unsanctioned contact between South and North Koreans, 137; US relations from 1966 to 1975 with, 1–2. See also Peace Corps–Korea volunteers; specific cities
South Vietnam: US troops increased in, Peace Corps and, 196. See also Vietnam War

CPSIA information can be obtained
at www.ICGtesting.com
Printed in the USA
BVHW032131030720
582856BV00002B/6

9 780295 748139